Public
Personnel
and
Administrative
Behavior

The Duxbury Press Series in Public Administration

Public Personnel and Administrative Behavior: Cases and Text
Peter Allan, Pace University, and Stephen Rosenberg, Baruch College, CUNY

Managing Government Organizations: An Introduction to Public Administration
Robert D. Pursley and Neil Snortland, University of Arkansas, Little Rock

Managing Public Systems: Analytic Techniques for Public Administration
Michael J. White, Ross Clayton, Robert C. Myrtle, Gilbert B. Siegel, and Aaron Rose, University of Southern California, Los Angeles

Statistics for Public Policy and Management
William F. Matlack, University of Pittsburgh

Essentials of Public Administration: A Text with Readings
Larry B. Hill and F. Ted Hebert, University of Oklahoma, Norman

Experiences in Public Administration
Dennis R. Briscoe, University of San Diego, and Gene S. Leonardson, Willamette University, Salem, Oregon

Public Bureaucracy: Values and Perspectives
James A. Medeiros, U.S. Public Health Service, and David E. Schmitt, Northeastern University, Boston

Managing Urban America: The Politics and Administration of America's Cities
David R. Morgan, University of Oklahoma, Norman

Of Related Interest

Policy Analysis for Public Decisions
Duncan MacRae, Jr., and James A. Wilde, University of North Carolina, Chapel Hill

Politics and the Bureaucracy: Policymaking in the Fourth Branch of Government
Kenneth J. Meier, University of Oklahoma, Norman

Public Policy and Politics in America
James E. Anderson and David W. Brady, University of Houston, and Charles W. Bullock, III, University of Georgia, Athens

An Introduction to the Study of Public Policy, 2nd Edition
Charles O. Jones, University of Pittsburgh

Introduction to Budgeting
John Wanat, University of Illinois, Chicago

Understanding Intergovernmental Relations: Public Policy and Participants' Perspectives in Local, State, and National Governments
Deil S. Wright, University of North Carolina, Chapel Hill

Duxbury Press, Monterey, California

Public Personnel and Administrative Behavior: cases and text

Peter Allan
Pace University

Stephen Rosenberg
Baruch College, CUNY

Public Personnel and Administrative Behavior: Cases and Text was prepared for publication by the following people:

Sponsoring Editor: Jean-François Vilain
Production Editor: Ellie Connolly
Copy Editor: Susan McCarthy
Cover and Interior Designer: Audrey Witt

Duxbury Press
A Division of Wadsworth, Inc.

Library of Congress Cataloging in Publication Data
Allan, Peter, 1926-
   Public personnel and administrative behavior.
   (Duxbury Press series in public administration)
   1. Civil service—Personnel management—Case studies. 2. Personnel management—Case studies.
I. Rosenberg, Stephen, 1943-   joint author.
II. Title. III. Series.
JF1601.A44   350.1   80-18906
ISBN 0-87872-287-4

Printed in the United States of America
1 2 3 4 5 6 7 8 9–85 84 83 82 81

Table of Contents

Preface

The idea for this casebook first came to us when we were reviewing the public sector human resources literature in connection with our research into managerial selection and performance appraisal. While there were a fair number of textbooks and books of readings in the field, there seemed to be no suitable casebook available and a definite scarcity of case materials in public sector human resources management. This casebook is intended to fill that gap.

In selecting these cases, we were guided by several considerations. First, the cases had to be *real*. We decided to draw on our experiences as well as on the experiences of colleagues. Accordingly, every case describes either an actual situation about which we had first-hand knowledge or an incident that was related to us by people who had lived through it. Second, the cases had to deal with *current* problems and with matters likely to be of concern in the foreseeable future. The cases address, for example, many of the issues that will be a focus of concern for personnel managers and that will be at the center of personnel reform efforts in the 1980s. Third, the cases had to be written so that students and practitioners could readily visualize the situation and place themselves within it. Fourth, the cases had to be sufficiently short so that they could be read and absorbed quickly.

We felt that obviating the need for lengthy study and preparation was an especially important consideration for instructors who wished to have students read and discuss a case during one classroom hour. This feature of the book makes it particularly applicable to training seminars and workshops. Finally, the cases had to be interesting and challenging to make for a rewarding learning experience. It is our hope that we have succeeded in meeting each of the criteria that we set for ourselves.

The cases have been selected to illuminate and bring to life the variety and complexity of practical problems and issues occupying human resources managers and to encourage the student without experience in the field to consider the pros and cons of various approaches and to think about workable solutions. The experienced practitioner will of course readily identify with the situations. By viewing the material in a somewhat different setting, the practicing human resources manager or technician should be stimulated to think of new approaches to familiar problems.

Each case is based on an actual occurrence. However, the names of the individuals and organizations, as well as the locations of the organizations, have been disguised. Although the cases are drawn from experiences in the public sector, many, if not most of the situations, could just as easily have occurred in other not-for-profit institutions or in private industry. Many of the issues raised by the cases transcend any boundaries that may be thought to exist among the sectors. Consequently, the cases may be useful for students of either public or private sector human resources management. This casebook is suited for use in graduate and undergraduate courses in human resources management and personnel administration to provide practical "real world" applications of various concepts. It is unlikely that all of the cases will be used in a one-semester course. Therefore, instructors will be able to select cases that best suit the approaches of their specific courses or that are of particular interest to them. This casebook could be used with a general human resources text, with a book of readings, or alone in training or development programs employing other instructional materials. For courses in organizational behavior, personnel psychology, or human relations, the book could well be used as a supplementary source of case materials or to expand the dimensions of the courses. Table 1, Cross-Reference Matrix, matches the chapters in this casebook

Table 1 Cross-Reference Matrix

Selected Texts	1 Selection and Recruitment	2 Assignment and Placement	3 Motivation and Incentives	4 Performance Evaluation, Discipline, and Layoffs	5 Training and Development	6 Line-Staff Relationships	7 Employee Relations	8 Organization Change and Job Design
				Chapters				
Beach, Dale, Personnel (New York: Macmillan, 1975)	8, 9, 10, 11, 12, 13	13, 18	17, 20, 21, 22, 26	12, 13, 20, 22, 23	14, 15	7	5, 6	8, 16, 19
Coleman, Charles J., Personnel (Cambridge, Mass.: Winthrop, 1979)	5, 6	3	13	9	10, 11		15	4, 11
Davis, Keith, Human Behavior at Work (New York: McGraw-Hill, 1977)	8	15, 16, 18, 23	3, 4, 5, 9, 25	15, 21, 22, 23, 25	11	9, 22	6, 16, 17, 19	6, 10, 11, 12, 14, 21, 24
Gibson, James L., Ivancevich, John M., and Donnelly, James H., Organizations (Dallas: Business Publications, 1979)			3, 4, 5, 14	3, 13, 15	17, 18	6, 7	19	3, 10, 11, 12, 17, 18, 19
Greenlaw, Paul S., Readings in Personnel Management (Philadelphia: W.B. Saunders, 1979)	Part II B	Parts I, II A	Parts IV A, B	Part III A	Part III B		Part V C	
Greenlaw, Paul S. and Biggs, William D., Modern Personnel Management (Philadelphia: W.B. Saunders, 1979)	4	3	9, 10	5	6, 7, 8	2	14	

Reference								
Hackman, J. Richard, Lawler, Edward E., and Porter, Lyman W., *Perspectives on Behavior in Organizations* (New York: McGraw-Hill, 1977)	1, 3, 4	4	1, 7, 8	7	4, 9	5	10	5, 6, 10
Hamner, W. Clay and Schmidt, Frank L., *Contemporary Problems in Personnel* (Chicago: St. Clair, 1977)	2 A, B, C, D, E 3, 10 A, B	10 B	5, 7A, B, 8	6, 10B	4		9	7A
Lee, Robert D., *Public Personnel Systems* (Baltimore: University Park Press, 1979)	5, 8		10, 11	6	7		12	3
Nigro, Felix A. and Nigro, Lloyd, G., *The New Public Personnel Administration* (Itasca: F.E. Peacock, 1976)	6, 7	7	5	8	9	3	10	2
Sayles, Leonard R. and Strauss, George, *Managing Human Resources* (Englewood Cliffs, N.J.: Prentice-Hall, 1977)	7, 8, 10, 11	5, 7, 9, 11	17	6, 11, 13, 17	9, 12, 14	2, 3, 5	4	14
Shafritz, Jay M. et al., *Personnel Management in Government* (New York: Marcel Dekker, 1978)	7, 8	7	12	13	13	3, 4	10, 11	
Stahl, O. Glenn, *Public Personnel Administration* (New York: Harper & Row, 1976)	7, 8, 9, 10	10	11, 12	12, 18, 22	13	24, 25	19, 20, 21	4
Wexley, Kenneth N. and Yukl, Gary A., *Organizational Behavior and Industrial Psychology* (New York: Oxford, 1975)	5, 8		10, 11	6	7		12	3
Wexley, Kenneth N. and Yukl, Gary A., *Organizational Behavior and Personnel Psychology* (Homewood: Richard D. Irwin, 1977)	11, 12	7	5, 6	4, 6, 10	13, 14	9	9	15

with chapters from selected texts that may provide additional background information for analyzing the cases. The selected texts are listed on the left of the matrix. The chapters from this casebook are listed on the top of the matrix. The chapters from each selected text that can best be used in conjunction with the casebook chapters are listed in the center of the matrix. For example, Chapter 1, Selection and Recruitment, corresponds to chapters 8, 9, 10, 11, 12, and 13 of *Personnel* by Dale Beach. Additional suggested readings to this casebook appear at the end of each chapter.

We are grateful to Professor William E. Steckman of the Graduate School of Business Administration, C. W. Post Center of Long Island University and Professor Melvin Zimet of the Department of Managerial Sciences at Manhattan College, both of whom read the cases and gave valuable comments and suggestions, as well as words of encouragement. We are indebted to Richard Gitlin for suggesting a number of case problems, some of which appear in this casebook. And finally, we are grateful to the following reviewers: James P. Pfiffner, California State University at Fullerton; Frederick S. Lane, Baruch College, CUNY; and Jeremy F. Plant, George Mason University.

Introduction

Human resources management is a field that has been undergoing rapid and extensive change. It has gone from a relatively neglected area of interest and study that has been held in relatively low esteem to a discipline considered of crucial importance. Rather than being a dormant field in which most, if not all, of the major problems seemed to have been solved, it has become a dynamic area filled with great challenges and formidable problems.

In the past the range and scope of personnel activities in the public sector were relatively restricted. In the view of many practitioners, personnel administration consisted of nothing more than the enforcement of civil service rules—that is, making sure that all personnel activities were carried out within the framework of the civil service system. This role restriction led to the perception that the personnel function was static rather than dynamic and to the belief that the strict application of civil service rules and the administration of formal, written tests would furnish the system with well-qualified employees and at the same time ensure justice, equity, and fairness for all.

In recent years there has been increasing appreciation of the complexity of human and organizational needs and the consequent necessity to adopt more sophisticated methods such as assessment centers, results-based performance evaluation systems, and performance-linked incentive systems. There is also evidence that employees are no longer willing to accept authority unquestioningly or to refrain from expressing their dissatisfaction with management's personnel policies and practices. Further, many of the techniques that had been used and seemingly perfected into the 1960s have been found to be inadequate. Methods of selecting employees, training approaches, and mechanisms for evaluating employee performance have come under attack. New concepts and new methodologies have had to be developed to meet new demands and new challenges.

The increased involvement of government at all levels in regulating various aspects of human resources management, particularly in promoting equal employment opportunity, has made the field more complex. Consequently, the jobs of human resources specialists have become more demanding. Increasingly, top management has turned to human resources staffs for guidance in solving complicated and potentially costly problems.

Another trend helping to focus attention on human resources management has been the concern expressed by Congress and the President about certain personnel practices in federal agencies. This concern resulted, in 1978, in the first major legislative reform of federal personnel practices in decades. But personnel reform efforts have not been confined to the federal government level. Attempts to change state and local government personnel systems were underway well before federal legislation was enacted. However, the impetus provided by the federal government is expected to spark additional personnel reform initiatives at the state and local levels.

In many ways, decisionmakers in public sector organizations are subject to a greater variety of pressures and constraints than their counterparts in the private sector. For public sector managers the model of the rational decision-making process is frequently not applicable. The rational model specifies that a manager must carefully make a diagnosis of the situation after gathering all appropriate facts, develop a comprehensive set of alternative solutions, analyze and evaluate each alternative by weighing the costs and benefits of each, make the decision, and then implement it. But the range of alternatives is often limited by available resources; evaluation of the alternatives may be well-nigh impossible because benefits cannot be identified, much less calculated; and decisions once made cannot be put into effect because of changing political and other pressures.

Further, the actions of public sector managers are circumscribed by a complex, detailed web of civil service laws and rules. Managers moving from the private sector to the public sector have found themselves baffled and frustrated by rigid civil service requirements that severely limit the manager's ability to hire, promote, discipline, and fire employees.

The manager is also subject to powerful and possibly conflicting and irreconcilable pressures from political leaders who wish to attain short-term results often at the expense of more meaningful long-term results, from minority groups seeking greater representation at all levels of the bureaucracy, from bureaucrats and organized groups of civil servants seeking to preserve the status quo at any price, from civic groups seeking to make the civil service more productive and responsive, from community groups seeking a larger share of public services, and from taxpayers seeking to hold down the costs of government.

Other managers experiencing the world of public sector employment for the first time are quickly made aware of the need to pay careful attention to the news media. Managers soon learn that a good press is often vital to the success of their programs. Further, while managers in the private sector can function in near anonymity, public sector managers' actions are subject to the close, continuing scrutiny of the press and the public.

There is no pat formula for evaluating the effectiveness or appropriateness of decisions. As students proceed to analyze the cases, they will develop skill and sophistication in making and evaluating decisions, and in time, general guidelines for effective decision making will suggest themselves. Among the characteristics that we believe to be associated with effective decision making are the following:

> Decisions must conform to the law and those rules and regulations that have the force and effect of law.
>
> Decisions must be free of even the appearance of conflict of interest.
>
> Decisions must not be arbitrary or capricious.

To gain acceptance, decisions must appear to be equitable, fair, and appropriate, and they must be able to withstand scrutiny by diverse groups.

In arriving at decisions, considerations must often be given to a variety of constituencies who may have contradictory aims and values.

Decisions must often take into account existing practices and long-standing traditions.

Decisions likely to produce immediate rather than long-range results may be preferred by the political leadership and powerful interest groups even though the immediate results may not be in the best long-range interests of the community.

Decisionmakers must correctly identify significant needs, key variables, and constraints in a situation.

In making decisions, it is essential to accurately anticipate the potential consequences, implications, and ramifications of contemplated actions.

Risks attached to various alternative courses of action should be realistically assessed.

Decisionmakers must take into account the characteristics and needs of the individuals who will be affected by the decision.

While decisions made in the past may be guides for present action, each decision must be responsive and tailored to the unique circumstances of a situation.

The considerations suggested above are not meant to be all-inclusive or exhaustive; the student may well develop additional guides for effective decision making.

The division of this book and the selection of cases reflect what we perceive will be the major topics of concern in the 1980s. The topical coverage also reflects the views of others in the field and parallels the subjects that might be covered in a course in human resources management in the public sector. We have attempted to provide flexibility by offering a choice of cases in each broad topical area. In order to cover a wide range of problems, we decided to include a large number of short cases rather than concentrate on a small number of lengthy ones. Even though the cases are short, they deal with controversial areas, are likely to stimulate considerable interest and discussion, and probably lead to a diversity of conclusions.

This book is divided into eight chapters, with introductory comments for each chapter. These comments help make the transition between sections of a course. The first and by far the largest chapter deals with personnel selection and is split into two sections: (1) selection methods and procedures and (2) equal employment opportunity problems. The emphasis placed on personnel selection indicates our judgment as to its present and probable future importance. The cases in Chapter 2 consider some problems organizations may have in assigning and placing people after they have been selected for employment. Chapter 3 presents cases in motivation and incentives. Chapter 4 contains problems in performance evaluation, discipline, and lay-offs, which are some of the most difficult and frustrating matters for the human resources manager. In Chapter 5 there are cases highlighting some training and development problems. The conflicts between line and staff departments and units, which are described in the cases in Chapter 6, are classic problems that continue to plague managers. Chapter 7 focuses on employee relations, a matter of growing concern for the human resources manager. The final chapter provides a variety of situations portraying the difficulties that accompany attempts to bring about organizational change.

To aid the student in analyzing the cases and in arriving at appropriate decisions, the federal government's *Uniform Guidelines on Employee Selection Procedures* (1978) and *Questions and Answers on the Uniform Guidelines* are included as appendixes to this text. Although the guidelines appear to be directed toward employee selection, they have an impact on other personnel activities such as training, assignment, performance evaluation, and so forth.

While the cases in each chapter have been selected to illustrate issues indicated by the chapter titles many can be fit into other categories. Human resources problems often are complex; they do not fall neatly into one specific classification or another.

A series of questions is presented at the end of each case to guide analysis and discussion. Many questions ask the case reader to make a decision or recommend a course of action; others ask for consequences or implications. Clearly, these questions are not exhaustive. Undoubtedly, additional questions and issues will be raised by instructors and students. Some instructors may choose not to use the questions but rather to follow the traditional case analysis approach. In either event, the student should look beyond the specific cases and consider the broader implications of the issues raised. The real value of the cases may well be in the broad principles or guides to behavior that can be extracted.

1 Selection and Recruitment

A combination of federal, state, and local legislation, guidelines on employee selection procedures, and recent court decisions have led employers to move in the direction of professionally developed selection procedures. The legal requirements surrounding the development and administration of formal tests have an enormous impact upon users in terms of cost, effort, and time. Because of the difficulty and expense involved in formal testing procedures, many employers in the private sector have abandoned them. Public sector employers, however, do not have this option; formal competitive tests are mandated by state and local merit system laws.

Selection, at least in the public sector, may involve a number of phases or steps. These usually include the determination of minimum qualification requirements (e.g., edu-

1

cation, experience, physical, and/or medical requirements), recruitment, the administration of one or more types of tests, the background investigation, the establishment of ranked lists of successful candidates, and the final selection from among these successful candidates. Discrimination on the basis of race, ethnicity, or other irrelevant criteria, whether intentional or not, may occur during any of these phases or steps.

According to the law, selection procedures should be directly related to jobs and should not discriminate against any group for non-job-related reasons. The possibility of disparate impact—that is, the possibility that a test will discriminate against a particular minority group—makes it advisable for employers to conduct a validation study for every examination that they give. Validation studies, however, are expensive, as is the need to maintain various kinds of documentation and data on the impact of selection procedures on protected classes of applicants. Public employers, particularly large ones that administer many examinations, may be hard put to meet these demands at a time of fiscal crises and taxpayer resentment against high levels of public spending.

Legal requirements in connection with selection stem mainly from three sources: Title VII of the Civil Rights Act of 1964, the federal government's *Uniform Guidelines on Employee Selection Procedures* (1978), and landmark court decisions. Of course, there may also be state and local statutes that mandate additional requirements.

The Civil Rights Act of 1964 prohibits discrimination on the basis of race, color, religion, sex, or national origin in hiring, firing, determining wages, seniority, promotions, benefits, and other working conditions. Thus, Title VII was intended to cover a broad range of employment practices. Judicial interpretations of the Civil Rights Act make it plain that claimants need only show the discriminatory effect or consequence of employment practices, not that the employer purposely or deliberately intended to discriminate.

Prior to 1972, Title VII applied only to private sector employers. The Equal Employment Opportunity Act (EEOA) of 1972, however, extended Title VII's coverage to public sector employers with fifteen or more employees. This act also empowered the Equal Employment Opportunity Commission (EEOC) to administer Title VII and to enforce its provisions in federal court. Title VII authorized the use of any professionally developed test for purposes of hiring provided it was not used to discriminate against minorities. In 1966 EEOC had adopted guidelines, later revised in 1970, to inform employers of what the law and good professional practice required in developing and administering selection procedures. Any procedure or test that had an adverse impact on protected groups was unlawful unless it could be justified. To justify a test that discriminated against minorities, the employer had to prove that the test predicted performance on the job.

The 1970 version of EEOC's guidelines expanded upon the job-relatedness principle and extended coverage to all selection procedures such as interviews, application blanks, and so forth. However, those new guidelines were criticized by public and private employers on a variety of grounds (e.g., the guidelines were not specific enough; they were so demanding that employers would be unable to comply with them; they conflicted with requirements of other federal agencies that had responsibility for providing equal employment opportunity; and so forth). Accordingly, revisions were proposed by various groups.

After prolonged discussions and several attempts to produce a set of guidelines that would be acceptable to affected agencies, a new set was adopted in August 1978 by EEOC, the Civil Service Commission, the Department of Labor, and the Department of Justice. Although the 1978 *Uniform Guidelines on Employee Selection Procedures* are complex and lengthy, it is worthwhile to highlight some of the significant points embodied in this document. The new guidelines are intended to reflect previous court decisions, professional testing standards, the experience of enforcement agencies, as well as the Equal Employment Opportunity Act of 1972. These guidelines have had an enormous impact on employer selection procedures.

The primary goal of the guidelines appears to be the avoidance of adverse impact in the employment process. If adverse impact against any group results from the use of a particular selection procedure, the burden then falls to the employer to justify the procedure as a business necessity. The guidelines are intended to cover selection procedures that are used as the basis for any employment decision. These decisions may include hiring, promotion, demotion, referral, retention, licensing, certification or any other decision related to employment.

The criterion for determining adverse impact is the so-called four-fifths (4/5), or 80 percent, rule of thumb. This criterion means that a selection rate for any group that is less than 80 percent of the rate for the group with the highest selection rate will generally be considered as evidence of adverse impact. Where adverse impact exists, the employer must justify the selection procedure by showing that it is valid—that is, that the selection procedure measures what it is supposed to measure.

A validation process attempts to establish a tie or relationship between the selection instrument and the ability to perform the job. The guidelines allow for the use of three different kinds of validation methods—content, construct, or criterion (see Appendix A). The first two methods, however, require a job analysis in order to identify the critical or important work behaviors required for successful performance of the job. The third method simply requires a review of job information to determine measures of work behavior. Content validation is the method most commonly used by public employers.

The selection instrument developed from the analysis should contain a representative sample of the needed critical work behaviors and, to the extent possible, should be an actual sample of the job. For example, if a particular job requires incumbents to write reports and report writing is a *significant* component of the job, the test should require candidates to write an actual report; or if typing from copy is an important part of the job, a typing performance test should be a component of the selection procedure.

Certain landmark court cases have given these guidelines the force of law, have provided certain interpretations of Title VII of the Civil Rights Act of 1964 and the 1972 Equal Employment Opportunity Act, and have had a tremendous impact on personnel administration. One of the most important of these cases is *Griggs* v. *Duke Power Company,* which was decided by the U.S. Supreme Court in 1971.

Black employees of the Duke Power Company had brought a class action suit under Title VII alleging that the company's practice of requiring the possession of a high school diploma and attainment of a passing score on an intelligence test and an aptitude test as a condition of employment and promotion constituted discrimination. Prior to 1965 black employees had been confined to the company's lowest paying jobs in the labor department. In 1965 the company allowed blacks to transfer to other departments provided that they possessed high school diplomas and passed the two tests. The same requirements applied to new employees entering every department of the company except for the labor department. The Supreme Court ruled that plaintiffs did not have to show discriminatory intent on the part of the company but only that certain employment practices had a disproportionate impact on blacks. If adverse impact was shown, the company would than have to prove that the practices were a reasonable measure of job performance. The EEOC guidelines on test validation, in the view of the Court, expressed congressional intent in regard to Title VII. The Court found that neither the high school requirement nor the tests bore any demonstrated relationship to successful performance of the job for which they were used. The requirements were therefore overturned.

In another landmark case, *Albermarle Paper Co.* v. *Moody,* even greater deference was given to EEOC guidelines. In this case plaintiffs brought a class action suit under Title VII alleging that the company had discriminated through its departmental seniority system and pre-employment testing program. The Court found that the company failed to validate its tests in accordance with EEOC procedures that the Court regarded as the administrative interpretation of Title VII.

Failure to satisfy the requirements of law may result in legal challenges and delay the filling of jobs that must be filled if government is to function. Legal challenges, in turn, may lead to alternative solutions imposed by the courts, such as hiring quotas that many may find unpalatable. Although some people may quarrel with the complex and difficult technical demands of equal employment opportunity guidelines, few would object to the notion that tests should be valid and nondiscriminatory. In this connection equal employment opportunity requirements may have a salutary effect in improving the quality of selection procedures by forcefully bringing to the attention of employers the need to adhere to good testing practices.

Even if no problems existed in regard to discrimination, employers would still face the problems that are inherent in a large variety of testing methods and procedures currently in use. Public employers are not wedded to the concept of formal written examinations; they also use assessment centers, practical tests, and evaluations of education and experience. Each of these methods has its own problems. Apart from the testing techniques themselves, public employers must also grapple with procedures that have been mandated by merit system rules—such as the use of ranked civil service registers, the use of the "one-of-three rule," the weight of seniority, and the background investigation—which may tend to complicate further the task of bringing competent people into the system. Ultimately, the central issue for public and private employers alike is whether the selection system results in the selection of qualified people.

Because of the emerging criticality of the selection problem, this chapter has been given a relatively heavy emphasis. For the sake of logical organization, the cases in this chapter have been divided into two sections. The first section, entitled "Selection Methods and Procedures," deals with problems arising out of and associated with the use of a variety of methods and procedures. The second section, entitled "Equal Employment Opportunity Problems," centers around the impact of equal employment opportunity requirements on selection procedures.

Cases in Selection and Recruitment

Section A: Selection Methods and Procedures

The Assessment Center
The Education and Experience Test
The Police Captain's Test
The Typing Test
The One-of-Three Rule
Civil Service Registers That Failed to Qualify
The Background Investigation

The Assessment Center

The city of Cragston, a major midwestern metropolis, had always used written promotion tests to select its lieutenants (the first level of supervision in the Fire Department). However, the Fire Commissioner had become increasingly concerned about the quality of the individuals who had been appointed from these promotion lists and had doubts that the multiple-choice promotion examinations could really measure the abilities needed for the position. The Field Performance Evaluation Program, under which lieutenants' performances at the scenes of fires were evaluated by superior officers, had revealed that a large number of lieutenants had displayed serious deficiencies in deployment of personnel, placement of apparatus, response time, maintaining the safety of members, and general crisis leadership. All newly appointed lieutenants were required to complete an extensive training program, but the training appeared to have little effect upon their subsequent performance.

The Commissioner had heard that a number of organizations in the private sector and some in the public sector had successfully used assessment centers in evaluating supervisory, managerial, and leadership abilities and felt that this approach might result in the selection of more effective lieutenants than did the multiple-choice tests that were being used. He therefore contacted the Alpha Corporation, a prominent national consulting firm with considerable experience in setting up assessment centers for various organizations.

At a meeting with representatives of the Alpha Corporation, the Commissioner explained that the Department was considering the use of an assessment center as an alternative to the traditional multiple-choice test. However, the Department had a very limited budget, and since there would probably be a fairly large number of candidates involved, the assessment process could not last beyond one day.

The Alpha Corporation offered the Commissioner an assessment package that had been used successfully in a large number of companies and some public jurisdictions. The package included a total of four exercises that could be conducted in the course of one day. In addition to the exercises, the Alpha Corporation would provide one day of training to a limited number of superior officers who would act as assessors at the assessment center on a temporary basis. As a result of their observations of candidates during the four exercises, the assessors would rate each candidate on a scale from 1 to 7 on each of 10 general abilities, which included planning, oral communication, written communication, leadership, and decision making. The price tag on the package was $50,000.

The Commissioner accepted the proposal of the Alpha Corporation. After the center became operational, all lieutenant candidates would pass through for assessment. The resultant ratings would be used as the major factor in ranking the candidates. After the center had been in operation for about two months, the Commissioner decided to sit in as an observer of a group of lieutenant candidates. The assessors were fire officers above the rank of lieutenant who had been assigned to the center temporarily when the center began functioning.

In the morning session the candidates participated in a career interview and an "in-basket" exercise. Prior to the interview each candidate filled out a personal history form. The interview itself was supposed to permit the assessor to obtain personal information about the candidate and to observe the candidate's behavior in a one-to-one situation. The Commissioner noted that the assessors did not seem to be interested in the answers to some of the probing personal questions; they did little to put the candidates at ease. Many of their questions dealt with personal habits and ways of handling family problems.

In the "in-basket" exercise, participants were asked to play a supervisory role in a private business organization and, in that role, to make a number of decisions that would be generated by problems coming into the supervisor's "in" basket. Several of the candidates complained out loud that the issues seemed to have no relationship to the job of fire fighting; most failed to become involved in their roles. Some of the assessors made little attempt to draw out the candidates as to the reasons for their decisions or to challenge the decisions they made.

The afternoon exercises consisted of a management decision game and a selection simulation. Both of these were group exercises that called for interaction among participants while the assessors observed. The game dealt with the problems of a textile manufacturing company; the selection simulation concerned a promotion decision in a telephone company. Throughout the exercises the assessors displayed a certain amount of impatience and boredom. They seemed anxious to return to their permanent assignments. They also expressed reservations about evaluating participants on the ten general abilities rather than on how they would perform specific tasks on the job.

After all the candidates had been assessed, a number of the best performing ones were appointed as lieutenants. Subsequent field evaluations revealed no significant difference between their performance and that of lieutenants appointed as the result of the multiple-choice tests. The Commissioner was greatly disappointed with the results.

1. Was the poor field performance of lieutenants necessarily due to weaknesses in the selection procedure used?
2. Evaluate the process the Commissioner went through (a) in adopting the use of the assessment center for selection of lieutenants and (b) in deciding to employ the services of the Alpha Corporation.
3. What information should the Commissioner have obtained from the Alpha Corporation before accepting their proposal?
4. Was the assessment package offered by the Alpha Corporation and accepted by the Commissioner an appropriate one? Explain.
5. What weaknesses of the Cragston Fire Department Assessment Center were revealed in the case description?
6. What modifications in the assessment center approach would deal with these weaknesses?

The Education and Experience Test

The Finance Department in a western state had reached a desperate stage. There were more than forty vacancies for accountants, and the lack of staff was affecting the Department's ability to function. Several other state departments that employed accountants were in the same situation. Accountants were in such great demand in the area that state agencies found it difficult to fill their openings.

The Commissioner of Finance contacted Juan Garcia, the state's Director of Personnel, and asked what could be done to fill the vacancies. Garcia told him that an examination (typically with written and oral subtest components) could be held but that this would take some time. The Commissioner raised the possibility of using an unassembled evaluation or rating of a candidate's education and experience. He reasoned that persons who had college degrees and experience in the field of accounting could probably perform the job. He also emphasized that professional people like accountants, especially in a field in short supply, might be unwilling to take formal written and oral tests. Garcia agreed to try the unassembled test.

After the one-month period that applications were accepted for the position of accountant had ended, Garcia found that more than 90 percent of the applicants had recently arrived in the United States from several foreign countries where English was not the official language. Further investigation revealed that the recent immigrants were having difficulty finding accountant jobs in the private sector and so were flocking to state jobs. On the other hand, native-born accountants were accepting more attractive opportunities in private industry.

After the applicants' education and experience were evaluated, the Department of Personnel established a register (a list of eligibles) of accountants and referred more than seventy of them to eight state departments. The largest number of these were employed by the Department of Finance. About a month later, Garcia received a call from the Commissioner of Finance, and the following discussion took place:

Commissioner: Juan, those new accountants are not working out well. They appear to know accounting theory and practice, but they can't communicate with their fellow workers or with members of the public with whom they must deal because their command of English is poor. What do we do?

Garcia: Terminate them during the probationary period. That's why we have the probationary period.

Commissioner: We can't do that. They've already indicated they would file complaints of racial and ethnic discrimination if we attempted to dismiss them.

Garcia received similar calls from all the departments to which the accountants had been referred. He pondered what course of action, if any, to take.

1. What can the departments or Garcia do?
2. What can Garcia do to prevent similar types of problems in the future?
3. If the state continues to attract candidates who are unable to communicate effectively in English, what can the departments do?
4. If the Commissioner followed Garcia's advice and terminated the accountants with a poor command of English, and if those accountants filed complaints of discrimination, would the Department be able to justify the terminations? Explain.

The Police Captain's Test

As a result of some retirements, the Police Department of the city of Henderson found itself with several vacancies in the rank of captain. The Police Commissioner ordered Deputy Chief Locke, the head of the Police Department's Personnel Division, to proceed to develop a promotion test in cooperation with the city's central Department of Personnel.

Locke's first task was to conduct a job analysis. Subsequently, a decision would have to be made as to the type of test to be given. Since performance ratings and seniority would be part of the examination process, a decision would have to be made for the weights to give each of them. On the issue of seniority, the top officials of the Department had expressed a strong preference for a very substantial weight for seniority (as much as 50 percent of the total score, with the remaining 50 percent of the score divided between the test and the performance rating). They felt that to function effectively as captain (who typically commanded a precinct), candidates needed a very wide range of knowledge and abilities that could only be acquired by long experience on the job, especially as a lieutenant, the next lowest rank.

Shortly after the top officials had expressed their view on seniority, Locke was visited by a representative of the Police Lieutenant's Association, the organization that represented the lieutenants in collective bargaining, and the following discussion took place:

Union representative:	I understand that the Department is preparing a new captain's test.
Locke:	Yes, that's right. We plan to hold the test about six months from now.
Union representative:	Well, I stopped by to say that my people are very concerned about this one. It has been about seven years since the last test. and some of them have been in the lieutenant's grade for a very long time. The majority of them feel that seniority should count for a lot on this test. After all, it's the only fair and objective way of deciding who should be promoted. Some of my people may not be very good test takers, but they've been on the job a long time and they're damn good cops.
Locke:	I understand how you feel, but this test has to be job related. The job analysis should determine how much weight to give seniority. We've got to look at the knowledge and abilities needed for the job.
Union representative:	I don't care about any job analysis. Everyone knows that good cops are developed by experience.
Locke:	All I can say is we are going to do our best to come up with a good, fair examination.

Shortly after the visit by the union representative, Locke was also visited by an official of the Shield Society, an organization representing black lieutenants. The following discussion occurred:

Shield official:	We understand that there is going to be a new captain's test and that seniority is going to have a lot of weight.
Locke:	That hasn't been decided yet. The weight will depend on the job analysis.
Shield official:	I want you to know that we're against giving seniority much weight in this test. Since most of our people have relatively little seniority in comparison with white lieutenants, a test with a heavy weight for seniority would discriminate against our members. It would also discriminate against

women and younger lieutenants in general. If a person demonstrates his ability by scoring high on the written test and has a good performance rating, why should he have a low position on the promotion register just because he has low seniority? What does seniority mean in any case? It doesn't really demonstrate ability to perform the job.

Locke: We'll take your views into consideration. Thanks for coming in.

Two months after the discussions with both representatives, Locke received a copy of the completed job analysis, which had been prepared by specialists from the Police and Personnel Departments. It gave very little guidance as to the appropriate weight for seniority. He pondered the question for a long time.

1. Evaluate the arguments made by the union representative and by the Shield official.
2. Evaluate the approach taken by Locke in developing the test for captain.
3. How should Locke proceed to decide on a weight for seniority?
4. Is Locke likely to satisfy both the union representative and the Shield official? Explain.
5. What are the long-range implications of accepting the argument in favor of seniority?

The Typing Test

In the city of Glassport, typists in various city departments had long been recruited and selected on the basis of an evaluation of education and experience possessed by candidates. Most candidates had diplomas from secretarial schools, and some had typing experience from other jobs.

More recently, many city departments had been complaining that new typists were unable to do the typing work they were asked to do. Testing specialists in the Glassport central Department of Personnel agreed to develop a practical typing test in which candidates would have to demonstrate their actual typing skills.

The test technicians constructed directives, memoranda, and letters that were similar to the kinds of materials that typists might be asked to produce on the job. Each of the facsimile documents was neatly typed and reproduced for the candidates so that they would have no trouble in reading or interpreting the material. Fifty candidates, who appeared for the first such practical test, were seated at typewriters and asked to type an exact copy of each facsimile document within a specified period of time.

Candidates' products were scored for speed and accuracy. Penalties were assessed for various kinds of typing errors. A minimum number of words had to be typed without error; there was a maximum number of errors allowed. The twenty top-ranking candidates who passed the test were referred to various city agencies for jobs and all were hired.

A month later the Department of Personnel again received complaints from the agencies to which the new typists had been referred. The agencies claimed that the new group of typists were no better than typists recruited through an evaluation of education and experience. The new typists were having trouble copying from original documents that contained numerous handwritten changes and symbols. Because they were having difficulty in interpreting the changes and symbols, the typists were slow and inaccurate. The agencies did admit that the typists' work was satisfactory when it involved straight copying of typed materials; however, this kind of work was not a significant part of their duties.

1. Why did the approach of the Department of Personnel fail to deal with the agencies' complaints?
2. What can the Department of Personnel do to respond to agency complaints?
3. What, if anything, can the agencies do to help solve the problem? Explain.
4. Is an evaluation of education and experience an appropriate selection method to use to hire typists? Explain.
5. For what kinds of jobs and/or hiring situations would it be appropriate to use the technique of evaluating education and experience?

6. What are the advantages and disadvantages of using evaluation of education and experience as the selection method?

The One-of-Three Rule

The Commissioner of the Department of Public Works of a large eastern state phoned his Personnel Officer, Martin Cohen, and the following conversation took place:

Commissioner: I've just met with an engineer named Martha Stone who seems to have the right background for that job vacancy we have to fill in the Division of Design. I believe she is number 6 on the Civil Engineer's list of eligibles. See if you can arrange for a certification from the Civil Service Commission right away. Get Stone on board as quickly as you can.

Cohen: We may have a problem, Commissioner. You know that there's a one-of-three rule in effect on Civil Service appointments in the state. If the first three candidates don't decline the job, we won't be able to reach Stone for appointment.

Commissioner: Then find out if the first three candidates will decline.

Cohen: I'll get to work on this right away.

Cohen canvassed the top three persons on the list by letter asking them if they would be interested in a Civil Engineer job with the Department. All three answered that they might be interested. Cohen reported the results of his inquiry to the Commissioner and informed him that since all three had not declined, Stone could not be reached for appointment.

Obviously irritated, the Commissioner responded that he didn't know all the intricacies of civil service law, but rather that it was Cohen's job to provide the solutions to personnel problems. He concluded by saying to Cohen, "All I know is that Stone has the perfect background for that big construction project that is just getting underway. I want you to do whatever is necessary to get her on staff."

Cohen answered, "I'll do the best I can."

1. What can Cohen or the Department do?
2. What can be done to prevent similar problems in the future?
3. What are the arguments for and against the one-of-three rule in making Civil Service appointments?
4. What are some alternatives to the one-of-three rule?
5. Are Civil Service unions likely to favor or oppose the one-of-three rule? Explain.

Civil Service Registers That Failed to Qualify

Harold Ferro, the Commissioner of Banking of a northern state, was visited one day in his office by Cynthia Rhodes, the Supervisor of the Audit Division. The following conversation took place:

Rhodes: Those new accountants we recently appointed from the list of eligibles established by the Civil Service Commission are next to useless. They just don't understand our bookkeeping and accounting procedures. Most of these people had all of their experience in the private sector.

Ferro: I know! We had the same problem with the financial analyst's register last year and with the clerk's list the year before. I am sick and tired of having the Civil Service Commission send us people who aren't trained to do the job. We would be better off selecting people off the street. I'll see if I can do something about this.

Ferro asked his secretary to get the Chairman of the Civil Service Commission on the telephone. The Chairman, Peter Brewer, came on the line and said, "Harold, what can I do for you?" The conversation continued:

Ferro: Those new accountants we recently hired aren't working out. You know, we've had the same problem with other registers. Can't you do something about sending us people who are able to do the job? There must be something wrong with your testing procedures.

Brewer: There's nothing wrong with our selection procedures. All of our tests are based on careful analysis of the jobs to be filled. In the case of titles like accountant, which are found in several agencies, we try to ensure that the examination reflects the job as it is performed in all of the agencies, not just in yours. I realize that this usually means that the examination is pretty general and that not all of the people on the list will meet the particular needs of your agency. So, you'll just have to make the best of it.

Ferro: *Something* has to be done!

1. What can Ferro do? How should he go about doing it?
2. What can the Civil Service Commission do?
3. Is the problem facing Ferro and Rhodes likely to be encountered in other state departments? Explain.
4. What is likely to be the effect on the Civil Service Commission's testing procedures if the duties of the accountant's job were increased to include responsibility for supervising a staff of bookkeepers and clerks? Explain.
5. Is the job analysis procedure used to develop the examination appropriate? Explain.

The Background Investigation

After passing a civil service examination, John Kempton was hired as an account clerk by the Unemployment Insurance Department of a southeastern state. Upon completing the required one-year probationary period, he was given permanent status. Six months later he was given a merit salary increase in recognition of his outstanding performance; Kempton had identified and corrected some serious bookkeeping errors, thereby saving the state thousands of dollars.

When he had completed two years of service, Kempton was called in by the state's central Department of Personnel for the routine verification of qualifications, which was required of all civil service appointees. Kempton arrived at the Department, and the investigator assigned to the case began by saying, "Mr. Kempton, we've been able to verify the experience you claimed on your application form. All we need is a copy of your high school diploma, and we can close your case." The conversation continued:

Kempton:	That's impossible. I can't give you a copy.
Investigator:	I don't understand.
Kempton:	I graduated from a high school in a small town in Ohio. That school burned down more than ten years ago and all of the records were destroyed. I lost my own copy of the diploma when I moved from Ohio. There is no way that I can produce a copy at this time.
Investigator:	Isn't there any way that you can produce proof of your graduation?
Kempton:	No way; you'll just have to accept my word for it.
Investigator:	Department rules and regulations don't allow us to accept your word for it. We have to see documentary proof. Since you can't prove that you graduated, I have no choice but to notify my superiors, who will probably tell your Department that you will have to be terminated.
Kempton:	That is grossly unfair, and I don't intend to take it lying down.

Kempton sued the state, alleging that in terminating him, the state was guilty of arbitrary and capricious action and of denying him his rights of due process. The arguments brought out in his petition read in part:

> The petitioner's inability to submit documentary evidence of his high school graduation is not in dispute. (A statement from the city of Lindstrom, Ohio, corroborating the destruction of such records is attached.) The key issue is that it took the Department of Personnel two years to get around to carrying out a background investigation of the petitioner. During this period the petitioner achieved permanent status by suc-

cessfully completing the required one-year probationary period. The petitioner's service was more than satisfactory, and he received three commendations (copies attached) and a merit salary increase in recognition of outstanding performance. The petitioner's qualifications are not relevant at this point. What is relevant is that petitioner passed a civil service test for his position, he passed a probationary period, and his work has been more than satisfactory since then. What further evidence is required to demonstrate his qualifications?

1. Evaluate Kempton's (petitioner's) arguments.
2. What should the Department of Personnel say in its defense?
3. Is Kempton likely to win the case? Explain.
4. Aside from being subjected to lawsuits such as the one in this case, what other kinds of problems could the Department of Personnel's procedures lead to?
5. Evaluate the Department of Personnel's procedures and rules.
6. In what way can delayed investigations cast doubt on the validity of the selection procedure?

Section B: Equal Employment Opportunity Problems

The Recruitment Campaign
The Age Discrimination Case
The Height Requirement
The Professional Careers Program
The Physical Test

The Recruitment Campaign

In the city of Lakeview, a minority group that accounted for 40 percent of this city's population held only 5 percent of the jobs in the Fire Department. This underrepresentation had several adverse consequences. First, it made it very difficult for the Department to "sell" its Fire Prevention Education Program to the minority community. The Department had virtually no relationships with minority community organizations, and the number of fire code violations in these areas was increasing. Fire Department personnel were generally greeted with suspicion by community residents. In addition, the state's Human Rights Commission as well as the U.S. Equal Employment Opportunity Commission had received several complaints alleging employment discrimination by Lakeview's Fire Department.

The Fire Commissioner was aware that an examination for fire fighter was planned for the near future, and he wanted to be sure that members of the minority group were well represented among the applicants. Although the Fire Department would have normally handled this kind of recruitment campaign itself, the Commissioner was especially sensitive in this case to possible charges of discrimination against the Fire Department. He therefore decided to turn the entire campaign over to the city's central Personnel Department, which had responsibility for preparing and conducting the examination as well. The Fire Department would not participate in any aspect of the campaign or examination. The Commissioner stressed to the Personnel Director that it was essential for the examination to be well publicized. He also emphasized the need for a thorough and intensive job analysis as the basis for the examination. The minimum qualification requirements, as well as the examination itself, had to be clearly related to and justified by the needs of the job. He did not want any element of the selection procedure to discriminate unfairly.

Since the city administration was concerned about the job discrimination charges, the sum of $50,000 was authorized for recruitment. Advertisements announcing the examination were placed in the city's major newspapers on a regular basis for one month prior to and during the application period. Several radio and television announcements were also used. The Personnel Department distributed leaflets to the city's high schools and colleges.

After the examination was conducted, the following results were tabulated:

1. Of a total of 5000 applicants, 500 were minority group members.
2. Of the 2000 candidates who received passing scores, 100 were minority group members.
3. Of the 200 top-scoring candidates (those who were most likely to be appointed fire fighters), 5 were minority group members.

1. Evaluate the foregoing results in terms of (a) the success of the recruitment campaign, (b) the impact of the examination on minority candidates, and (c) the quality of the minority candidates who applied for the test.
2. What might have led to these results?
3. Should the Fire Department have participated in the recruitment campaign and/or preparation of the examination? Explain.
4. What might have been done to bring about different results?
5. What is likely to happen now?

The Age Discrimination Case

The Department of Personnel of the city of Hamilton announced that it would receive applications for the title of Computer Systems Analyst Trainee. The Department had attempted to hire experienced systems analysts in the past but had been unsuccessful in competing with the private sector. A decision was therefore made to recruit recent college graduates with appropriate majors and train them on the job. Candidates were required to have a bachelor's degree with a concentration in Computer Sciences, Management Sciences, or Mathematics. The degree had to have been obtained within the preceding three years. There were no experience requirements.

Dorothy Reilly, who was forty-five years old and who had been looking for a systems analyst job, was surprised to find that she was not eligible for the job. She had received her degree fifteen years previously and been away from the job market for some time. The recency of degree requirement, in her view, would tend to discriminate against older people and was not really related to the needs of the job. She therefore decided to submit a discrimination complaint to the city's Human Rights Division, which was responsible for handling complaints under the city's ordinance barring age discrimination in employment.

The Division summoned Reilly and Richard Chang, an official of the city's Personnel Department, to appear before the Division for an informal hearing on the complaint. The Division's hearing officer asked Reilly to begin.

Reilly: I fail to see how the issue of when I received my degree is related to ability to perform the job. In college, my major was mathematics; I also took a couple of courses in operations research. After I received my degree, I went to work as a mathematician with a computer firm; after working with the company for two years, I left to raise a family. Now that my children are older, I feel ready to go back to work. Why should I be penalized because I raised a family? I feel physically fit and mentally alert. I refuse to accept the idea that a twenty-one-year-old who graduated from college last June is necessarily more capable than I am.

Chang: We have very good reasons for insisting upon candidates who obtained their degrees within the last three years. First, computer sciences and the other fields are rapidly changing. The training that Mrs. Reilly received more than fifteen years ago is almost entirely obsolete. Computer technology has been revolutionized within the past fifteen years. We want people who are reasonably up-to-date. We also have to remember that this is a training position. We're going to make an investment in these trainees, and we want people who will stay with the city long enough to give us a return on our investment. Frankly, older people won't be able to offer us the same number of years as young people will.

Reilly: I want to address myself to Mr. Chang's so-called reasons. Although I received my degree fifteen years ago, I kept up with the field by reading journals and other publications. I'm at least as up-to-date as recent college graduates are. Besides, does anyone really have to be up-to-date? This job is an entry-level training position. People who possess a basic competence will be given all the skills they need while they are on the job. As to the issue of "a return on the city's investment," statistics show that young people have a far higher turnover rate than older people. The average person stays with his or her first job for less than two years. If I enter the city service now, it is likely that I will continue to work until age sixty-five. Assuming that I stay with the city (and frankly, at my age, I don't want to start job hopping), the city will get twenty productive years out of me. Can the city expect this kind of return on its investment from recent college graduates? I think not.

1. Evaluate the arguments presented by Reilly and Chang.
2. If you were the hearing officer, what ruling would you make? Explain.
3. What steps could the Department of Personnel take to justify this type of recruiting decision in the future?
4. Assume the hearing officer rules in favor of Reilly and that the ruling is final. What should the Department of Personnel do?
5. What additional points could have been presented either by Reilly or by Chang?

The Height Requirement

The city of Santa Elena, a major urban center in the Southwest, announced that it was accepting applications for its upcoming police officer's examination. The minimum requirements in the official announcement specified that all candidates had to be at least 5 feet 6 inches tall.

Jose Diaz, a Mexican-American, had expected to apply for this examination, but he was only 5 feet 5 inches tall. After reading the official examination announcement,

Diaz went before the U.S. District Court in an attempt to remove the height requirement. His arguments included the following:

> The city of Santa Elena has engaged in a discriminatory practice in violation of Title VII of the Civil Rights Act of 1964 by imposing a qualification requirement that is not related to the job of police officer. The following pattern of discrimination can be identified:
>
> 1. The height requirement most adversely affects Hispanic individuals who have a lower average stature than the population at large.
> 2. The selection by the city of Santa Elena of a minimum height of 5 feet 6 inches is an arbitrary decision, not a bona fide job requirement.
> 3. Meeting the minimum height requirement reveals nothing about the candidate's ability to do the job.
> 4. The physical test can be used to test for physical attributes such as strength and agility.
>
> I therefore ask that the height requirement be eliminated and that I be allowed to take the police officer examination.

In asking that Diaz's complaint be dismissed, the response of the city of Santa Elena included the following points:

> Although the height requirement cannot be shown directly to be necessary to do the job of police officer, high-ranking officials in the Police Department feel that a minimum height is critical to successful performance in the police officer's job. We have studies indicating that shorter police officers are twice as likely as taller officers to become involved in violent incidents or to use their firearms.

1. Evaluate the arguments made by Diaz and the city of Santa Elena.

2. How could the city go about demonstrating the need for a height requirement? What kind of evidence could be presented?

3. Could Diaz's arguments be made for female applicants to the Santa Elena police force? Explain.

The Professional Careers Program

Elmington County decided to hold a single examination to fill a variety of entry-level professional positions in various county agencies. The county hoped to attract recent college graduates without experience but with high potential. Because minority group members were greatly underrepresented in Elmington's professional and managerial ranks, a special effort was to be made by the central personnel agency to recruit minority group members.

Usually, candidates were required to pass a written test to demonstrate their qualifications. Since, in the past, minority group members had not done as well as majority candidates on written tests, the Department of Personnel decided to offer an alternative to candidates who did not wish to take the written test. They would be permitted to present their college grade point average for evaluation in lieu of the written test. In addition, academic honors, awards, and extracurricular activities would be given substantial weight in the final examination scores of all candidates. It was reasoned that by de-emphasizing the written test and allowing consideration of academic performance, those minority group candidates who had done relatively well academically would rank high on the list of eligibles.

To increase the pool of minority group applicants, recruiters were sent to several of the black colleges in the South. College seniors were interviewed and encouraged to apply. Those students who wished to submit their academic credentials in lieu of the written test were told that they could apply by mail. The recruiters gave special attention to students who were in the top 10 percent of their class.

When the application period ended, the Elmington Department of Personnel had received about 1,000 applications. From ethnic information provided voluntarily by the applicants, the Department learned that 400 of the 1000 applications came from minority group candidates. Department executives were optimistic that minorities would be well represented among successful candidates.

When the final register of successful applicants was established, it was found that some 500 candidates passed. Of these, 150 were minority group members. However, of the top 100 eligibles on the register, only 5 were members of minority groups. This result dismayed the management of the Department since a register of only 100 persons was deemed sufficient to fill county needs for professional jobs in the foreseeable future.

1. Evaluate the Department's alternative to the written test.
2. Evaluate the Department's recruitment effort in the South.
3. What other recruitment measures could the Department have attempted?
4. Should the Department have waited until the application period was over before tabulating results? Explain.
5. What might the county do in the future to provide greater representation of minority group members at the top of the register?

The Physical Test

The Civil Service Department of a populous eastern state decided to conduct a civil service test for audiovisual aide technicians in the training divisions of various state departments. Although many of the positions in this title were filled, some of the incumbents did not hold their jobs on a permanent civil service basis but rather had only temporary appointments. The projected examination would provide the temporary incumbents with the opportunity to acquire permanent status by passing the test and would supply additional people to fill vacancies.

As a preliminary to the actual preparation of the examination, a job analysis was conducted. The analysis revealed that, among other required abilities, technicians had to be able to lift and carry different types of audiovisual equipment weighing up to fifty pounds. The Civil Service Department, therefore, decided to have a qualifying physical test in which candidates would have to lift and carry (for a specified distance) a fifty-pound object equivalent in size to the equipment.

Many women candidates, some of whom had scored extremely well on the written test, which was also part of the examination, failed the qualifying physical test. Several of them went to court seeking to invalidate the physical test. They claimed that the physical test discriminated unfairly against women. They made the following arguments:

1. Many of the female candidates who failed the physical test had already been performing the job successfully on a temporary basis. The physical test, therefore, was not related to the actual requirements of the job.

2. Audiovisual aide technicians did not really have to lift and carry equipment by themselves; it was almost always possible for them to get the help of other staff in carrying it from location to location.

In opposition to these arguments, the Civil Service Department stated that the physical test did not unfairly discriminate against women because it was "strictly related to the requirements of the job." The Department's statement read in part:

> It has always been the responsibility of the audiovisual aide technician to bring all necessary equipment to the location where training was being conducted. We acknowledge that it has sometimes been the practice for female technicians to ask male technicians to assist them or to carry the equipment for them. This is not a desirable situation because it unfairly adds to the burdens of the male technicians who receive no additional compensation for such extra services. Further, there is no assurance that such assistance will always be available; if it is not, the job will not be done.

1. Evaluate the arguments of the litigants and of the Department.
2. Evaluate the procedure followed by the Department in deciding to have a physical test.
3. What do you think was the decision of the court? What should it be in your opinion? Why?
4. Suppose the court ruled against the Department and invalidated the physical test. What should the Department do when hiring audiovisual aide technicians in the future?
5. For what other types of jobs are similiar arguments likely to be made?
6. Assume that the agency was aware of the practice of male technicians helping female technicians lift equipment and made no attempt to prevent it. Would this informal practice have affected the decision of the court?

Suggested Readings for Chapter 1

Adler, Seymour. "Using Assessment Centers in Smaller Organizations." *Personnel Journal* 57, no. 9 (September 1978):484–87.

Allen, Lawrence. "Test Transportability and the Uniform Guidelines." *Public Personnel Management* 8, no. 5 (September–October 1979):309–13.

American Psychological Association. *Standards for Educational and Psychological Tests.* Washington, D.C., 1974.

Anastasi, Anne. *Psychological Testing.* 4th ed. New York: Macmillan, 1976.

Bemis, Stephen E. "Systems for Measuring and Assessing Adverse Impact." *Public Personnel Management* 7, no. 6 (November–December 1978):354–57.

Biddle, Richard E. *Discrimination: What Does It Mean?* Chicago: International Personnel Management Association, 1973.

Boyles, Wiley, R. "Court-Ordered Affirmative Action." *Public Personnel Management* 7, no. 6 (November–December 1978):394–98.

Byham, William C., and D.W. Bray. *Administering an Assessment Center.* Pittsburgh, Pa.: Development Dimensions Press, 1973.

———, **and Carl Wettengel.** "Assessment Centers for Supervisors and Managers, an Introduction and Overview." *Public Personnel Management* 3, no. 5 (September–October 1974):352–64.

Campion, James E. "Work Sampling for Personnel Selection." *Journal of Applied Psychology* 56, no. 1 (February 1972):40–44.

Cronbach, Lee J. *Essentials of Psychological Testing,* 3rd ed. New York: Harper & Row, 1970.

Division of Industrial and Organizational Psychology, American Psychological Association. *Principles for the Validation and Use of Personnel Selection Procedures.* Dayton, Ohio: The Industrial–Organizational Psychologist, 1975.

Donovan, Jerome, ed. *Recruitment and Selection in the Public Service.* Chicago: International Personnel Management Association, 1968.

Dunnette, Marvin E. *Personnel Selection and Placement.* Belmont, Calif.: Brooks–Cole Publishing, 1966.

Educational Testing Service. *An Investigation of Sources of Bias in the Prediction of Job Performance, A Six-Year Study: Proceedings of International Conference.* Princeton, N.J.: 1972.

Equal Employment Opportunity Commission, et al. "Uniform Guidelines on Employee Selection Procedures (1978)." *Federal Register* 43, no. 166 (August 25, 1978):38291–309.

_____. "Adoption of Questions and Answers." *Federal Register* 44, no. 43 (March 2, 1979):11996–12009.

Gatewood, Robert D., and Lyle F. Schoenfeldt. "Content Validity and EEOC: A Useful Alternative for Selection." *Personnel Journal* 56, no. 10 (October 1977):520–25.

Great Lakes Assessment Council. *Legal Aspects of Personnel Selection in the Public Service.* Chicago: International Personnel Management Association, 1973.

Grosman, Harry. "The Equal Employment Opportunity Act of 1972, Its Implications for the State and Local Government Manager." *Public Personnel Management* 2, no. 5 (September–October 1973):370–79.

Holt, Thaddeus. "Personnel Selection and the Supreme Court." In W.C. Hamner and F.L. Schmidt, *Contemporary Problems in Personnel.* Chicago: St. Clair Press, 1977.

Horstman, Dee Ann S. "New Judicial Standards for Adverse Impact: Their Meaning for Personnel Practices." *Public Personnel Management* 7, no. 6 (November–December 1978):347–51.

Howard, Ann. "An Assessment of Assessment Centers." *Academy of Management Journal* 17, no. 1 (March 1974):115–34.

Klimoski, Richard J., and William J. Strickland. "Assessment Centers—Valid or Merely Prescient." *Personnel Psychology* 30 (Autumn 1977):353–61.

Ledvinka, James, and Lyle F. Schoenfeldt. "Legal Developments In Employment Testing: Albemarle and Beyond." *Personnel Psychology* 31, no. 1 (Spring 1978):1–13.

Levine, Marvin J. "An EEO Overview for Personnel Managers." *Training and Development Journal* 33, no. 1 (January 1979):60–63.

Miner, John B. "The Selection Interview." In W.C. Hamner and Frank L. Schmidt, *Contemporary Problems in Personnel.* Chicago: St. Clair Press, 1977.

Nigro, Lloyd G., ed. "Affirmative Action in Public Employment." *Public Administration Review* 34, no. 3 (May–June 1974):234–46.

Norton, Steven D. "The Empirical and Content Validity of Assessment Centers vs. Traditional Methods for Predicting Managerial Success." *Academy of Management Review* 2, no. 3 (July 1977):442–53.

Robertson, David E. "New Directions in EEO Guidelines." *Personnel Journal* 57, no. 7 (July 1978):360–63.

Rynecki, Steven B. "Age Discrimination: An Update of Recent Amendments." *Public Employee Relations Counselor* (International Personnel Management Association) 1, no. 1 (October 1978):19–26.

_____. "Bakke: What's the Outlook for Affirmative Action?" *Public Employee Relations Counselor* 1, no. 1 (October 1978):1–18.

Schmidt, Frank L., et al. "Job Sample vs. Paper-and-Pencil Trades and Technical Tests: Adverse Impact and Examinee Attitudes." *Personnel Psychology* 30, no. 2 (Summer, 1977):187–97.

Shaeffer, Ruth G. *Nondiscrimination in Employment: Changing Perspectives, 1963–1972.* New York: The Conference Board, 1973.

_____. *Nondiscrimination in Employment, 1973–1975.* New York: The Conference Board, 1975.

_____. *Staffing Systems: Managerial and Professional Jobs.* New York: The Conference Board, 1972.

Sherman, Mitchell. "Equal Employment Opportunity: Legal Issues and Societal Consequences." *Public Personnel Management* 7, no. 2 (March–April 1978):127–33.

Tallent, Stephen E. "A Legal Perspective on the Bakke Decision." *Personnel Journal* 58, no. 5 (May 1979):296–302.

Taylor, Vernon R. *Essentials of Effective Personnel Selection.* Chicago: International Personnel Management Association, 1972.

_____. *Test Validity in Public Personnel Selection—Public Employment Practices Bulletin No. 2.* Chicago: International Personnel Management Association, 1971.

U.S. Civil Service Commission. *Job Analysis for Improved Job-Related Selection, A Guide for State and Local Governments.* Washington, D.C.: 1975.

Wanous, John P. "A Job Preview Makes Recruiting More Effective." *Harvard Business Review* 53, no. 5 (September–October 1975):16, 166–68.

Wisner, Roscoe W. "The Kirkland Case—Its Implications for Personnel Selection." *Public Personnel Management* 4, no. 4 (July–August 1975):263–67.

Wollock, Stephen. "Content Validity: Its Legal and Psychometric Basis." *Public Personnel Management* 5, no. 6 (November–December 1976):397–408.

Wright, Grace H., ed. *Public Sector Employment Selection: A Manual for the Personnel Generalist.* Chicago: International Personnel Management Association, 1974.

Zashin, Elliot M. "Affirmative Action, Preferential Selection and Federal Employment." *Public Personnel Management* 7, no. 6 (November–December 1978):378–93.

2 Assignment and Placement

Assignment and placement are a logical outgrowth of the selection process. In the public sector people are often selected for a job title or class of positions rather than a specific vacancy or position. Appointees must therefore be placed in a particular position and be given appropriate, specific assignments. It may also be necessary to reassign employees as a result of changes in the organization and its mission or as a result of changes in their abilities, attitudes, or performance. Effective assignment and placement require rational, systematic procedures for assessing organizational staffing needs and for matching jobs with employees' capabilities. The ultimate objective of such procedures should be to meet the organization's staffing needs in the most efficient manner while assuring full utilization of each employee's talents.

The quality of an organization's system for assignment and placement of employees has serious implications for both the organization and the employee. On the one hand, the extent to which assignment procedures provide qualified people to meet the demands of organizational roles has a significant impact on overall organizational effectiveness. On the other hand, the extent to which the roles themselves provide people with appropriately challenging and satisfying work and career development opportunities has an important effect on employee motivation and performance.

Positions to be filled by new employees without prior specific training must be carefully designed. For example, initial assignments should be structured so that new employees have opportunities to develop needed skills and are absorbed into the organization without disrupting it. However, an effective assignment system requires more than proper design of jobs and determination of the skills needed to fill them. Organizations must also be able to assess the strengths and capacities possessed by individual employees. This assessment includes recognition of individual needs and personal idiosyncracies that may be more important than the degree of skills possessed. Many organizational problems such as poor performance, lack of discipline, and lack of motivation can be traced to a mismatch of the person and the job.

Systematic and rational assignment procedures usually include a method for determining knowledge, skills, abilities, and other characteristics needed to perform the duties of particular positions. This type of "position analysis" differs somewhat from job analysis, where the focus is on common characteristics or similarities found among a number of positions in a class. Even though all positions in a class may be similar in some respects, there may also be significant differences that call for special care in matching people to positions.

Once the requirements of each position have been determined, rational assignment and placement systems must also provide a method for determining the qualifications possessed by employees. The degree of "fit" between the person and the position is determined not only by knowledge, skills, and abilities possessed by a person, but also by personality characteristics and idiosyncrasies that affect the person's adjustment to the organizational environment.

There are several potential sources of information about qualifications possessed by employees. One of these sources is the application form or personal history questionnaire completed by the employee at the time of hiring. Information about past training and experience can be translated into skills, knowledge, and abilities. Another source of information is past performance appraisals, which can be excellent indicators of an employee's strengths and deficiencies. However, care must be taken in using performance appraisals from past employers because the appraisals may be invalid. Appraisals may suffer from rater subjectivity or failure to focus on the truly critical elements of the job.

Some organizations have used assessment centers to identify employees' capabilities for purposes of assignment and placement. Under the assessment-center concept, employees participate in a number of exercises that simulate on-the-job situations. A number of trained assessors observe employees' behavior throughout the exercises and arrive at judgments concerning each employee's capabilities.

Although the probationary period is a continuation or extension of the initial selection procedures, it is also extremely valuable for purposes of assignment and placement. The probationary period represents an opportunity to see how well someone fits into various organizational roles. During this learning period the new employees can be rotated through a number of different assignments, and the extent to which they adjust to these new roles can be observed at first hand. Supervisors have the opportunity not only to evaluate the extent to which employees possess required knowledge, skills, and abilities but also to observe the interplay and impact of personality factors that affect performance on the job.

Assignment systems often include provisions for career development. A planned sequence of assignments is structured to enable employees to develop the knowledge, skills, and abilities required for performance in progressively higher positions. Each assignment provides employees with experiences that help them perform at higher levels. Plans for individual employees, however, may vary because of differences in previous experience and in personal goals. The successful use of assignments for purposes of career development assumes that the organization has adequate information about qualifications required for a variety of positions as well as qualifications possessed by employees.

In order to accomplish the proper matching of people with positions, some organizations have developed employee rosters or skills-inventory systems. Many of these systems are computer based and provide for coding of information about employee skills and capabilities in a format that facilitates matching people with position requirements. Unfortunately, in establishing, maintaining, and utilizing these systems, organizations have experienced problems in:

> Identifying the kind of information about employee skills that should be included;
>
> Selecting a method for entering employee information into the system;
>
> Assuring the reliability of information in the system;
>
> Keeping information in the system up-to-date;
>
> Retrieving information quickly;
>
> Justifying the heavy investment in this type of system on the basis of the results actually produced.

Because of these problems and others, some employers have abandoned skills-inventory systems after a trial period.

The filling of organizational slots does not complete the assignment and placement process. Once an employee has been assigned to a position within an organization unit, the unit's supervisor may have considerable latitude in assigning specific tasks, in distributing the unit's workload, and in specifying the conditions under which the work is to be accomplished. In assigning work, the supervisor must consider unit needs and individual strengths and needs, as well as equity to employees. But it is not enough for a supervisor to be equitable; employees themselves must perceive that the work is fairly distributed if the supervisor wants to avoid employee resentment and dissatisfaction.

As in other types of personnel decisions, the employer must take care not to discriminate unfairly against employees when placing or assigning them. Not only is it against public policy to discriminate on the basis of race, sex, or other irrelevant criteria, but it is also against the employer's best interest to discriminate unfairly. Discriminatory practices may also have the effect of limiting the choices that an employer has in making decisions and thereby may result in less than optimal utilization of the organization's human resources.

Cases in Assignment and Placement

Sex Discrimination on the Night Shift
The Management Trainee Program
The Misfit
The Achiever
The Skills-Inventory System

Sex Discrimination on the Night Shift

The Police Department of the city of Driftwood employed a number of clerks to carry out a variety of clerical functions in virtually all divisions and bureaus of the Department. There was approximately the same number of female clerks and male clerks. It was the practice in the Police Department to assign only male clerks to the night shift. Men with the least seniority were assigned to work nights.

For a long time the practice of assigning only men to the night shift had been accepted without opposition. Jack Dunn, one of the men assigned to the night shift, asked to be transferred to the day shift. His wife had recently started working during the day, and because of their different shifts, they were seldom home at the same time. The Department's Personnel Officer told Dunn that such a shift change would not be possible because Dunn had less seniority than any of the men working the day shift. Dunn responded that several of the women on the day shift had less seniority than he had. The Personnel Officer explained that it was not the Department's practice to assign women to the night shift even though they might have less seniority than the men.

Dunn was determined to challenge this practice. With the support of several other male clerks assigned to the night shift and with some legal assistance, he submitted the following complaint to the city's Human Rights Commission, which was responsible for enforcing the city's ordinance prohibiting discrimination on the basis of sex, age, and race:

The Police Department has engaged in discriminatory employment practices based on sex in violation of Driftwood's Civil Rights Ordinance. This complaint is supported by the following facts:

1. *The Police Department has two shifts for clerks—a day shift and a night shift. The day shift is considered to be the more desirable assignment, especially since the areas in which the clerks must work are deserted and dangerous at night.*

2. There are no women assigned to the night shift. All women are assigned to the day shift regardless of their seniority. The remaining day-shift positions are filled by men on the basis of seniority. Those men with the highest seniority are assigned to the day shift. The Department therefore operates dual assignment systems—one for men and another for women.

3. Although the night shift is more hazardous and more disruptive of family life, no additional compensation is paid to those men assigned to the night shift. In addition, even though only male clerks are subject to night assignments, male and female clerks are paid at the same rate.

4. Whenever male clerks assigned to the night shift have asked for reassignment to the day shift, the Department has responded that this could only be accomplished by displacing women on the day shift and that it was not the Department's policy to assign women to the night shift.

The Department responded to Dunn's complaint with the following statement to the Human Rights Commission:

The Department denies that its practice constitutes discrimination. The complainant has conceded that the areas in which clerks are required to work are dangerous. Statistics show that a woman is much more likely to be assaulted or mugged. Male employees simply do not face a similar level of risk. In this regard departmental practice is quite similar to practices followed by other organizations of the same type throughout the country.

The Department also denies the complainant's contention that being subject to night *assignment fundamentally alters the nature of the male clerk's job and entitles the clerks on the night shift to additional compensation. The duties, responsibilities, and job expectations of clerks are exactly the same whether they are assigned to the day shift or the night shift.*

We therefore ask the Commission to dismiss the petitioner's complaint.

1. Evaluate the Department's system for assigning men and women to the two shifts.
2. Evaluate the arguments of Jack Dunn and of the Department.
3. What do you think would be the female clerks' views of the matter?
4. What is likely to be the ruling of the Human Rights Commission?
5. What would be a fair ruling to make in this case?
6. Is a complaint dealing with shift or work assignments covered by the federal government's 1978 *Uniform Guidelines on Employee Selection Procedures?* Explain.

The Management Trainee Program

In order to upgrade the quality of its professional and managerial staff, the Department of Civil Service of a large midwestern state decided to recruit outstanding recent college graduates under a new Management Trainee Program. This program called for advancement of trainees to a higher salary at the end of a six-month traineeship period. The higher salary was considerably above the salary normally paid to entry-level professional and managerial employees after six months of service and above the salary of some employees with several years of experience.

Five of the new management trainees were assigned to various units in the Bureau of Recruitment and Examining. Anne Tierney, Chief of the Bureau, asked the experienced employees in the Bureau to give the trainees guidance and assistance to help them with their new jobs. Tierney also assigned a special project to each of the trainees. They were to gather information and statistics and report personally to Tierney at the end of two weeks.

After two weeks had passed, each of the trainees reported that they had not been successful in obtaining the information required for their projects. They complained that the experienced people had given them no assistance. Tierney, upset that the experienced staff was not doing what she had asked, called a meeting of the Bureau's experienced staff. She began by saying, "The new people depend on you veterans to learn the job. I thought I made it clear that I wanted you to help them with their new assignments. What happened?"

Sharon Jones, one of the most outstanding employees in the Bureau, responded, "Why should we help them learn the job? They receive special benefits under the Management Trainee Program; in six months they will be earning more than we are; and we have been working here for two years. It's just not fair! All of us have the same qualifications as the trainees, only we've been here much longer."

Tierney replied, "I understand how you feel. These newcomers were given the opportunity to take a special examination. Most of you weren't eligible because you received your degrees too many years ago; but I promise you that everyone will have promotion opportunities."

During the next few months, the trainees were given regular assignments in assisting to conduct recruitment campaigns and to prepare tests. The experienced staff continued to ignore them or to provide only limited amounts of information and assistance. Consequently, the trainees had to ask their unit supervisors, as well as Tierney, to obtain even the most basic information needed to carry out their jobs. Tierney pondered what action to take in order to resolve this problem.

1. Were the reactions of the experienced employees predictable? Explain.
2. Evaluate Tierney's handling of the situation.
3. If this program is continued, what is likely to be the effect on the Bureau of Recruitment and Examining?
4. What should Tierney do now?
5. Assuming the Management Trainee Program is continued, what might be done to prevent a recurrence of this situation?

The Misfit

Steven Roth was hired by the Department of Social Services of a large western city from a personnel technician list of eligible candidates. The Department found him to be slow in processing the necessary forms and in taking care of the many administrative details involved in hiring applicants for the Department. Various unit supervisors who came in contact with Roth found that it was difficult to deal with him. He was perceived as overly "theoretical," "academic," and "ivory towerish." Within three months the Department terminated him without giving a reason. This action was permissible during the six-month probationary period.

Since the full probationary period had not been exhausted, Roth arranged to have his name restored to the list of eligibles, thereby making himself eligible for referral to another department. Shortly thereafter, Roth was offered another position in the central Department of Civil Service. The hiring officer of the Department assigned Roth to the Work Programs Division that offered temporary summer and part-time city jobs to students in the poorer areas of the city. His supervisor, Victor Valdez, telephoned Roth's former supervisor in the Department of Social Services, who advised Valdez to supervise Roth closely.

It was June, and Valdez was under great pressure to process and place as many summer program participants as possible. Because Roth was slow in processing and referring applicants, he soon fell behind in his work and accumulated a backlog. Some of the applicants complained that Roth was standoffish and snobbish. He also occupied a great deal of Valdez's time in asking questions about processing procedures and in engaging in discussions about the long-term possibility of computerizing the application process. Valdez seriously considered terminating Roth before the end of the probationary period.

At about this time Valdez had lunch with Peter Walsh, the Department's Director of Test Development, and the following discussion took place:

> Walsh: I was recently talking to that new technician of yours; I believe his name is Roth. Did you know that he has quite a background in statistical analysis and computer applica-

	tions? In fact almost all of his experience has been in statistical and computer work. I believe he's just gotten into personnel work because he needed a job badly.
Valdez:	No, I didn't know. As a matter of fact, I've been considering terminating him. He's not working out at all; he's slow, he's very theoretical, and the applicants have been complaining about him. I am rapidly running out of patience with him.
Walsh:	We could sure use someone like him for a job I've got to fill in my shop. We're developing tests for computer systems analysts and I need subject matter experts. We've also been under pressure to come up with a computer program for analyzing the results of our multiple-choice tests in terms of reliability, difficulty level, and so forth; the information could help improve our tests. Roth's background might be ideal. As you know, our list of eligibles for personnel technicians seldom has people with his background. The more usual applicant has verbal skills and training in personnel management and organizational behavior. Would you object if I arranged for Roth to transfer to my unit?
Valdez:	I hope you realize that Roth has almost completed probation. If he completes probation in your unit and then doesn't work out, you'll have to keep him. Let me warn you—even if he does seem to have the theoretical background you need, he's a slow worker and he doesn't get along with other people.
Walsh:	I'm willing to take a chance on him.
Valdez:	OK. I'll cooperate in the transfer, but don't say I didn't warn you.

1. Evaluate the practice of permitting a terminated probationer to restore his name to the list of eligibles and thereby to make himself eligible for referral to other departments.

2. Was the hiring officer of the Department of Civil Service correct in hiring and placing Roth in the Work Programs Division? Explain.

3. If you were Walsh, would you have asked for Roth to be transferred to your unit? Why or why not?

4. Evaluate Valdez's handling of Roth.
5. Evaluate Walsh's handling of the transfer of Roth.
6. Did Roth's apparent lack of success in his first two assignments indicate anything about the validity of the selection procedure used to hire him?

The Achiever

Janet Strauss was reassigned, because of a reorganization, from the Classification Bureau to the Bureau of Test Development and Examining in the Civil Service Department of a large western state. Her new supervisor, Jim Pappas, was quite impressed with her. She was conscientious, productive, inventive, and resourceful. Her work was extremely accurate and usually submitted far in advance of deadlines. Whenever she finished an assignment and had some slack time before another could be started, she asked Pappas if he had any work he wanted her to do in the interim. From time to time, Pappas did have some rather pressing jobs that had to be done. Accordingly, he welcomed her volunteering on those occasions. As far as Pappas was concerned, Strauss was the best employee in the Bureau.

Although most of Strauss's previous assignments had been of the type that called on her to work independently, Pappas now found it necessary to assign her to a two-member team responsible for developing a police officer's test, which was a major and important test development project. The other member of the team was Maria Torres, one of the better employees in the Bureau.

One week after Pappas made the new assignment, Torres came into Pappas's office in an obvious state of agitation.

Torres: You've got to do something about getting me off this project with Janet. She is absolutely impossible to work with. Not only is her manner patronizing, but she has embarrassed me in front of the Police Department officials we interviewed for the upcoming test. She behaves as though she is a third-grade elementary school teacher and I am one of her pupils. She is also totally inflexible in her approach to the work; she has never taken any of my ideas into consideration. You know as well as I do that a lot of judgment goes into test development and that I've had some really good ideas and insights in other tests I've worked on.

Pappas: Maria, I can only say that I'm surprised. I had no idea that Janet behaved in this way. She's always struck me as a highly efficient and productive employee who is very much committed to her work.

Torres: I can only repeat that she is impossible to work with.

Pappas: All right, Maria. You can pitch in on the typist examination, and I'll assign someone else to work with Janet.

Attempts at assigning Strauss to work with two other employees yielded the same results. Each in turn complained to Pappas and asked not to be assigned to work with her. Finally Pappas called Strauss into his office and the following discussion took place:

Pappas: Janet, several of the other people in the Bureau have been complaining about you. They say that you're overbearing, patronizing, and unwilling to consider their viewpoints.

Strauss: Mr. Pappas, I had no idea that they felt this (Breaking way about me. Why didn't they tell me? I've out in only tried to do my best. You know I've altears) ways tried to be helpful.

Pappas: Look, Janet. We have to be able to work together in this Bureau because most of our jobs take more than one person if they are to be done on time or at all. I wish you would make an effort to get along with the other people.

Strauss: I'll do my best.

1. Evaluate Pappas's actions after speaking to Torres.
2. Evaluate Pappas's discussion with Strauss.
3. Should Pappas continue to assign Strauss to work with other people in the Bureau? Why or why not?
4. Should Pappas arrange to have Strauss meet with Torres and the other complaining employees? Explain.

5. Suppose that after assigning Strauss to work with other people, Pappas receives the same kinds of complaints. What could Pappas do?

The Skills-Inventory System

The Police Commissioner of the city of Brookfield became increasingly concerned about the periodic need to go outside of the Police Department to other city departments for staff with special qualifications to handle special projects. The Commissioner knew that members of his Department had a wide variety of skills and training backgrounds that could be used in many of the special projects. However, he had no way of identifying these people quickly. The existing procedure for obtaining qualified outside or internal staff entailed a great deal of expense for the Department as well as lengthy delays in carrying out the projects.

The Commissioner was aware that several organizations in both the public and private sectors had had some success with computer-based skills-inventory systems. He therefore ordered the Department's Personnel Division to develop such a system for the Police Department and to have the new system fully operational within six months.

The Chief of the Personnel Division learned about a system utilized in the state government that could be adapted for use by the Police Department. The state's system appeared to be quite simple and easy to install. The employee merely checked off on a form which skills he or she possessed within thirty different categories. For example, the form asked the employee: Check the following computer languages you are familiar with.

( ) COBOL
( ) FORTRAN
( ) BASIC
( ) RPG

Using the state's system as a model, the Personnel Division prepared a questionnaire that was distributed to all employees in the Department. The information contained in the completed questionnaires was coded and placed on computer tapes. Completed questionnaires were eventually received for all of the 3000 employees in the Department, and this information was computerized.

Three months after the installation of the new system, the Commissioner received a letter from Pierre Marsot, Chief of Police of the city of Marseille, France, who said that he would be visiting the city of Brookfield and that he would appreciate a tour of its police facilities. Marsot also indicated that he spoke very little English and would need the services of a French-speaking guide. The Commissioner saw this situation as an opportunity to test the new skills-inventory system. He therefore asked the Personnel Division to have the system provide a list of the employees in the Department who spoke French.

Within an hour after the Commissioner made his request, the Personnel Division provided him with a list of ten employees who had indicated a knowledge of French on the skills-inventory questionnaire. The Commissioner asked one of his assistants to interview all ten employees on the list and to select the most suitable one to serve as interpreter and guide. The assistant discovered that six of the ten individuals were no longer with the Department: one had died; two had retired; and three had resigned. Of the four employees still with the Department, three indicated that they had studied French in school some time ago, but they could not actually speak and understand the language. The fourth employee indicated that he must have checked off French by accident; he had no knowledge of the language. The Commissioner was disturbed when the assistant reported the results of the interviews.

1. Evaluate the Personnel Division's approach to developing and establishing the system.
2. What shortcomings in the skills-inventory system were identified by this test of the system?
3. What can the Chief of Personnel do to correct the problems identified by this test of the system?
4. What are the most difficult problems to overcome in order to make an employee skills-inventory system fully operational?
5. Evaluate the Commissioner's analysis of the need for the system and his decision to install the system.

Suggested Readings for Chapter 2

Burack, Elmer H., and James W. Walker. *Manpower Planning and Programming.* Boston: Allyn and Bacon, 1972.

Coleman, Charles J. "Personnel: The Changing Function." *Public Personnel Management* 2 (May–June 1973):186–93.

Dela Montague, Robert P., and James B. Weitzul. "Performance Alignment: The Fine Art of the Perfect Fit." *Personnel Journal* 59, no. 2 (February 1980):115–17, and 131.

Ference, Thomas P., James A. Stoner, and E. Kirby Warren. "Managing the Career Plateau." *Academy of Management Review* 2, no. 4 (October 1977):602–12.

Gilbreath, Jerri D. "Sex Discrimination and Title VII of the Civil Rights Act." *Personnel Journal* 56, no. 1 (January 1977):23–26.

Leach, John J., and William A. Murray. "The Career Contract: Quid Pro Quo between You and Your Boss." *Management Review* 68, no. 10 (October 1979):20–28, and 51–52.

Lee, Robert D., Jr., and William M. Lucianovic. "Personnel Management Information Systems for State and Local Government." *Public Personnel Management* 4, no. 2 (March–April 1975):84–89.

Martin, Robert A. "Skills Inventories." *Personnel Journal* 46, no. 1 (January 1967):22–28.

Morgan, Marilyn A., Douglas T. Hall, and Alison Martier. "Career Development Strategies in Industry—Where Are We and Where Should We Be?" *Personnel* 56, no. 2 (March–April 1979):13–30.

Schein, Edgar H. "The Individual, the Organization, and the Career: A Conceptual Scheme." *Journal of Applied Behavioral Science* 7, no 4 (July–August 1971):401–26.

_____. "Organizational Socialization and the Profession of Management." *Industrial Management Review* 9, no. 2 (Winter 1968):1–15.

Wanous, J. P. *Organizational Entry: Recruitment, Selection, and Socialization of Newcomers.* Reading, Mass.: Addison-Wesley, 1980.

3 Motivation and Incentives

Once people have entered the organization and have been assigned to positions, the organization must see that they are motivated to perform well. Motivation of employees cannot be taken for granted. The organization and individual supervisors must take deliberate steps to insure that their employees view their jobs as satisfying experiences and to provide rewards for good performance. The rewards must be built into the system, and employees must view the rewards as worthwhile. It must be clear to employees that a certain level of performance in fact results in the reward, that the reward must be valued by the employees, and that the reward must be indeed provided when the desired behavior is manifested.

Employees' desires to satisfy certain of their needs influence their behavior. Managers and supervisors can motivate their subordinates by doing things that satisfy the subordinates' needs while channeling the subordinates' behavior toward the attainment of organizational goals. Motivators are perceived rewards that promise the satisfaction of one or more needs. The promise of satisfaction induces the individual to perform well.

Human needs are quite complex and varied. They include purely physical needs (e.g., hunger and thirst), social needs (e.g., the desire to be loved and to be accepted), and ego needs (e.g., the desire to achieve and to have one's achievements recognized). Different needs occur in different individuals at different times and in varying intensities. Needs can be heavily influenced by the environment. The satisfaction of one need may intensify the desire to satisfy other needs. Organizations must learn that no one action, incentive, or program motivates everyone; motivation depends on the situation. The specific needs that the organization must appeal to depend at least in part on the personalities, wants, and propensities of the individuals.

Motivation is more complex than the mere satisfaction of needs. In addition to placing a value on a particular reward, people must perceive that their actions actually lead to the attainment of the reward and that the reward is equitable in light of the effort required to attain it. Their perceptions of the probability of receiving a reward and of the amount of effort necessary to attain it are affected to some extent by their past experiences, especially if they have done the job before. The lesson for organizations seems to be that desired behavior should lead to a particular reward and that the value of the reward should be intimately related to the amount of effort required to reach a goal.

Some people have emphasized the motivational value of the work itself and have felt that organizations should pay particular attention to intrinsic rewards (i.e., rewards that arise from performing the job, such as a feeling of achievement). According to this view special efforts should be made by organizations to build into the content of a job features such as autonomy, discretion, control, challenge, and opportunity for growth. It is probably safe to assume that a substantial proportion of people in our highly individualistic and competitive society would respond favorably to these types of job-content factors.

Although most private sector organizations have considerable flexibility in building motivating conditions into the work environment, public sector organizations usually have a number of constraints that may interfere with their ability to provide a motivating environment. Many facets of organizational life in the public service are circumscribed by laws, rules, regulations, and procedures. Many of these requirements force the public sector organization in the direction of equal treatment of employees and limit its flexibility in making allowances for individual needs, desires, and achievements.

In public sector organizations salary increases are usually given in practice to entire classes of employees; merit salary increases in recognition of individual achievements are limited and discouraged by virtue of the elaborate paperwork associated with these increases and by the strict definitions of conditions under which they may be given. Similarly, advancement or promotion are more often a function of seniority and scores on formal tests than of actual performance on the job. Job duties are narrowly defined, and formal classification actions are required to build more autonomy and discretion into a job. Attempts by individual supervisors to build up their subordinates' jobs or to increase the responsibilities of their subordinates might result in out-of-title complaints from unions or adverse findngs from position-classification auditors.

Criteria or standards of performance used as the basis for granting rewards must be meaningful and fair. Employees should view such standards as attainable. The mere use of numbers or quantities, if inappropriate or unrealistic, can have a demotivating effect. When inappropriate numerical standards are imposed from the top, they are likely to have an adverse effect upon the quality of performance, even though the numerical standards may ostensibly be met. Whenever possible, employees should play a role in formulating performance standards. Participation in itself may be a valuable motivator.

Management should cultivate an organizational climate in which employees are encouraged to submit their ideas and suggestions; otherwise, valuable contributions to the attainment of organizational goals may not be forthcoming. However, the mere existence of formal incentive or suggestion programs does not guarantee employee participation. Overly elaborate or bureaucratized incentive programs may backfire and perhaps inhibit employee contributions.

Cases in Motivation and Incentives

The Productivity Campaign
The New Incentive Program
The Suggestion Program
The New Health Inspector

The Productivity Campaign

When a new governor took office in a Middle Atlantic state, William Baldwin was appointed to head up a Department of Personnel that consisted of 200 employees. Baldwin's appointment came in the midst of a series of newspaper reports criticizing the large number of "provisional" employees —that is, persons appointed without first passing a competitive examination—in state government. The press viewed the provisional employees as patronage appointments.

In his first week on the job, Baldwin called the chiefs of the Department's five major bureaus into his office.

Baldwin: The Governor is extremely concerned about productivity, and for that matter so am I. Also, the newspapers have been having a field day with us because of the number of provisional employees in state service. We all know that the Department of Personnel hasn't produced examinations quickly enough to replace all of the provisionals with permanent employees from civil service lists. Last year the Bureau of Examinations administered 100 examinations. This year I intend to raise that total to 200 examinations. We will in the next twelve months hold an examination for every title in which there are provisional employees serving. Replacement of provisional employees by permanent ones will be the number one priority of this Department. I intend to double the size of the Bureau of Examinations by transferring staff from other bureaus. The other bureau chiefs will be expected to maintain their current levels of output in spite of the reductions in staff. As far as I'm concerned, you people in areas such as training have been overstaffed; you will continue to provide the same level of service in areas such as training courses offered and so on.

Mary DeMarco:
(Director of
Classification)
I think we can reach your output goals without a massive reallocation of staff and without putting extreme pressure on existing staff. As you know, many of our titles have related duties and qualification require-

ments. Why don't we experiment with giving common examinations for a number of related titles? The work load will certainly be reduced.

Baldwin: We don't have the time to experiment with new ideas and techniques. Staff will be transferred to the Bureau of Examinations. I expect you bureau chiefs and your staff to meet these production goals. I suspect that the people in the Department of Personnel have been underworked for too long. I'm only asking for an honest day's work for a day's pay.

In the following twelve months, none of the bureau chiefs attempted to contribute ideas or suggestions to Baldwin. At the end of the year, however, the Department's annual report indicated that the Bureau of Examinations had produced 210 examinations for the year, while output levels in areas such as training courses given, new titles established and classified, and so forth were maintained at previous levels.

1. Assume that, contrary to Baldwin's belief, the Department was not overstaffed. Explain how the bureaus, other than the Bureau of Examinations, might have been able to maintain their previous level of output in the face of their loss of personnel.
2. What effect are Baldwin's attitudes and policies likely to have on the Department in the long run? Why?
3. What results might have been achieved with input from the bureau chiefs? Why?
4. What is the Governor's reaction likely to be when he reviews the Department's annual report?
5. What is Baldwin likely to do about the Department's goals for the following year?
6. What are the main dangers in overemphasizing quantified goals?

The New Incentive Program

Michael Bradshaw was a permanent accountant working for the Department of Finance and Taxation of a large southern state. Bradshaw's job consisted primarily of conducting tax audits. In carrying out his assignments, he was hard-working and extremely thorough. Bradshaw's supervisor, Carol Brent, had complimented him on these qualities several times but had so far been unable to provide any monetary rewards in recognition of his service.

The Commissioner of the Department was concerned about the lack of incentives for accountants in his department. All accountants were paid at the same basic rate and received the same cost-of-living and longevity salary adjustments, even though productivity among the accountants varied considerably. The Commissioner therefore decided to initiate a new incentive program. Under this program those accountants whose performance placed them in the top 10 percent of the accountants in the Department would receive special merit salary increases at the end of the year. Performance was to be judged on the basis of the average number of audits completed per month for the twelve-month period.

At the time the new program was announced, Brent called Bradshaw into her office, and the following discussion took place:

> Brent: Mike, I'm sure you've heard about the new incentive program. You know that I think a lot of your work, and I've been trying to find a way to reward you. This new program might now provide me with the means. I just wanted to tell you to keep up the good work. I know that you'll do well at the end of the year.
>
> Bradshaw: I'll certainly do my best. If anyone in this Department deserves a raise, it's me.

Bradshaw felt very encouraged by the new program. He knew that his performance was a cut above that of most of the department's accountants. Besides, he really needed the money now. He had just purchased a new home and his wife was expecting another child. He therefore redoubled his efforts. Several of his audits were responsible for uncovering major discrepancies that lead to $5 million in additional tax collections by the state.

At the end of the year, Brent asked Bradshaw to come to her office. In an apologetic tone Brent said, "Mike, your performance during the past year has been nothing short of outstanding. You've recovered more funds than any other accountant in the Department. Unfortunately, you were not selected for a merit salary increase because the number of audits you averaged per month did not place you in the top 10 percent. You have to understand that we're bound by the criteria that were established by the Commissioner. I wish I could do something, but that's the way things have worked out."

Bradshaw was speechless.

1. Why was Bradshaw speechless?
2. Evaluate the criteria for judging performance.
3. How is Bradshaw's work likely to be affected the following year? Explain.
4. Is the situation better or worse than it was before the initiation of the incentive program? Explain.
5. Could Brent be criticized for what happened? Explain.
6. What, if anything, should (a) Brent and (b) the top management of the Department do now?

The Suggestion Program

The Mayor of the city of Northville asked the Department of Personnel to initiate a suggestion program for employees of all city departments in order to stimulate the flow of cost-saving ideas from city employees. Roy Svensson, who already had some experience in suggestion programs in another city, was assigned responsibility for planning and administering the new program.

Svensson and other Department of Personnel executives felt that city departments failed to consider employees' ideas seriously. To overcome this problem, it was decided to centralize administration of the program in a new unit headed by Svensson. Svensson's plans for the new program included the following provisions:

1. All employee suggestions would be submitted directly to the Department of Personnel. The anonymity of those making the suggestions would be preserved until their suggestions were accepted or rejected.

2. Each suggestion would be referred to the appropriate city department for evaluation. For example, a suggestion to improve fire services would be referred to the Fire Department. Answers from departments would then be referred to Svensson's unit.

3. Svensson's unit would review each departmental response for completeness, fairness, and appropriateness of award. If, for example, the reasons for nonacceptance of a suggestion were unclear, if the rejection was unreasonable in the unit's judgment, or if the award was deemed too high or too low, the response would be returned to the department for further work.

4. The final response would be sent from Svensson's unit, with a thank you letter, to the person who had made the suggestion.

5. The actual amount of the award given for adopted suggestions would be linked to the savings expected to be achieved by the suggestion, with a maximum award of $5,000.

To get the program under way, Svensson's unit prepared and distributed pamphlets, posters, and suggestion forms to the Suggestion Coordinator (one was appointed in each city agency). In the first six months of operation, Svensson's unit received an average of 100 suggestions per month. Unfortunately, many of the suggestions submitted were not usable; the adoption rate was only 3 percent. In addition as many as one-half of the departmental evaluations had to be sent back to the departments for further work. Because suggestions had to be referred back to the departments and because Svensson had only one clerk reviewing departmental evaluations, delays of up to four months in giving final answers to the people making suggestions were quite common.

In the seventh month of operation, the number of suggestions declined to fifty. In his conversations with several departmental coordinators, Svensson sensed that participation had fallen because employees didn't like the long delays in getting final answers. Svensson assigned another clerk to review departmental evaluations; the waiting period was reduced to six weeks. By the end of the twelfth month, however, average participation had fallen to thirty suggestions per month.

1. Evaluate the provisions of Svensson's new program.
2. Why did the number of suggestions continue to decline?
3. What might Svensson do to increase participation in the program?
4. In addition to assigning another clerk to review departmental evaluations, what else could be done to reduce the long delays?

The New Health Inspector

Manuel Alvarez was appointed as an inspector in the Health Department of a large county on the West Coast. The job involved the inspection of restaurants and other food service establishments in order to insure that they were adhering to the county's health code and to report code violations. Before he was allowed to assume his regular duties, Alvarez had to go through a six-week training program run by the Department for all new inspectors. His instructors remarked that he was one of the best trainees to pass through the program in a long time.

At the conclusion of the program, Alvarez was assigned to accompany an experienced inspector for a one-week period so that he could observe how inspections were actually conducted. Alvarez immediately noticed that the experienced man, Joseph Edwards, conducted the inspections in a leisurely and almost casual fashion. At the end of the first day, Edwards had completed five inspections; it seemed to Alvarez that it would have been possible to conduct at least twice that number. Only four inspections were completed on the second day. On the third day, when Alvarez decided to broach the subject with Edwards, the following conversation took place:

Alvarez: Joe, I don't understand why we're doing the inspections so slowly. If we speeded up, I'm sure we could do twice as many inspections a day. I also see that you're letting a lot of minor violations go by.

Edwards: We get paid the same amount whether we do five inspections per day or ten. What's the use in killing ourselves? I've been in this department a long time, and there's no percentage in going out of your way to do extra work. The supervisors don't care as long as you make the minimum number of inspections, which has always been four inspections a day. As far as the minor violations go, what's the point? If we report them, they only mean a lot of paperwork for us and have no real effect on the way these restaurants operate.

Alvarez: I don't agree with you, Joe. I think that our supervisors want us to do a good job and will recognize us for it.

Edwards: You'll find out what the score is!

Alvarez turned out to be one of the most productive and effective inspectors the Department had ever employed. He ultimately averaged twelve inspections per day and led the Department in citations issued for code violations. By the end of the year, Alvarez was waiting for some sign of recognition, and when none appeared, he stopped in to see his supervisor, Arthur Jensen, the Chief Inspector. The following discussion took place in Jensen's office:

Alvarez: You must be aware of the fact that I led the Department in the number of inspections conducted and in the citations issued. I think I deserve some kind of reward.

Jensen: I agree with you, Manny. You're one of the best inspectors who has ever worked for me. But you know that we're limited in what we can do.

Alvarez: There are some vacancies in the senior inspector grade.

Jensen: You know that we can promote people only after they pass civil service tests. The next test for senior inspector won't be given until next June.

Alvarez: What about a temporary appointment? I know that your recommendation swings a lot of weight with the Commissioner.

Jensen: It's no good. Because of budgetary problems, we've got a hiring freeze on for the
next eight months. We aren't allowed to fill
those senior inspector vacancies.

Alvarez: What about a merit salary increase? These
are sometimes given for outstanding performance.

Jensen: You're right, but the county Budget Office
demands a lot of documentation for all such
increases. The last two requests that our
Commissioner sent through were turned
down by Budget. But I'll send a recommendation to the Commissioner. That's the best
I can do.

Alvarez: Thank you, Mr. Jensen. I really appreciate
it.

Two weeks later, Alvarez was informed
that the Commissioner had refused to submit the request to the
Budget Office. The Commissioner told Jensen that he didn't want
to give the Budget Office another opportunity to turn him down.

1. What effect is the Commissioner's action likely to have on
   Alvarez?
2. How is the Commissioner's action likely to affect Jensen?
3. What, if anything, should Jensen do?
4. What effect is the Commissioner's action likely to have on
   the other inspectors?
5. What, if anything, should be done to change the Health
   Department's system of incentives and rewards for its inspectors? Explain.
6. What does the case reveal about motivation and incentives
   in the civil service? What should be done to change civil service procedures?

Suggested Readings for Chapter 3

Egbert, Wallace G. "Employee Suggestion Systems." In Carl Heyel, ed., *Handbook of Modern Office Management and Administrative Services.* New York: McGraw-Hill, 1972. Pp. 7–81.

Elbing, Alvar O., Herman Gadon, and John R.M. Gordon. "Flexible Working Hours: The Missing Link." *California Management Review* 17, no. 3 (Spring 1975):50–57.

Ford, Robert N. *Motivation through the Work Itself.* New York: American Management Association, 1969.

Golembiewski, Robert T., and Carl W. Proehl. "Public Sector Applications of Flexible Work Hours: A Review of Available Experience." *Public Administration Review* 40, no. 1 (January–February 1980):72–83.

Greene, Charles N. "The Satisfaction–Performance Controversy." *Business Horizons* 15, no. 2 (1972):31–41.

Herzberg, Frederick. "One More Time: How Do You Motivate Employees?" *Harvard Business Review* 46, no. 1 (January–February 1968):53–62.

———. *Work and the Nature of Man.* Cleveland, Ohio: World Publishing Co., 1966.

Kearney, William J. "Pay for Performance? Not Always." *MSU Business Topics* 27, no. 2 (Spring 1979):5–16.

Kerr, Steven. "On the Folly of Rewarding A, While Hoping for B." *Academy of Management Journal* 18, no. 4 (1975):769–83.

Maslow, Abraham H. "A Theory of Human Motivation." *Psychological Review* 50, no. 4 (July 1943):370–96.

———. *Motivation and Personality.* New York: Harper & Row, 1954.

McClelland, David, and David H. Burnham. "Power Is the Great Motivator." *Harvard Business Review* 54, no. 2 (March–April 1976):100–10.

Meyer, Herbert H. "The Pay-for-Performance Dilemma." *Organizational Dynamics* 3, no. 3 (Winter 1975):39–50.

Owen, John D. "Flextime: Some Problems and Solutions." *Industrial and Labor Relations Review* 30, no. 2 (January 1977):152–60.

Rock, Milton L., ed. *Handbook of Wage and Salary Administration.* New York: McGraw-Hill, 1972.

Reuter, Vincent G. "Suggestion Systems: Utilization, Evaluation, and Implementation." *California Management Review* 19, no. 3 (1977):78–89.

4 Performance Evaluation, Discipline, and Layoffs

Performance evaluation is one of the most critical areas of human resources management. It can provide organizations with valuable information for making assignments, granting rewards, and identifying training needs; it can also provide feedback for performance improvement. Yet, implementation of objective, valid, and workable performance evaluation systems is one of the most intractable problems in the entire human resources area. Despite the publication of numerous volumes on performance evaluation, a valid, reliable, and easily administrable performance appraisal system applicable to a broad spectrum of jobs has yet to be developed. Perhaps it never will be.

There are a wide variety of performance evaluation systems in use today among both private and public employers. Each of these systems has strengths and weaknesses.

Some of the better-known approaches include graphic-rating scales, essay or open-ended approaches, behaviorally anchored rating scales, critical incidents, and management by objectives.

Graphic Rating Scales. This type of performance evaluation system is still the most commonly used approach in the country. Certain general dimensions, traits, or characteristics such as quality of work, quantity of work, reliability, cooperativeness, dependability, initiative, and so forth are listed on a performance evaluation form. Next to each characteristic is a range of performance levels that may be described in terms of unsatisfactory, satisfactory, above average, and outstanding. Between five and nine levels are used. The rater merely checks the box next to the appropriate performance level. This kind of system is fairly simple to administer; one standard form is used for everyone. However, it is not a job-specific system—that is, the rating factors are not tailored or related to specific jobs. No performance standards are communicated in advance or at the time of evaluation to the individual employee, and the ratings are subject to errors of leniency and subjectivity. The dimensions being rated are not clearly defined. Ratings also tend to be unreliable since different raters may give different ratings to the same employee.

Essay or Open-Ended Approaches. Essay appraisals are also a common method of evaluating employee performance. Raters are asked to describe in narrative form the employee's strengths, weaknesses, and potential. Although this method is easy to administer, no specific performance standards are communicated to the employee. Ratings under this approach can be extremely subjective, do not necessarily focus on the most significant aspects of performance, and make comparisons between employees almost impossible.

Behaviorally Anchored Rating Scales. In this approach the major activities or tasks of the job are identified, and a number of behavioral statements describing job performance are developed for each activity. Each behavioral statement is "anchored" by job experts to points on a scale that ranges from excellent performance to unacceptable performance. The rater is asked to select the statement that best characterizes the performance of the employee being evaluated from the statements describing each activity. This system is based on actual job behaviors that have been identified as important. Because the statements are specific, the ratings should be reliable. However, development of the scales requires considerable time and effort, and there is a question as to whether the amount of time and effort required yields results that are clearly superior to simpler systems.

Critical Incidents. In this method the rater records significant incidents of the employee's good and poor performances as they occur throughout the rating period. These incidents are then discussed with the employee at appraisal interviews. Since the interviews focus on specific performance rather than on personality traits, they tend to be quite constructive in identifying performance problems as well as methods for improving performance. This approach, however, requires that supervisors write down performance incidents on a regular basis, and this process can become time consuming. Also, performance standards are not necessarily set and communicated to the employee in advance.

Management by Objectives (MBO). Objectives or performance goals are set individually for each employee at the beginning of the evaluation period. The employee is usually involved in the goal-setting process, and this participation encourages employee commitment to attaining these goals. Establishing goals in advance helps clarify exactly what the employee is responsible for accomplishing during the evaluation period. Further, the factors or objectives used as the basis for evaluation are job specific. Focusing on actual performance generates information useful for performance improvement and employee development. However, a results-based approach, while appropriate for managers who have some degree of control over ultimate end results, may have limited utility for lower-level employees who lack control over their jobs. Also, the system is not appropriate for employees who do not wish to participate in the goal-setting process. Further, experience indicates that employees usually require a fair amount of training and preparation before they can successfully articulate objectives, and some organizations may be unwilling or unable to make this kind of investment. Another weakness of this approach is that managers may focus on short-term goals when long-term goals are more significant. There is also a tendency for managers to ignore or overlook important managerial responsibilities that support the attainment of organizational objectives. For example, managers may ignore employee development in the process of attaining production goals. The case, "The Commission's Management by Objectives Program" in Chapter 8, describes how one public jurisdiction installed an MBO program that included a performance evaluation system based on results.

One of the major problems associated with the evaluation of performance is the subjectivity that is inherent in most systems. The absence of clear and objective performance criteria and a lack of common understanding of performance expectations inevitably lead to controversy, disagreement, and even ill will between those who are evaluating and those who are being evaluated. Even if a system is reasonably objective, it may still fail because of the manner in which it is implemented.

For any system to have even a chance of success, employees must know what is expected of them. In many systems there is a failure to communicate performance standards. This type of failure will turn performance-review sessions and appraisal interviews into unproductive and uncomfortable situations for everyone concerned.

Sometimes it becomes necessary for a supervisor to initiate disciplinary action when an employee is unmotivated, unwilling, or unable to perform in a satisfactory manner. Allowing an unsatisfactory employee to continue in his or her position can have a serious impact on the morale of others in the unit and on the effectiveness of the unit. Most public service systems provide extensive protection for employee rights and tenure; any disciplinary action has to be carefully documented and justified. A supervisor who seeks to remove an employee for incompetence must be prepared to provide specific details about the employee's failure to meet performance standards. Specific incidents should therefore be recorded at the time they occur.

In attempting to make employees conform to certain standards of behavior or conduct, for example, in the areas of attendance and punctuality, organizations sometimes institute highly structured control programs. Such programs, however, may or may not result in desired outcomes. If the programs fail to get at the root causes of the undesirable kinds of employee behavior, they will probably work only for a short time, if at all.

Even when employees are performing satisfactorily, it may be necessary in times of fiscal constraint or shifts in priorities to terminate some employees. In such situations objective, rational, and equitable systems for bringing about reductions in the work force may lessen the impact on the organization and may help ease the pain of separation for the employee.

Cases in Performance Evaluation, Discipline, and Layoffs

The Performance Rating System That Failed to Perform

The Appraisal Interview

The Insubordinate Employee

The Absence-Reduction Program

The Layoff

The Performance Rating System
That Failed to Perform

Top executives in the city of Tolden decided that performance should be a factor in the promotion of city employees. Until then promotion had been entirely a function of employees' scores on written tests and seniority. Under the new performance rating system developed by the city's Department of Personnel, those employees who attained ratings of satisfactory or higher would have a number of points added on to their scores on the written tests and on to their seniority ratings. Hence, their promotion opportunities could be significantly affected by their performance ratings. The performance rating form shown here was designed by the Department of Personnel to be used by supervisors to rate all city employees.

Under the new system supervisors would only have to explain or support ratings other than that of satisfactory. A supervisor rating an employee as satisfactory would merely have to check "satisfactory" under section 2 (Rating Category). Supervisors were required to conduct appraisal interviews with each employee being evaluated. Although employees were required to sign the form, their signature did not mean that they agreed with the rating but merely that they had been told what the rating was.

After the first round of ratings was completed, the Department of Personnel found that 98 percent of all city employees had been rated as satisfactory. The Department also found that the existence of the system, especially the appraisal interview at the end of the rating period, generated conflict, controversy, and friction between supervisors and their subordinates. A large number of employees indicated that they resented being rated as merely "satisfactory." In addition, every employee who was evaluated as less than satisfactory submitted a formal appeal.

1. Should the Department of Personnel have anticipated that supervisors would rate so many employees as satisfactory? Explain.
2. Should the Department have expected employees being rated to react as they did? Explain.
3. What are the strengths of the city's system?
4. What are the weaknesses of the city's system?

City of Tolden
Employee Performance Rating

Period Covered by Rating: From_____To_____

1. Employee's Name_____Title_____

   Department_____Unit_____

   Supervisor's Name and Title_____

2. Overall Rating Category (check one):

   _____Outstanding   _____Needs improvement

   _____Superior   _____Unsatisfactory

   _____Satisfactory

3. Check one or more of the following categories that best describe other than satisfactory performance by the employee during the rating period:

   Above Satisfactory

   _____1. Quantity of work

   _____2. Quality of work

   _____3. Initiative/ resourcefulness

   _____4. Cooperation/ dependability

   _____5. Alertness

   _____6. Contribution of ideas

   _____7. Supervisory/ administrative effectiveness

   Below Satisfactory

   _____1. Neglected duty

   _____2. Acted insubordinately

   _____3. Lack of alertness

   _____4. Inefficiency

   _____5. Violation of rules

   _____6. Inadequate quantity or poor quality of work

   _____7. Excessive latenesses or absences

4. Explain reasons for each category checked above in section 3. Include all details needed to support your evaluation.

   _____

   Signature of employee and date

5. What might be done to improve the effectiveness of the new system?

6. What other system(s) could the city have adopted?

The Appraisal Interview

The supervisors in the Department of Public Works in a large northeastern state were preparing to submit annual performance appraisals of their subordinates. Tim Brown, the Supervisor of the Accounts Division, scheduled an appraisal interview with Joan Logan, one of the senior clerks in his Division. While Brown felt that Logan was a good worker, he was concerned about Logan's tardiness in completing audits of payment vouchers.

Brown began the interview by saying, "Joan, your work has always been very accurate, but I can't give you a superior rating this year. You've been late on almost all of your audits. You know that we have very tight deadlines around here, and the Commissioner has been on my back about these audits."

Logan, who was visibly upset, responded, "It's not my fault if the Commissioner is on your back! Why take it out on me? You know I've always done good work. In addition to my regular work, I've been handling the vouchers for the Construction Fund. Then, you ought to remember, about two months ago, you assigned the Highway Fund vouchers to me. All in all, I've been putting out a lot more work than anyone else in the Division, and you know that my work is always accurate. There is just no way that I can do the job right and get all of the audits done on time."

Brown answered, "I know you've had a big work load this year. But I have no choice in the matter. We have to get those audits out on time. If you try harder, I know that you can do it, Joan. Put a little more effort into the job, and maybe I can do better on your performance rating next year. Will you try harder?" Brown got up from his chair to signal the end of the interview. Logan also rose and said in conclusion, "What do I have to do to get a good rating around here?"

1. What is the fundamental problem in this situation?

2. Evaluate the supervisor's handling of the interview.

3. Was Logan's behavior during the interview predictable? Explain.
4. Is it likely that Logan will try harder in the future? Explain.
5. What is the proper approach to handling an appraisal interview?
6. Did Brown and Logan have the same understanding of what kind of performance was expected of Logan? Explain.

The Insubordinate Employee

Ellen Brody had been employed as a typist with the Department of Parks of a midwestern state for two years. Within that period she had been transferred no less than six times. Her superiors and peers attributed these transfers to her uncooperative attitude and to her behavior that at times bordered on the insubordinate. She attempted to pick and choose her assignments, frequently handed her work in late, and sometimes submitted work that was so sloppy it had to be retyped.

Under normal circumstances she would not have been retained past the six-month probationary period. However, Tom Szabo, her superior during her probationary period, was under very intense work pressures. Also, Szabo was not sure how quickly he could get a replacement if he were to recommend terminating her, and in his view some output was better than no output. After eight months the pressure on Szabo's unit subsided. By this time Brody was creating conflicts and resentment among her co-workers, who frequently had to do some of her work over again. The morale and effectiveness of the unit was being adversely affected, and Szabo had to do something about her. However, Brody was now a permanent employee, and formal charges would have to be brought against her in order to have her dismissed. The state's Civil Service Commission, which reviewed appeals from Department of Parks decisions, almost never concurred with such termination actions. Szabo therefore arranged to have Brody transferred to another unit as the only practical solution to the problem.

The same situation repeated itself five more times. In each case the supervisor held numerous discussions with Brody in an effort to get her to change her work habits. All of these efforts were in vain; Brody refused to change her ways. She was eventually transferred to Rose Sullivan's unit. Sullivan had heard about the typist's work behavior, and in an effort to start out on the right foot, she spoke to Brody on the first day that she arrived in Sullivan's unit. She began, "Ellen, welcome aboard! I hope that you'll be happy here. I like to have good working relationships with all of the people in my unit. I know that you have had some problems with supervisors in the past, but let's forget the past and start out fresh."

Brody responded, "Problems? I haven't had any problems. All of those supervisors had it in for me. They tried to exploit me, but I wouldn't let them. I know that I do good work."

Sullivan was determined to give Brody a fair chance. Within a short time, however, the old pattern repeated itself. Brody became insubordinate, refused those assignments she didn't like, submitted work late, and so forth. In line with a new policy directive issued by the Commissioner of Parks, under which all supervisors were encouraged to take disciplinary action against incompetent or insubordinate employees, Sullivan decided to prefer charges against Brody and to recommend her dismissal. She first attempted to gather evidence that could be used in the departmental hearing. She asked Tom Szabo and Brody's other supervisors if they would submit evidence or testimony in the case. All of the other supervisors indicated that they had no specific evidence, could not recollect any of the details or incidents that had involved Brody, and did not want to get involved. Sullivan had to go it alone. She sat down and attempted to recall details of the past six months. What she remembered she wrote down in the form of a report. She submitted the report to the departmental Hearing Board and gave oral testimony at the hearing on Brody's case. The Board sustained Sullivan's charges and ordered Brody's termination.

Brody appealed to the state's Civil Service Commission after she was terminated. The Commission, citing a lack of documentation as the basis for its decision, overturned the departmental Hearing Board's decision. Brody was reinstated in her job. The Commissioner of Parks decided to have her placed in a position where she could do little damage to the Department.

1. Evaluate Tom Szabo's decision to retain Brody at the end of her probationary period.
2. Was Szabo correct in transferring Brody to another unit? Explain.

3. Evaluate Sullivan's approach to preparing charges against Brody.
4. Was the Commissioner of Parks correct in placing Brody where she could do little damage to the Department?
5. What might (a) supervisors and (b) the Department do to prevent similar cases from recurring?
6. What implications does this case have for broad-based reform of personnel policies and practices at all levels of government?

The Absence-Reduction Program

The Mayor of the city of Hartville had become quite concerned about excessive use of sick leave in most city departments. A recent newspaper story had indicated that city employees used as much as 50 percent of the sick leave that they accumulated each year. The Mayor ordered Herbert Haller, the city's Personnel Director, to develop a program to reduce the use of sick leave by the city's work force.

Haller had served as vice president of the National Bank of Hartville, the leading bank in the area, before being appointed Personnel Director. At the bank he had been successful in reducing absenteeism by introducing an absence-reduction program. Drawing upon his experience at the bank, Haller formulated a four-step program designed to aid supervisors in detecting at an early stage the beginning of poor attendance habits, in initiating necessary corrective actions, and in encouraging good attendance. Under the program supervisors maintain for each employee a record on which all of the employee's absences are recorded. A distinction is made between supported and unsupported sick-leave absences. A supported absence is one for which the employee provides written evidence of illness from a doctor, hospital, or so forth. A sick-leave absence is recorded as unsupported if no verification is submitted from an appropriate medical authority. Space is also provided for recording details on the absence and for summarizing discussions between the employee and supervisor. The program's four steps are as follows:

1. Preliminary Investigation. When an employee has an unsupported sick-leave absence before or after a weekend or holiday or a second unsupported sick-leave absence during the week, the supervisor asks the employee why he or she was absent when the employee returns to work. The supervisor notes on the employee's absence record the results of the investigation and includes any comments of the employee.

2. Initial Warning. When an employee has a second unsupported sick-leave absence before or after a weekend or holiday or a third unsupported sick-leave absence during the week, the supervisor interviews the employee when the latter returns to work and records on the employee's absence record what took place at the interview. During the interview the supervisor reviews the employee's previous sick-leave absences, advises the employee that continued absences will not be tolerated, and warns the employee that medical confirmation may be required for all future absences and that if the employee does not provide such evidence when it is required, the employee will not be paid for the days absent.

3. Second Warning. When an employee has a third unsupported sick-leave absence before or after a weekend or holiday or a fourth unsupported sick-leave absence during the week, the supervisor discusses the case with his or her superior. Then the supervisor meets with the employee when the latter returns to work and repeats the warning given at the initial-warning interview. The matters discussed at this meeting are also written on the employee's absence record by the superior.

4. Final Warning. When an employee has a fourth unsupported sick-leave absence before or after a weekend or holiday or a fifth unsupported sick-leave absence during the week, the supervisor reviews the case with the agency's second highest ranking executive (usually the individual in charge of day-to-day operations of the agency). When the employee returns to work, the supervisor makes the following statement verbatim to the employee: "Your attendance is still unsatisfactory. This is your final warning that you will not be paid for any future sick-leave absences unless they are supported by written medical evidence." The supervisor enters this final warning statement and a summary of the discussion on the employee's absence record.

Haller submitted a summary of the program to the Mayor. The Mayor received it very favorably and suggested that Haller install the program on a pilot basis in his own Department even though the Department of Personnel had one of the better attendance records in the city. If the program succeeded there, it would be extended to other city departments.

When the program was installed, all of the Personnel Department superiors were given an orientation to the new program and were told that the records they kept on their employees would be reviewed periodically by an assistant to the Personnel Director to ensure that the procedures were being followed uniformly. A week before the program went into effect, each employee in the Department was issued a memorandum that described the program briefly.

1. How were the Department's employees likely to react to the new program?
2. How were the Department's supervisors likely to react to the new program?
3. What were the likely effects of the program on employee sick-leave absences?
4. Evaluate the approach taken to install the program.
5. Evaluate the features of the four-step program that was developed by Haller.
6. Is the program likely to have an impact on the Department in areas other than absenteeism? Explain.

The Layoff

Jane Cooke was one of the first blacks to be hired by the city of Grandville. She was near the top of the list of eligibles for a secretary-typist position and appeared to have a great deal of potential. She began work on January 1 as secretary to one of the supervisors in the Public Health Department. The Department was especially pleased to hire Ms. Cooke because until then there had been no other black secretaries in the Department. In fact there were few black secretaries in the city government even though blacks comprised 20 percent of the city's population.

For the following five months her performance was exemplary. Her completed work was almost always free of errors. When her supervisor, Paul Glenn, asked her to stay late, she complied willingly and cheerfully. On June 1, one month before the end of her probationary period, Glenn called her into his office and said, "Jane, I am really happy with your work. I realize you've only been here a short time, but your performance has been so outstanding that as soon as your probationary period is over, I will recommend you for a merit salary increase."

On June 15, Glenn received a notice that Jane Cooke would be laid off effective July 1. The city had been experiencing fiscal difficulties and the Mayor had ordered the Public Health Department to cut its budget by $500,000 through layoffs. The Department had decided that in some cases one secretary could do the secretarial work for two supervisors. Glenn then asked Cooke into his office, and the following discussion took place:

> Glenn: I'm sorry, Jane, but I have a layoff notice here for you. State law mandates layoffs strictly on the basis of seniority by job category, and you're the secretary with the least seniority in the Department. I want you to know that I hate to lose you.
>
> Cooke: Mr. Glenn, I don't understand. Two weeks ago you told me that my performance was outstanding and that you were recommending me for a salary increase. Why is this happening to me? Can't you do anything? I really need this job.
>
> Glenn: I discussed your case with the Commissioner, but there's nothing we can do. We're hamstrung by state law on this.

Two weeks later a new secretary, who was white and who had survived the layoffs, was assigned to Glenn. She was late to work on the first day of work for Glenn and continued to be late from time to time. The quality and quantity of her work was minimally adequate. When asked to work after 5 P.M., she always had a pressing reason why she could not.

1. What could Glenn or the Department have done to prevent Cooke's layoff?
2. What can be done in the longer run to prevent employees like Cooke from being let go at times when layoffs are unavoidable?
3. What justification is there for the use of seniority as the criterion in layoffs?

4. What are the drawbacks to using seniority as the sole basis for layoffs?

5. Does the use of seniority in layoffs interfere with the accomplishment of social goals such as the provision of equal employment opportunity?

6. In what other personnel decisions is seniority sometimes a factor? Is the use of seniority more justified in those decisions than in layoff decisions? Explain.

Suggested Readings for Chapter 4

Allan, Peter, and Stephen Rosenberg. "The Development of a Task-Oriented Approach to Performance Evaluation in the City of New York." *Public Personnel Management* 7, no. 6 (January–February 1978):26–32.

_____. "Formulating Usable Objectives for Manager Performance Appraisal." *Personnel Journal* 57, no. 11 (November 1978):626–29, 640, and 642.

Boncarosky, Leon D. "Guidelines to Corrective Discipline." *Personnel Journal* 58, no. 10 (October 1979):698–702.

Campbell, J. P., et al. *Managerial Behavior, Performance, and Effectiveness.* New York: McGraw–Hill, 1970.

Cowan, Paula. "How Blue Cross Put Pay-for-Performance to Work." *Personnel Journal* 57, no. 5 (May 1978):250–55.

Cummings, L.L., and Donald P. Schwab. *Performance in Organizations, Determinants, and Appraisal.* Glenview, Ill.: Scott, Foresman, 1973.

Feild, Hubert S., and William H. Holley. "Performance Appraisal—An Analysis of State-wide Practices." *Public Personnel Management* 4, no. 3 (May–June 1975):145–60.

Haynes, Marion G. "Developing an Appraisal Program." *Personnel Journal* 57, no. 1 (January 1978):14–19.

Holley, William H., and Hubert S. Feild. "Performance Appraisal and the Law." *Labor Law Journal* 26, no. 7 (July 1975):423–30.

_____, **and Mona J. Barnett.** "Analyzing Performance Appraisal Systems: An Empirical Study." *Personnel Journal* 55, no. 9 (September 1976):457–59, and 463.

Kearney, William J. "Behaviorally Anchored Rating Scales—MBO's Missing Ingredients." *Personnel Journal* 58, no. 1 (January 1979):20–25.

Koontz, Harold. *Appraising Managers as Managers.* New York: McGraw–Hill, 1971.

_____. "Making Managerial Appraisal Effective." *California Management Review* 15, no. 2 (Winter 1972):46–55.

Lacho, Kenneth J., G. Kent Stearns, and Maurice F. Villere. "A Study of Employee Appraisal Systems of Major Cities in the United States." *Public Personnel Management* 8, no. 2 (March–April 1979):111–25.

Lazer, Robert. "The Discrimination Danger in Performance Appraisal." *Conference Board Review* 13, no. 3 (March 1976):60–64.

_____, **and Walter S. Wikstrom.** *Appraising Managerial Performance: Current Practices and Future Directions.* New York: The Conference Board, 1977.

Levinson, Harry. "Appraisal of What Performance?" *Harvard Business Review* 54, no. 4 (July–August 1976):30–48.

Locher, Alan H., and Kenneth S. Teel. "Performance Appraisal—A Survey of Current Practices." *Personnel Journal* 56, no. 5 (May 1977):245–47, and 254.

McGregor, Douglas. "An Uneasy Look at Performance Appraisal." *Harvard Business Review* 35, no. 3 (May–June 1957):89–94.

Mayer, Herbert H., Emanual Kay, and John R.P. French, Jr. "Split Roles in Performance Appraisal." *Harvard Business Review* 43, no. 1 (January–February 1965):123–29.

Oberg, Winston. "Make Performance Appraisal Relevant." *Harvard Business Review* 50, no. 1 (January–February 1972):61–67.

Oberle, Rodney, L. "Administering Disciplinary Actions." *Personnel Journal* 57, no. 1 (January 1978):29–31.

Saso, Carmen, and Earl Tanis. *Disciplinary Policy and Practices.* Chicago: International Personnel Management Association, 1973.

Schwab, Donald P., Herbert G. Heneman, III, and Thomas A. DeCotiis. "Behaviorally Anchored Rating Scales: A Review of the Literature." *Personnel Psychology* 28, no. 4 (Winter 1975):549–62.

Swanson, Stephen C. "The Effort of the Supreme Court's Seniority Decisions." *Personnel Journal* 56, no. 12 (December 1977):625–27.

Thomas, John Clayton. "Budget-Cutting and Minority Employment in City Governments: Lessons from Cincinnati." *Public Personnel Management* 7, no. 3 (May–June 1978):155–61.

U.S. Office of Personnel Management. *Employee Performance Evaluation—A Practical Guide to Development and Implementation.* Washington, D.C., 1980.

_____. *Performance Evaluation Workbook and Supervisory Training Guide for State and Local Governments.* Washington, D.C., 1980.

van Adelsberg, Henri. "Relating Performance Evaluation to Compensation of Public Employees." *Public Personnel Management* 7 no. 2 (March–April 1978):72–79.

5 Training and Development

Even if an organization took steps to ensure that people were properly selected, assigned, motivated, and appraised, there would still be no assurance that its employees were being utilized effectively. Changes in the internal and external environment of an organization (e.g., legislative or financial), as well as career interests of employees, create a need for employee training and development that is a regular part of organizational life.

People entering an organization do not bring with them all of the skills that they need to be effective performers. People are transferred, jobs change, and employees are advanced. Organizations must be prepared to supplement and strengthen the knowledge and skills that employees bring with them. Performance appraisal may reveal the need for the development of additional skills and abilities (e.g., written communication or conference leadership). Many of these needs may be met through training. The way in which training programs are developed and carried out is critical to their success in improving performance.

Most organizations carry out two types of training and development activities. One type helps people to perform their current jobs more effectively. The other type prepares people to perform higher-level or future assignments. In the former case the benefits are sometimes quite obvious and reveal themselves in the form of improved performance on the current job. In the latter case the returns may not be as obvious. Nevertheless, from the viewpoint of the organization's long-term effectiveness, training for future assignments is just as significant as training for current duties. What the organization does to prepare staff for advancement affects the organization's ability to fill key positions and to carry out its mission effectively in the future. From the viewpoint of the individual employee, the existence of career development programs and actual opportunities for advancement may be regarded as evidence of the organization's interest in the careers of its employees. Such programs and opportunities may have a motivational effect on an employee's current performance and may encourage long-term commitment to and identification with organizational goals.

Training and development are too often perceived by organizations as solely staff activities—that is, specialized functions that lie outside the boundaries of the regular job of a manager. In organizations in which much of the training is carried out by a specialized unit, line managers may see the training not only as an activity that has no direct benefit but also as something that interferes with the productivity of the unit by taking people away from the job. Although the process of developing and training subordinates is a critical management activity, managers are rarely evaluated on the training they provide to subordinates. Training activities are often among the first activities that are cut back in times of austerity. Part of the reason that training is accorded such a low status in many organizations is that it is sometimes difficult to demonstrate tangible benefits from training.

The evaluation of results is perhaps the most difficult part of the training process. Evaluation is complex, expensive, and unreliable. Consequently, in some cases training practitioners resort to methods of evaluation that consist of nothing more than asking participants what they think about the training program. In other cases evaluations of completed training activities depend on supervisory appraisals of employee performance that are not necessarily objective in themselves. In some cases results may not be readily apparent; in other cases results may only be realized in the long term. Managers, particularly in the public sector, are often concerned with the resolution of immediate problems; if something has to be sacrificed, it will be an activity that has a payoff only in the future.

Since management does not continue to support an investment in training unless some benefits are obtained, training specialists must make sure that programs actually meet genuine needs and are responsive to management goals. Training and development programs cannot be developed in a vacuum; they must be tailored to a specific organizational setting and based on a rigorous analysis of performance needs. It should be possible as a result of such an analysis to determine whether training is really needed. A careful analysis of performance may reveal a need for changes in management practices and procedures or job design, rather than a need for a training program. All too often training programs are proposed as remedies for organizational ills when other kinds of solutions are needed.

In recognition of the variety of training and nontraining solutions available for solving organizational problems, training and development practitioners have begun to place more and more emphasis on the analysis of performance to insure that appropriate solutions are identified. Even when a training solution is called for, a formal course of instruction may be inappropriate. Approaches other than formal courses, such as on-the-job experiences, may be the most effective means of attaining the training objectives. If the need for a formal course in indicated, it is probably best to avoid the indiscriminate use of prepackaged programs. It is preferable to tailor a course to the specific training needs of the organization.

If a certain type of formal training program is needed and conducted, the mere completion of the program does not guarantee that those people completing it will change their behavior or apply what they have learned. Provision must also be made for establishing an organizational climate that supports changes in behavior and application of new skills. There have been too many cases in which people have gone through training programs, have been exposed to new ideas and approaches, and have returned to apply them to an organization that was not receptive to them. In such cases it would have been far better not to have "trained" the people at all.

Cases in Training and Development

The Training Needs Assessment Study
The Management Development Program
The Training Course
Improving Managerial Skills through Training

The Training Needs Assessment Study

Alice Foster, Director of Training for a large eastern state, became aware of the availability of federal financial grants that aid states and localities in assessing their training needs. Several of the larger state agencies were surveyed by Foster's staff concerning their possible interest in carrying out such an assessment. The Department of Social Services was the only agency that expressed interest in an intensive department-wide study of its training needs. The Commissioner of Social Services, in responding to Foster's inquiry, stated, "This kind of study will be very useful to us. I've always felt that we've needed training in several areas."

Foster enlisted the cooperation of a local university in preparing the grant application; the university was expected to assist in conducting the assessments. The Department of Social Services was selected as the target agency. Two months were spent in preparing the grant application. Three months later, Foster was notified that the grant had been awarded and that her unit could start work under the grant the following month. Several members of the training unit were assigned to work on the assessment project with university staff members. The project staff interviewed a large sample of employees and first-line supervisors in the Department of Social Services. Extensive discussions were also held with management personnel at various levels of the Department.

Information derived from interviews and discussions was carefully analyzed, and the conclusions of the project staff were summarized in a seventy-five-page report. The report detailed the training needs of each major segment of the organization at all levels. Recommendations included formal skills training courses, on-the-job developmental experiences, active coaching by supervisors, and some fundamental changes in supervisory and managerial practices.

Soon thereafter, copies of the report were submitted to the Commissioner and the Personnel Director of the Department of Social Services. Foster expressed her readiness to meet with both of them to discuss the actions recommended in the report, as well as her training unit's possible role in implementing some of the recommended changes. Both Social Services officials said that they would contact Foster about a meeting as soon as they had digested the report. Weeks and months passed and

Foster did not hear from either of them, nor did they ever return her telephone calls when she attempted repeatedly to contact them.

1. Why did the Commissioner apparently lose interest in the project?
2. Evaluate the approach of the Director of Training to assessing the Department's training needs.
3. What should the Director of Training have done to ensure the success of the project?
4. What should the Director of Training do now?
5. What lessons does this hold for other areas of personnel management?
6. Which of the recommendations contained in the report are least likely to receive a favorable reaction from the Commissioner?

The Management Development Program

The new administration in the city of Middlevale had campaigned on a platform of improved delivery of services by charging that the city's managers were not doing an effective job. Consequently, the Training Director of the central Department of Personnel was called on to do something about upgrading the skills of the city's managers. The Training Director decided to develop a city-wide management skills training program for senior-level managers.

As a first step, the Training Director asked the head of each city agency for suggestions about what kind of training courses would be useful for high-level managers. After reviewing the responses of all of the agency heads, the Director decided that the program would include courses in basic supervisory skills, electronic data processing, management by objectives, program planning, and project management. The actual content of the courses would be based upon materials that had been developed by a prestigious national management consulting organization and that had been used in several large corporations and agencies of the federal government. The instructors, in large part, would be supplied by the same consulting organization.

The Training Director's staff solicited nominations from each city agency for participants in the first course of the program. Twenty agencies submitted a total of 100 nominations. There were, however, only 25 openings in the course. The Training Director accepted the nominees submitted by the agencies and filled course openings on a first-come, first-served basis while trying to give each agency at least one place.

After the first day of the course, the instructors reported that many of the participants had no idea why they were sent. Some of them did not even know the name of the course they were attending. The instructors also reported that many of the participants were low-level staff people with no line supervisory or managerial responsibilities. In many instances their jobs had nothing to do with the areas in which they were being trained.

1. Evaluate the Training Director's approach to developing the program.
2. Evaluate the method used for filling places in the course.
3. On what basis did agencies appear to have selected nominees for the course?
4. What might have led to the situation reported by the instructors?
5. What should the Training Director do to prevent the situation from recurring in future courses?
6. What results would you expect the training course to produce? Why?

The Training Course

The civil service examinations prepared by the Department of Personnel of Ocean View County, a metropolitan area on the East Coast, had faced a number of challenges in court. To help improve the quality and job-relatedness of these examinations, the Department decided to give a course on test construction to all of its test technicians. Elements of the course, such as principles of good test construction and the avoidance of ambiguity in the use of language, were based on a review of past examinations and on the identification of commonly occurring errors. Attendance at the course, which was scheduled for six hours per week for a period of six weeks, was compulsory for all test technicians.

The Department decided on a formal course of classroom study because the technicians were not being trained on the job by their supervisors. Some of the technicians had received similar training a number of years before. However, the newer technicians had received no training in test construction; whatever skills they possessed had been acquired haphazardly.

The technicians, many of whom had many years of experience in test construction, did not see that their testing skills needed improvement. Several of them stated, "We prepare test items, turn them over to our supervisors, and never hear about them again. If anything were really wrong, we'd hear from our supervisors."

Before the technicians began the course, their supervisors and assistant supervisors were given a somewhat abbreviated version of the course. The reason for training the supervisors as well as the technicians was to sharpen their testing skills, which management believed were weak. The trainers also wanted to apprise them of what their subordinates would be taught so that the supervisors could reinforce the classroom training on the job.

During the training course for supervisors, it was clear that they resented it and viewed it as an implied criticism of their work. The supervisors felt that the course taught them nothing that they did not already know. Further, they expressed skepticism concerning the technicians' need for the course and the consequences of removing the technicians from their regular duties for such a large block of time.

The course evaluation sheets that the technicians filled out at the end of the course indicated that most of them had benefited from it; most of them agreed that the course had been a good learning experience and that they got a lot of new ideas for preparing tests that they would like to apply on the job. The trainers encouraged them to apply the new ideas on the job. However, analysis of a number of tests prepared in the six-month period after the end of the technicians' course revealed that there was practically no change in the quality of tests that were produced.

1. What might account for the difference between the course evaluations and the lack of improvement in test quality?
2. What might explain the lack of improvement in the quality of the tests?
3. Could the Department have attempted to improve test quality by means other than the training course?
4. What might the Department do now to improve the quality of the tests?
5. In light of this experience, what approach would you recommend for introducing and conducting any future courses of this kind? Explain.
6. Evaluate the method used to develop the course.

Improving Managerial
Skills through Training

With the blessing of the Mayor, the Pennington central Department of Personnel developed and scheduled an in-service training course for managers from the various city departments. The course, entitled "Developing Your Managers," was designed to help managers develop their subordinate managers' skills. When the Department of Personnel solicited nominations for attendance at the course, Doris Phillips, the Commissioner of Social Services, nominated Donald Moss, her Director of Client Payments. Moss was happy to attend the course since he felt that his own developmental and coaching skills could use some upgrading and that his subordinate managers would benefit from his improved skills.

The course met for two mornings a week and lasted for twelve weeks. It consisted of seminars and workshops. Moss was exposed to approaches and techniques for assessing individual training needs, formulating individual development plans, and using on-the-job developmental experiences that would improve managerial skills. At the end of the course, Moss felt that he had learned a great deal and was resolved to put his new knowledge and skills to immediate use.

Moss began to meet with his subordinate managers, as individuals and as a group, on a regular basis. Their development needs were assessed, plans were formulated, specific assignments were given to individual managers, and feedback was provided on their progress. Most of the managers reacted quite positively to the new development activities. Although the meetings consumed a good deal of time, Moss felt that the new program would ultimately pay off by producing better managers and a better managed Client Payments Division.

During one of the meetings, Moss received a telephone call from the Commissioner, and the following conversation took place:

Phillips: Don, you and your people have to get to work right away on implementing the new eligibility standards. This will probably entail rewriting almost all of our procedures to meet the new state requirements. The revision has to be done right away. State auditors are coming in, and we stand to lose state reimbursement if we haven't revised our procedures by the time the auditors arrive. Incidentally, I've had some trouble in getting hold of you during the past few weeks; you always seem to be at meetings. Is there something going on that I should know about?

Moss: As a matter of fact, I've been putting into effect some of the concepts and techniques I learned in that training course. I know that a lot of my time has been spent in meetings, but this is an investment that will pay off in the long run by producing better managers in my Division.

Phillips: Look, Don, we don't have time for new management theories in this Department. We have a lot of work to get out, especially in your Division, which is usually the busiest in the Department. If we had the luxury of unlimited time, you might be able to try out some of this new stuff to see if it works. But, if we don't get those procedures revised in time, the Mayor will come down on my head.

1. Was Phillips being unfair to Moss? Explain.
2. What could Moss have said in response to Phillips' remark, "... we don't have time for new management theories in this Department"?

3. Is Moss likely to succeed in applying what he learned in the training course? Explain.
4. Why did the Commissioner nominate a key manager like Moss to attend the training course?
5. Did Moss really need the training? Is the training likely to help him do a better job?

Suggested Readings for Chapter 5

Barlett, C. J. "Equal Employment Opportunity in Training." *Public Personnel Management* 8, no. 6 (November–December 1979):398–405.

Brown, F. Gerald, and Kenneth R. Wedel. *Assessing Training Needs.* Washington, D.C.: National Training and Development Service Press, 1974.

Bureau of National Affairs. "Planning the Training Program." *Personnel Management: BNA Policy and Practice Series.* Washington, D.C., 1975.

Byers, Kenneth T., ed. *Employee Training and Development in the Public Service.* Chicago: International Personnel Management Association, 1970.

Campbell, John P., et al. *Managerial Behavior, Performance, and Effectiveness.* New York: McGraw-Hill, 1970.

Claycombe, W. W. "An Evaluation of Supervisory Skills to Determine Training Needs." *Personnel Journal* 55, no. 3 (March 1976):116–20.

Cooke, Kathleen. "A Model for the Identification of Training Needs." *Public Personnel Management* 8, no. 4 (July–August 1979):256–61.

Couch, Peter D., and George S. Strother. "A Critical Incident Evaluation of Supervisory Training." *Training and Development Journal* 25, no. 9 (September 1971):6–11.

DiLauro, Thomas J. "Training Needs Assessment: Current Practices and New Directions." *Public Personnel Management* 8, no. 6 (November–December 1979):350–59.

Dooley, Arch R., and Wickham Skinner. "Casing Casemethod Methods." *Academy of Management Review* 2, no. 2 (April 1977):277–89.

Fisher, Delbert W. "Educational Psychology Involved in On-the-Job Training." *Personnel Journal* 56, no. 10 (October 1977):516–19.

Gilbert, G. Ronald, and John V. Sauter. "Executive Development: The Federal Executive Institute's Executive Development Program." *Public Personnel Management* 8, no. 6 (November–December 1979):407–15.

Goodacre, Daniel. "The Experimental Evaluation of Management Training: Principles and Practice." *Personnel* 52, no. 6 (May 1975):534–38.

Gordon, Michael E. "Planning Training Activity." *Training and Development Journal* 27, no. 1 (January 1973):3–6.

Hill, Alfred W. "How Organizational Philosophy Influences Management Development." *Personnel Journal* 59, no. 2 (February 1980):118–20, and 148.

Hyde, A. C., and Jay M. Shafritz. "Training and Development and Personnel Management." *Public Personnel Management* 8, no. 6 (November–December 1979):344–49.

Inderlied, S. D., and D. L. Bates. "A Practical Approach to Determining Training-Solvable Problems." *Personnel Journal* 59, no. 2 (February 1980):121–25.

Jobe, Ernest D., W. Randy Boxx, and D.L. Howell. "A Customized Approach to Management Development." *Personnel Journal* 58, no. 3 (March 1979):150–53.

Kellog, Marion S. *Closing the Performance Gap: Results-Centered Employee Development.* New York: American Management Association, 1967.

Mandt, Edward J. "A Basic Model of Manager Development." *Personnel Journal* 58, no. 6 (June 1979):395–400.

Nadler, Leonard. "Support Systems for Training." *Training and Development Journal* 25, no. 10 (October 1971):2–7.

Odiorne, George S. *Training by Objectives: An Economic Approach to Management Training.* New York: Macmillan, 1970.

Pomerlau, Raymond. "The State of Management Development in the Federal Service." *Public Personnel Management* 3, no. 1 (January–February 1974):23–27.

Salinger, Ruth D. *Disincentives to Effective Employee Training and Developent.* Washington, D.C.: U.S. Civil Service Commission, 1973.

Steiner, Richard, and Frank Kelly. "A Key Factors Approach to Assessing Management Development." *Personnel Journal* 55, no. 7 (July 1976):358–61.

Stockard, James G. "A Training Strategy for Decentralized Organizations." *Public Personnel Management* 2, no. 3 (May–June 1973):200–04.

Tracey, William R. *Evaluating Training and Development Systems.* New York: American Management Association, 1968.

Warren, Malcolm W. *Training for Results: A Systems Approach to the Development of Human Resources in Industry.* Reading, Mass.: Addison-Wesley, 1969.

Wolfe, Joseph. "Evaluating the Training Effort." *Training and Development Journal* 27, no. 5 (May 1973):20–28.

Zeira, Yoram. "Is External Management Training Effective for Organizational Change?" *Public Personnel Management* 2, no. 6 (November–December 1973): 400–07.

_____. "Job Rotation for Management Development." *Personnel* 51, no. 4 (July–August 1974):25–35.

6 Line-Staff Relationships

The terms *line* and *staff* describe two different types of roles and relationships often found within organizations. The two terms are used to characterize individuals, units within organizations, or even entire departments or agencies. Line authority implies the direct exercise of a full range of managerial authority and control over subordinates in the context of a hierarchical chain of command; staff authority is only advisory or supporting. For example, the counsel to the Department of Highways can only give legal advice to the Department's bureau chiefs; the counsel cannot tell them what to do. The staff role that the counsel is playing in dealing with the bureau chiefs is advisory. However, if the counsel has attorneys working for him or her, the counsel also exercises line authority over his or her own subordinates.

Units that are not directly responsible for carrying out an organization's basic mission or parts of the mission and that provide advisory or supporting services can be characterized as staff units. In a Department of Highways, for example, the Personnel Division is a staff unit; it provides supporting services (e.g., the recruitment of needed personnel for the other units of the Department). On the other hand, the Bureau of Highway Maintenance, which carries out the Department's basic mission of maintaining the jurisdiction's highways, is a line unit.

Similarly, some entire departments within a public jurisdiction are essentially line in nature while others are staff. For example, departments such as Highways, Parks, Health, Police, and Fire, which provide direct services to the public, are line agencies. Departments such as Personnel, Budget, and Purchase, which provide supporting services to other agencies, are staff agencies. In complex, modern organizations, line managers are unlikely to have all of the knowledge and expertise that they need to function effectively. Specialized staff individuals, units, or departments help line managers carry out their jobs by providing expertise to the line managers in a number of technical areas.

One long-standing and perennial source of conflict in public and private sector organizations arises from line-staff relationships. Line managers and departments responsible for the delivery of services often perceive the activities of staff organizations as impediments to the achievement of their own goals. Some of these attitudes on the part of line managers stem from unsatisfactory experiences in dealing with staff units. In many cases staff organizations have fostered unfavorable attitudes among line people by their lack of sensitivity to line needs, by their arrogance, and by their self-serving behavior.

Even when staff units do not exhibit these types of behavior, line organizations may see little value in their services, especially if line managers view the staff role as one that imposes standards, procedures, rules, and regulations—that is, exercises control rather than provides services. Although staff departments ordinarily come into existence to provide services to line organizations, circumstances may force the staff department to take on control responsibilities.

Because of a need for central coordination, control, and uniformity in areas such as interpretation of labor

contracts and time and leave policies, staff organizations sometimes develop functional authority—that is, the right to tell line
managers what to do in certain specific areas of work. Since
granting unrestrained functional authority to staff units may have
the effect of demoralizing and undermining the position of line
managers, such grants of authority should be carefully considered and made sparingly.

There is something inherently contradictory
about assigning both advisory and control functions to the same
staff unit. One role tends to compromise the other, and there is serious doubt as to whether any staff unit can perform both roles
effectively. Nevertheless, staff organizations such as central personnel departments are often assigned both roles by statute—that
is, they are required to assist operating agencies in setting up and
maintaining personnel programs, and at the same time are required to audit agency programs to ensure that they meet certain
standards. There may not be any simple answer to this problem of
contradictory roles, but it is desirable to assign only one of the two
roles to any staff organization to avoid potential role conflict.

One of the chronic complaints of managers
in line departments is that they lack the freedom to manage because their activities are circumscribed by staff organizations.
However, even when line managers are given authority, they may
be reluctant to accept it when faced with the responsibility that
the authority entails. Although line managers may desire to have
authority over their own employees, they may also find it convenient to blame staff organizations for actions or events that are
not popular among their own personnel.

Line-staff relationships are often beset with
friction, conflict, and outright hostility. This antagonism may be
due in some cases to the fundamental differences in orientation
and attitude between line and staff people. Although it is perhaps
an oversimplification, line people can be characterized as
"locals" who tend to identify with the goals, standards, and interests of their employer, while staff people can be characterized
as "cosmopolitans" who tend to identify with the goals, standards, and interests of their profession rather than with their particular employer. Line people may come to see staff people as
"ivory-tower" philosophers and planners, not doers. To some extent the nature of such relationships can be improved—that is,

both types of personnel can be rotated between line and staff roles, and a greater effort can be made to involve line people in decisions that concern them even when the staff people possess authority in the area.

Another problem arises from role ambiguity. The chief executive of the organization fails to define clearly the boundaries of the staff unit's authority. The staff unit is unsure of how far beyond its advisory role it may go. Top management's failure to clearly define the limits of the staff unit's authority may be a deliberate tactic intended to foster competition between line and staff units, but this tactic only sows the seeds of conflict between the units and has the effect of undermining the position of the staff people. Role ambiguity does not foster the development of an effective working relationship between the two types of units.

Sometimes, experts from outside the organization are employed in a staff capacity to develop certain programs for use by line managers. In such situations the employing organization should make sure that the consultant capitalizes upon the resources and expertise that already exist within the organization. Even when staff people possess the needed expertise, they may be isolated from the mainstream of the organization simply because they are outsiders. There is a natural tendency for organization members to treat outsiders with suspicion and distrust. The consultant should attempt to rapidly establish effective working relationships with organization members. In this regard top management can pave the way by indicating its unreserved support for the consultant's project.

Cases in Line-Staff
Relationships

The Personnel Forum
The Decentralized Personnel System
**Auditing Line Department
Performance**
**Improving Adherence to Payroll
Procedures**
The Job Analysis Manual

The Personnel Forum

In a northeastern state, relations between the central Personnel Department and operating agencies had become strained. Increasingly, there were signs of friction, suspicion, and misunderstanding between them. In order to promote better understanding and cooperation and improved coordination of personnel policy, the Governor asked Margaret Libby, the state's Personnel Director, to convene on a monthly basis a forum of top-ranking personnel officers from all state agencies. The forum would be used to discuss common problems, exchange information, and reach agreement on personnel policies that affect the state as a whole.

Libby wanted only high-ranking officials to attend the forum. She therefore issued an invitation to the Assistant Commissioners who were responsible for personnel and administrative services in each of the state's twenty agencies. All twenty Assistant Commissioners, some with supporting staff, came to the first meeting of the forum. Libby began the meeting by describing the purposes of the forum. She then asked the participants if there were any problems they wanted to discuss.

Anita Suarez, the Assistant Commissioner of Recreation, indicated that she wished to speak.

> Suarez: We just received a directive from the Personnel Department that requires employee attendance to be recorded from now on by means of a time clock and punch cards. We have work locations throughout the state that include parks, picnic grounds, supply depots, and garages. It would be very expensive for us to install and maintain time clocks in all of these locations. We've used a system of sign-in and sign-out sheets for years. All of our people are used to this system, and we've had no problem with it.
>
> Libby: There has to be a standardized state-wide system for controlling employees' time. It's too easy to falsify the kinds of sheets you have been using.
>
> Suarez: Our system works very well. Everyone understands it. Also, the supervisor maintains control by placing a red line after the signature of the last worker that reports in

on time. Anyone who signs after the red line is obviously late. The system works and I don't see why we have to change it.

Libby: I don't think that this is worth arguing about. I'm sorry, but we're going ahead with the time clocks.

Steve Bentley, Assistant Commissioner of Highways, asked to be recognized.

Bentley: Why is the Personnel Department holding up the approval of our Department's new incentives program?

Libby: We sent guidelines to all agencies a couple of months ago about the kinds and amounts of incentives that would be appropriate. For example, we just can't go along with the idea of offering special incentives for good attendance and punctuality.

Bentley: We studied our agency needs for eight months before we came up with this program. You know that we've got special morale and motivation problems in Highways. These incentives were designed to deal with some of these problems.

Libby: I'm willing to have members of my staff meet with your staff next week to figure out how your program can be modified to meet the guidelines' requirements. . . .

I would like to bring up a few points before we go on. First, I am not satisfied with the way your monthly staffing reports have been completed. My people tell me that they have to keep sending the reports back to your departments for corrections. This wastes a lot of my staff's time and effort. I want you to make sure the reports are accurate when they are submitted. Also, my staff informs me that the report forms GP 101-A have not been coming in on the first of every month when they are due. Instead, they've been arriving on the twelfth or fifteenth of the month. This is just not acceptable. I'd like you to tell your staff to get the reports in on time.

Libby then asked the participants if there were any other problems they wished to discuss. Since no one offered any, Libby scheduled the next meeting and then brought the session to a close. On the following month about half the agencies were represented by their Assistant Commissioners; low-ranking personnel represented the other agencies. The meeting was carried on in much the same way as the first one was. In succeeding months few, if any, Assistant Commissioners attended. Libby considered discontinuing the forum.

1. Was there a need for the forum? Explain.
2. Were the problems and topics discussed at the forum appropriate? Explain.
3. Was Libby correct in inviting only high-ranking officials to the forum? Explain.
4. Do the interactions at the forum meetings help to explain the reason for the strained relations described at the beginning of the case? Explain.
5. Why did the Assistant Commissioners stop coming to the forum?
6. What, if anything, should Libby do or refrain from doing? Why?

The Decentralized Personnel System

Managers in the line agencies in the city of Southport had long complained that they lacked the decision-making authority that they needed in the personnel area; consequently, they felt handicapped when attempting to carry out their line responsibilities. Every personnel action, from initial recruitment and selection to promotion and allocation of positions, needed the advance approval of, or was performed directly for, the line agencies by the city's central Department of Personnel. The frustrations engendered by a highly centralized personnel system had led to a considerable amount of friction and antagonism between the line agencies and the central Department of Personnel.

In response to strong pressures from various civic groups, Southport's City Council amended the city's personnel ordinance to shift primary responsibility for all personnel activities from the central Department of Personnel to the line agencies themselves. The central Department of Personnel was to confine itself primarily to setting standards and guidelines for line agencies, to providing technical assistance to them, and to post-auditing agency programs for adherence to standards.

To assist the line agencies in assuming their new responsibilities, the Department of Personnel issued detailed guidelines and manuals for each area of personnel. Extensive training was also provided, and each agency received help in establishing its own personnel unit. To further ensure that agencies possessed the capability for assuming their new responsibilities, they were asked to submit detailed plans and timetables for implementing each personnel function to the central Department of Personnel. In time all of the agencies' plans were submitted and approved by Personnel.

After initial successes in decentralizing some minor personnel functions, Personnel Director Robert Weiss moved to decentralize the administration of promotion tests, which is an important and sensitive activity. On February 1, he therefore issued the following memorandum to all agencies:

> Pursuant to the new provisions in the law, all agencies will be responsible for administering their own promotion tests beginning on April 1 of this year. This responsibility will include job analysis, test development, test administration, test rating, and the handling of candidate appeals.
>
> While the Department of Personnel is prepared to provide some technical assistance in all phases of the testing process, it should be understood that the operating agencies will have primary responsibility for the administration of these tests.

The day after the memorandum reached the agencies, Weiss received a telephone call from Frank McMahon, the Police Commissioner, and the following conversation took place:

McMahon: Bob, I just received your memo on promotion tests. I knew it was coming eventually, but I don't think we're ready for it yet. You know that there is a police captain's test scheduled for September and that this test will probably be the most difficult one for us to develop. If the test is not prepared properly, candidates will be very unhappy and will possibly challenge it in court. Even highly trained personnel selection specialists with long years of experience would find this test a challenging assignment. I am asking you to postpone indefinitely giving us responsibility for promotion tests.

Weiss: I understand your problem, but if I make an exception for you, I'll have to do the same for the other agencies.

McMahon: I don't want to pressure you, but if I have to, I'll go to the Mayor with this.

Within the next several days, Weiss received similar calls from the Environmental Protection, Public Works, and Social Services Commissioners. None of them was willing to accept responsibility for the tests. Weiss was dismayed; after all, the public had mandated decentralization of personnel testing.

1. Evaluate Weiss's approach to decentralizing test administration. Could he have introduced decentralized testing in a fashion that would have been more acceptable to line agencies? Explain.

2. When would the Police Commissioner be prepared to assume responsibility for promotion tests? Explain.

3. What should Weiss do now?

4. What does this case suggest about decentralization of authority to line managers?

5. What does this case suggest about the centralization of authority in staff departments?

6. What types of personnel functions are line agencies more likely to accept without resistance?

Auditing Line Department Performance

On January 1, the Department of Correction of a large western state embarked on a management by objectives (MBO) program. Under the terms of an agreement with the Office of the Governor, the top management of the Department of Correction was authorized within limits to grant merit increases to those managers who attained the best results at the end of each six-month evaluation period. Managerial performance was to be assessed through a results-based performance appraisal system, which was installed at the same time as the MBO program itself. Part of the system called for the completion of appropriate forms by the managers and their superiors that specified the objectives that managers were to meet, together with standards for judging performance. The agreement gave the state's central Department of Personnel responsibility for auditing the operation of the performance evaluation program and for reporting its findings and recommendations to the Governor.

On July 1, six months after the program began, the Commissioner of the Department of Correction announced that eight managers had been outstanding performers and that they would receive substantial merit increases. A few days later, the Deputy Director of the Department of Personnel sent the following letter to Carl Hansen, Deputy Commissioner of the Department of Correction, who was responsible for the implementation of the MBO program:

> *Dear Mr. Hansen:*
>
> *Under the terms of the MBO agreement, we plan to send one of our senior staff members, Henry Chin, to your Department on July 15 to audit your Department's managerial performance appraisal system. Mr. Chin will require the following for his audit:*
>
> 1. *A sample of ten completely filled out performance evaluation forms;*
> 2. *Arrangements for interviews with four managers who were rated and with the managers' superiors who did the actual rating.*
>
> *If the July 15 date is not suitable, please let me know; otherwise, Mr. Chin will be at your office on that date.*
>
> *Thank you for your cooperation.*

On July 15, when Chin arrived at Deputy Commissioner Hansen's office, the following discussion took place:

Hansen: I can't show you any rating forms because the first group of forms were returned to the raters as being unacceptable. It's also pointless to carry out the interviews because no final ratings were completed. However, I would be happy to try to answer any of your questions.

Chin: If no performance evaluations were satisfactorily completed, how were you able to determine who should be given merit increases?

Hansen: We don't really need a formal performance appraisal system to tell us who the good performers are. We know which managers get results. Besides, we have an equity problem here. Some of these managers were making less money than their unionized subordinates even though the managers were doing excellent work for years.

Chin: If you don't have rating forms that I can look at, may I at least see copies of the statements of objectives and performance standards for some of your managers?

Hansen: Unfortunately, most of the statements were also returned to the raters for revision. I really don't have any complete ones to give you.

1. If you were Chin, how would you evaluate the implementation of the Department of Correction's managerial performance appraisal system? Comment on the Department's motives for implementing the system.

2. If you were Chin, what recommendations would you make to the Deputy Director of Personnel on the Department of Correction's performance appraisal system?

3. Evaluate Hansen's statement: "We don't really need a formal appraisal system to tell us who the good performers are. We know which managers get results."

4. Evaluate the approach of the Department of Personnel in carrying out its audit function with the Department of Correction.

5. What lessons should the central Department of Personnel draw from this experience when it attempts to implement a performance evaluation system in other agencies?

6.   What role, if any, should the Office of the Governor play in the MBO program audit?

Improving Adherence
to Payroll Procedures

The city of Bedford had a partially decentralized payroll system. Each city agency had its own payroll division and initiated all payroll changes that reflected hirings, resignations, retirements, overtime charges, and so forth. Each agency payroll was audited by the Department of Audit and Control before paychecks were issued. Unfortunately, agency payroll clerks were making frequent errors and were not following all of the procedures that were mandated by the Department of Audit and Control.

In order to reduce costly payroll errors and to insure that agency clerks followed proper procedures, the Mayor of Bedford engaged a consulting organization, the Urban Institute, to prepare a manual of procedures that would be used by all agency payroll clerks. The Urban Institute was a local think tank that employed a number of part-time consultants from the local university to augment its force of full-time consultants. Although the consultants had little familiarity with actual city operations, they were acknowledged experts in the fields of accounting and management. To start the project off, one of the consultants, Sally MacDonald, scheduled a visit with Charles Wang, the Chief of Payroll in the Department of Audit and Control. The following discussion took place:

Wang: You said you were from the Urban Institute and wanted to talk about our payroll procedures. Why is the Urban Institute interested in our payroll procedures?

MacDonald: We've been commissioned by the Mayor's office to study your procedures and then to design a manual that could be used by payroll clerks in the operating agencies. I understand that the agency payroll clerks have been making a great many errors.

Wang: You can say that again! But, I don't think that any manual is going to solve the problem. The people in my office are pretty good. Although the system is fairly complex, they understand it. Their expertise has only

	come after long years of experience. The agency clerks aren't going to develop this expertise from a manual.
MacDonald:	You may be right, but I'm sure that a manual of standardized procedures will at least improve the situation. I'd like to talk to a number of people in your office. In fact I'd like to start with you. Could you outline briefly how the system works?
Wang:	Well, the basis of our system is the Form DAC–53 and the sixty-eight codes that designate the various kinds of payroll actions . . . .
MacDonald: *(interrupting)*	Excuse me. What's a DAC–53 form?

MacDonald continued her discussion with Wang and eventually spoke also with four subordinate supervisors and six payroll clerks, all of whom seemed reluctant to be of assistance. In some instances the information she received seemed to be contradictory and in other cases seemed incomplete. Consequently, she returned to the Department several times in an attempt to clarify some points. After six months of work, a manual was produced and distributed to all city agencies.

1. Evaluate the approach that was taken by the Mayor in his attempt to improve the performance of the payroll clerks in the agencies.

2. Evaluate the approach that was used by the Urban Institute to carry out the project.

3. How accurate is the new manual likely to be?

4. Assuming that the new manual accurately sets down existing procedures, is its issuance likely to bring about any improvement in the job performance of the payroll clerks? Explain.

5. Why were the employees to whom MacDonald spoke reluctant to be of assistance?

The Job Analysis Manual

The Personnel Department of a southwestern state had seen some of its civil service examinations upset by the courts for lack of job-relatedness. Courts had ruled that the tests seemed to bear little, if any, relationship to the abilities that were needed to perform the jobs. The head of the Department, Personnel Director Alan Buckley, was determined to do something about this situation. He therefore asked Vera Zabriskie, the Department's Chief of Research, to prepare for the personnel technicians who developed the tests detailed guidelines on how to conduct job analyses that could be used as the bases for the tests. Examinations supported by thorough job analyses would be much better able to withstand court challenge.

Zabriskie's research staff was responsible for conducting research into and developing new testing approaches for use by the various testing units of the Department. Her staff also analyzed the results of tests that were prepared by these units. In addition the research unit provided assistance and technical information to the testing units upon request. In short it was a staff unit that was providing service, advice, and guidance to the line units, sometimes on its own initiative and sometimes at the request of the line people.

Zabriskie assigned some of her staff to develop what was to become the Personnel Department's job analysis manual. Literature in the field was surveyed and requests were sent to a large number of public jurisdictions for copies of their manuals and procedures. Materials on job analysis were also obtained from the federal government.

Six months later a preliminary version of the manual was ready. Since the manual was to be used by the Department's testing units, it was important to obtain their reaction to this first version. Zabriskie gave copies of the draft version to the chiefs of the Department's five testing units, as well as to the agency's top executives. The testing chiefs were asked to read the manual carefully and make comments and suggestions.

Zabriskie received very detailed comments from the chiefs and incorporated most of the suggestions into the manual. The final version of the manual was more than 100 pages in length and was quite rigorous in terms of its requirements for sample size, interviewing, formulation of task statements, documentation, and other essential elements. Eight months after she received the assignment, Zabriskie presented a copy of the final version of the manual to the Personnel Director. Buckley congratulated Zabriskie on a job well done and directed that the manual be issued to all testing staff. Each test technician received a copy of the manual with the following memorandum signed by the Personnel Director:

Effective immediately, all testing techni-
cians will use the procedures contained in
the attached manual for conducting job
analyses. It is vital that we be able to select
the best qualified individuals by developing
job-related tests.

If you have any questions about these proce-
dures, feel free to contact Vera Zabriskie,
who is prepared to provide every assis-
tance. Your cooperation in this critical mat-
ter is appreciated.

In the five months following the issuance of the manual, Zabriskie received no inquiries on the new job analysis procedures. One day she was called to the Personnel Director's office. Buckley started by saying, "Vera, I'm really disappointed in you. You assured me that the new job analysis procedures would make our tests more job related and able to withstand legal challenges. I've just learned that the court ruled our last police officer examination invalid because of an inadequate job analysis. We'll now have to develop a new examination. This will cost us a lot of money, to say nothing of the delay that will occur in filling police officer jobs."

Zabriskie responded, "I'm at a loss to explain what happened. I'll talk to Ken Suzuki, head of the Police Testing Unit, and get back to you."

Zabriskie visited Suzuki at his office and asked to see a copy of the job analysis in question. The analysis fell far short of what the new procedures required. Zabriskie asked, "Why didn't your staff follow the new manual?"

Suzuki answered, "What manual? Oh wait, you people issued something about six months ago, didn't you? I seem to recollect that it was very complicated and detailed. We really didn't have the time for that sort of thing. This last police examination had a very tight deadline." Zabriskie left Suzuki's office dismayed and wondered what had gone wrong.

1. Why wasn't the job analysis manual used as it was intended to be used?
2. What could Zabriskie have done that she did not do?

3. What could Buckley have done to promote the use of the manual?

4. What should Zabriskie do now?

5. What if Zabriskie found that Suzuki's staff had followed the new procedure faithfully? What should she have done?

6. What are the broader implications in this case for staff roles in public or private sector organizations?

Suggested Readings for Chapter 6

Allen, Louis A. "The Line-Staff Relationship." *Management Record* 17, no. 9 (September 1955):346–49.

Beach, Dale S. *Personnel, the Management of People.* New York: MacMillan, 1970.

Bowen, Don L., and Merrill J. Collett. "When and How to Use a Consultant: Guidelines for Public Managers." *Public Administration Review* 38, no. 5 (September–October 1978):476–81.

Boynton, Robert E., and Harold C. White "Functions of Personnel Administration: Management's View in a Federal Installation." *Public Personnel Management* 2, no. 1 (January–February 1973):29–36.

Browne, Philip, and Robert Golembiewski. "The Line-Staff Concept Revisited." *Academy of Management Journal* 17, no. 3 (September 1974): 406–17.

Dalton, Melville. "Conflicts Between Staff and Line Managerial Officers." *American Sociological Review* 15, no. 3 (June 1950): 342–50.

Foulkes, Fred K. "The Expanding Role of the Personnel Function." *Harvard Business Review* 53, no. 2 (March–April 1975):71–84.

Frankenhuis, Jean Pierre. "How to Get a Good Consultant." *Harvard Business Review* 55, no. 6 (November–December 1977): 133–39.

Guthrie, Robert R. "Personnel's Emerging Role." *Personnel Journal* 53, no. 9 (September 1974):657–58.

Kline, Eliot H., and C. Gregory Buntz. "On the Effective Use of Public Sector Expertise: Or Why the Use of Outside Consultants Often Leads to the Waste of In-House Skills." *Public Administration Review* 39, no. 3 (May–June 1979):226–29.

Meyer, Herbert E. "Personnel Directors Are the New Corporate Heroes." *Fortune* 93, no. 2 (February 1976):84–88.

Mitchell, James M., and Rolfe E. Schroeder. "Future Shock for Personnel Administration." *Public Personnel Management* 3, no. 4 (July–August 1974):265–69.

Rehfuss, John. "Managing the Consultantship Process." *Public Administration Review* 39, no. 3 (May–June 1979):211–14.

Ritzer, George, and Harrison M. Trice. *An Occupation in Conflict: A Study of the Personnel Manager.* Ithaca, N.Y.: Cornell University Press, 1969.

Rosenblum, Robert, and Daniel McGillis. "Observations on the Role of Consultants in the Public Sector." *Public Administration Review* 39, no. 3 (May–June 1979):219–26.

Schleh, Edward C. "Using Central Staff to Boost Line Initiative." *Management Review* 65, no. 5 (May 1976):17–23.

Sorenson, James E., and Thomas L. Sorenson. "The Conflict of Professionals in Bureaucratic Organizations." *Administrative Science Quarterly* 19, no. 1 (March 1974):98–106.

7 Employee Relations

In addition to dealing with employees as individuals, employers must frequently deal with them collectively as members of unions or associations. In some cases employees join organizations that have been accorded collective bargaining rights; in other cases employees belong to organizations or associations that have not been granted legal recognition. What is significant from the viewpoint of human resources management is that employees who become members of an employee organization may take on its values and adopt its objectives. Union objectives may be in accord with or sharply at variance with the objectives of the employing organization.

The right of public employees to organize and to bargain collectively did not gain general acceptance until the late 1950s. Until that time public employees were viewed as a breed apart from other employees. It was widely believed that granting bargaining rights to public employees was an illegal surrender of state sovereignty. According to this view all decisions on public policy or public expenditures ought to be made by the elected officials who represent the community at large. To do anything else would be "undemocratic."

Since the late 1950s, however, membership in public sector employee organizations has increased dramatically. Employees have come to perceive organized collective action as an effective and appropriate means of advancing their interests and of protecting their rights in the face of large, impersonal, and bureaucratized organizations. Along with the phenomenal growth in union membership, there has also been increasing acceptance of the idea that labor relation practices in the public sector should resemble many of those practices that are found in the private sector. Consequently, the scope of matters that are covered under collective bargaining has broadened substantially in many jurisdictions, and many techniques for conflict resolution have been adapted from the private sector.

Even though private and public sector labor practices have been converging to some extent, there are still significant differences between the two. Public sector negotiations occur in a different context than private sector negotiations do. Chief executives and their negotiators must always be aware of political constituencies (e.g., a cost-conscious public opposed to overly generous settlements, cost-cutting legislators, and unions that may have substantial electoral power as well as political influence). Public sector negotiations themselves are not necessarily insulated from outside influences. Union leaders can undercut the negotiating position of public executives by appealing directly to legislators. The negotiating position of the employer may be predetermined by a budget deficit. Even a settlement once arrived at by management and labor can be overturned by a legislative body. The very existence of oversight bodies can tempt employers to agree to concessions that they ordinarily would not agree to because they know the concessions will be rejected later on.

Proponents of public employees' right to strike generally see no essential differences between employment in the public sector and employment in the private sector. If some services in the public sector are vital, these proponents would argue that some services such as private hospitals in the private sector are also vital. The strike weapon is in their view the most effective weapon available to workers. They would also argue that the strike threat is the only way to ensure that labor's voice is heeded by management in the collective bargaining process and that management bargains in good faith.

Even stringent legislation that bars certain types of union activity such as strikes may not succeed in its purpose. The record of antistrike legislation in preventing strikes has been uneven at best. In the public sector this is an especially serious problem. Many of the services provided by public agencies are essential. Employee strikes have the potential of crippling the ability of entire communities to function. The citizenry should not be expected to endure the chaos that is engendered by such strikes. In the long run the best way for a public employer to avoid strikes is to cultivate good labor-management relationships.

Many employee organizations are in a position to exercise significant influence upon the outcome of the employer's programs. There is a need for union understanding, cooperation, and support even if management is convinced that its actions in a particular area do not fall squarely within the scope of collective bargaining.

Employer attitudes and tactics can lead to unintended consequences, such as formation of unions where none existed previously. Employer attitudes may also influence the nature of working relationships with formally recognized unions. If unions perceive management actions as being arbitrary or threatening, they can be expected to oppose or obstruct the attainment of organizational goals. Union attitudes may be particularly significant when an employer is contemplating major organizational changes or the installation of new programs. In these cases union resistance may result in the failure of the programs.

Cases in Employee Relations

The Slowdown
The New Performance Evaluation System
The Mayor's Snoopers
The Professional Union

The Slowdown

The city of High Ridge was negotiating a new contract with the union that represents its transit workers. Negotiations, however, were not going well. The union was insisting upon a substantial cost-of-living increase to offset the high rate of inflation, and the city just did not have the funds to meet the union's demands. Stuart Reston, the city's Personnel Director and Chief Labor Negotiator, saw that the union was becoming increasingly impatient and feared the possibility of a strike. Union members were applying increasing pressure on the top union leadership to obtain real salary gains.

Reston met with the Mayor of High Ridge on the status of the negotiations, and the following conversation took place:

Reston: The union won't budge. Maybe we should meet them halfway.

Mayor: I was elected on a platform of fiscal austerity, and I refuse to cave in to the union. If I met the union demands even halfway, it would unbalance the budget. I can't afford that right now.

Reston: You also can't afford a transit strike right now. These people may not be far from a job action.

Mayor: I don't think we have to worry about that. The state's Slater Law imposes heavy financial penalties on any public employee who engages in a strike or other job action. The individual transit workers won't risk these fines no matter what the union says.

Reston: Things have gone pretty far. I'm not sure that the Slater Law will deter workers from striking.

On the following day when the old contract expired, the union broke off negotiations. Reston received a telephone call from the Mayor who began by saying (in an excited voice):

Mayor: "Stu, our transit system is in a chaotic state. None of the printed schedules is being followed. We have thousands of commuters stranded throughout the city. The transit workers are engaging in a slowdown. Start imposing Slater Law fines on them. That will get them back to work soon enough.

Reston: I can't apply the Slater Law in this situation.

Mayor: What do you mean you can't apply the law? These people are engaging in an illegal strike.

Reston: As far as I can see, they are engaging in a "rule book" slowdown. This means that they observe minimum distances between trains, spend a full five minutes at "catch-up" stops, and scrupulously observe all safety rules. We can't fine them for following the official operating rules.

Mayor: Something has got to be done!

1. Evaluate the Mayor's and Reston's handling of the situation.
2. What can Reston do now?
3. What does the slowdown suggest about the operating rules and their application?
4. What lessons does the slowdown provide for the future?
5. Was the Mayor bargaining in good faith? Did the city's fiscal condition really prevent the mayor from making any further concessions to the union? How much should the ability to pay affect a public jurisdiction's negotiating position?
6. What does the case suggest about the efficacy of legislative solutions to labor relations problems?

The New Performance Evaluation System

The Department of Highways in Livonia, a major Midwestern city, decided to install a new performance evaluation system for nonmanagerial staff. To ensure that the new system was job related, objective, and acceptable to the employees (most of whom belonged to a union), the Department decided to ask each employee for information about the work that he or she did and for suggestions about appropriate performance standards for evaluating the work. Supervisors would also be asked to supply information about the various jobs in the Department. The Department's Personnel Division wanted employees to play a major role in formulating the criteria that would be used to evaluate them. This system was a marked departure from the previous system in which employees played no part in developing rating criteria. Therefore, the new system was seen by management as being more beneficial to employees.

As a first step in obtaining the information, the Personnel Division prepared a questionnaire that was distributed to all employees; it included brief instructions, asked each employee to write down what he or she did, and asked them to return the completed questionnaire to the Division.

Upon receiving the questionnaire, some employees showed it to their union representatives. Union leadership stated that it did not understand why the agency asked employees to supply information about their jobs and took the position that performance evaluation was a supervisory responsibility, not a rank-and-file function. The union therefore advised the employees not to complete the form. The Department then warned all employees that failure to complete the form might result in disciplinary action.

1. Should the employees' and the union's responses to the new system have been anticipated by the Personnel Division? Explain.

2. Why did the employees and their union misinterpret the Department's motives for using the questionnaires?

3. What should the Personnel Division have done to introduce the new system?

4. Evaluate the union position according to which performance evaluation is a supervisory responsibility and not a function of rank-and-file employees.

5. What can the Department do now to resolve this problem other than to threaten to take disciplinary action?

6. Should the fact that the Department is unionized affect the manner in which a new system is introduced? Explain.

7. What implications does this case have for managers who are involved in the introduction of new systems?

The Mayor's Snoopers

The city of Harbor Point had recently experienced a major scandal that involved the acceptance of large bribes by some building inspectors. The Mayor of Harbor Point, Andrew Washington, was determined to restore honesty and integrity to city government. He called together his top cabinet officials and announced that he would appoint an Internal Affairs Officer (IAO) in each city agency. The Internal Affairs Officers would have sweeping investigatory powers to uncover cases of corruption and incompetence among city employees. Each IAO was also empowered to assess disciplinary penalties up to and including the removal of any employee who failed to cooperate with the IAO or a member of the IAO's staff in an investigation. This new program, which would be promulgated in the form of an executive order, contained the following additional features:

1. Each IAO was to have a staff of confidential investigators whose identities would not necessarily be known to agency employees.

2. Employees were required to report any occurrence of corruption, incompetence, or unethical behavior on the part of superiors, subordinates, or fellow employees. Any employee that had knowledge of questionable behavior on the part of another employee and failed to report such behavior would be subject to removal.

3. The IAO or members of the IAO's staff could interview any employee directly and without the knowledge of the employee's supervisor.

4. Each IAO was to report directly to the Mayor and was not subject to the authority of the head of the agency in which the IAO worked.

After the Mayor finished outlining the program, Edward Griffin, the city's Director of Personnel and Labor Relations, asked to be recognized and said, "Mr. Mayor, there are some agencies, such as Finance and Taxation, that we've never had any problem with. Appointing an IAO in this kind of agency is going to have a disastrous effect on morale. Some of these people pride themselves on their honesty and integrity."

Mayor: Ed, what you're saying is basically true, but we can't afford any more scandals like the one we had with the Housing Department. Although there has never been any problem with Finance and Taxation in the past, who's to say what will happen in the future? The very presence of these IAOs may serve to keep people honest.

Griffin: There's another problem. Disciplinary proceedings are a mandatory item for collective bargaining under our city-wide contract, and this new program provides for penalties and informal disciplinary proceedings. The unions may insist upon negotiating the actual procedures. If we don't involve them in this program, they may file an unfair labor practice complaint with the State Employee Relations Board. The whole program could be jeopardized if we get an adverse ruling from the Board. Incidentally, what has the union's initial reaction been?

Mayor: Frankly, I haven't consulted with the union. I believe that the matters addressed by this program lie outside the scope of collective bargaining. The disciplinary proceedings and penalties that come under the authority of the IAOs do not fall within the normal range of disciplinary matters that are covered by the contract.

1. Evaluate the features of the IAO program.
2. How are the employees of agencies such as Finance and Taxation likely to react? How are city employees in general likely to react?
3. What is the union's reaction likely to be?
4. While the IAO program was primarily established in an attempt to weed out or discourage corruption, what other purpose might it serve? Should this have been stressed by the Mayor?

5. Could the way in which the program was promulgated affect its subsequent success? Explain.
6. Are there alternative approaches to combating corruption other than an IAO-type program? Explain.

The Professional Union

Walter Riordan, the Commissioner of Taxation of a north central state, had been dealing informally with the Professional Association of Accountants (PAA), even though accountants, under state law, were excluded from collective bargaining. Although the organization represented only 40 percent of the accountants in his department, Riordan had found it convenient to settle certain matters that concerned accountants through some type of organization.

The state recently instituted a productivity improvement program that required all salary increases for state workers to be offset by productivity increases. Each department was expected to achieve certain productivity savings, and each department head was expected to reach agreement on such measures with each group of employees within their department.

Riordan quickly met and negotiated productivity agreements with each of the collective bargaining groups within the Taxation Department. The largest of these groups, which represented the clerical and secretarial employees, insisted that the Commissioner also negotiate an agreement with the accountants. The clerical employees wanted the accountants to contribute their share toward reaching the Department's productivity and money-saving goals.

Since Riordan could not negotiate with each accountant individually, he called a meeting with representatives of the PAA. Susan Pierce, the President of the PAA, together with two other officers, appeared at Riordan's office. The following conversation took place:

Riordan: To serve as the basis for next year's salary increase, I want your organization to sign an agreement with me. Here's what I propose: At our busiest times during tax season, your members would voluntarily agree to work overtime up to a maximum of ten hours a month without submitting claims for pay. In return your people can take an equal amount of time off during our slack periods. This extra working time during tax season would provide the increased production to offset the cost of the salary increase.

Pierce: Although it sounds reasonable, why should we sign a new agreement with you when you haven't lived up to all of our agreements in the past? As a matter of fact, you haven't treated our members as professionals. You recently imposed very strict time controls and encouraged supervisors to give clerical tasks to accountants rather than attempt to obtain additional clerical staff. At the same time you have made disparaging remarks about accountants by alleging that the work they are doing is really routine bookkeeping and not professional accounting work.

Riordan: I'm sick and tired of hearing the word *professional*. What does it mean? As far as I'm concerned it's nonsense. All of us are paid to get a job done, regardless of what the individual's job title is. I want you to know that I can order the accountants to work voluntary overtime and at the same time withhold your salary increase. Your members aren't covered by any collective bargaining agreement.

Pierce: Order the overtime! But you can be sure our members will submit claims for overtime pay.

Riordan: I don't like your attitude. Get out of my office!

Shortly after the meeting with Pierce, Riordan convened a meeting of all accountants in the Department and made the following statement:

> An organization purporting to represent the accountants in this Department has refused to sign a productivity agreement with me. If no agreement is reached, all of you will be denied your salary increases. I called all of you here today because I don't believe that

the organization represents a majority or even a substantial number of accountants in this Department.

In exchange for your salary increases, I am simply asking you to work overtime for a maximum of ten hours a month on a voluntary basis. As you can see, this is a reasonable offer. If the PAA really represented your interests, it would not have turned it down.

Riordan then answered questions and heard various comments from the accountants. When there were no further questions, Riordan asked, "Would all those in favor of abiding by this arrangement signify their agreement by raising their hands?" More than 90 percent of the accountants present voted in favor of Riordan's offer.

1. What effect were the events described in this case likely to have on the PAA and the size of its membership?
2. How were the future relationships between Riordan and the PAA likely to be affected?
3. Could Riordan have taken any other approach in dealing with the accountants? Explain.
4. Evaluate Riordan's remarks about "professional" accounting work.
5. Relate Riordan's and Pierce's attitudes toward "professional" work to the likely attitudes of the clerical and secretarial employees.
6. What would explain the difference between Pierce's position and remarks and the vote of the accountants?
7. Even if an employer is not required by law to bargain collectively with particular groups of employees, does the employer still have an obligation to treat these employees fairly? Explain.

Suggested Readings for Chapter 7

Aboud, Antone, and Grace Aboud. *The Right to Strike in Public Employment.* Ithaca, N.Y.: Cornell University Press, 1974.

Anderson, Arvid, and Hugh D. Jascourt, eds. *Trends in Public Sector Labor Relations.* Chicago: International Personnel Management Association, 1975.

Atwood, Jay F. "Collective Bargaining's Challenge: Five Imperatives for Public Managers." *Public Personnel Management* 5, no. 1 (January–February 1976):24–31.

Chamot, Dennis. "Professional Employees Turn to Unions." *Harvard Business Review* 54, no. 3 (May–June 1976):119–27.

Federal Labor Relations Council. *Labor-Management Relations in the Federal Service.* Washington, D.C.: U.S. Civil Service Commission, 1971.

Feigenbaum, Charles. "Civil Service and Collective Bargaining: Conflict or Compatibility?" *Public Personnel Management* 3, no. 3 (May–June 1974):244–52.

Heisel, Donald W. *New Questions and Answers on Public Employee Negotiation.* Chicago: International Personnel Management Association, 1973.

Hoffman, Eileen B. *Unionization of Professional Societies.* New York: The Conference Board, 1976.

Horton, Raymond D. *Municipal Labor Relations in New York City: Lessons of the Lindsay-Wagner Years.* New York: Praeger, 1973.

Jascourt, Hugh D. *Public Sector Labor Relations: Recent Trends and Developments.* Lexington, Ky.: Council of State Governments, 1975.

Lewin, David, and Raymond D. Horton. "The Impact of Collective Bargaining on the Merit System in Government." *The Arbitration Journal* 30, no. 3 (September 1975):199–211.

Liston, Robert A. *The Limits of Defiance: Strikes, Rights, and Government.* New York: Franklin Watts, 1971.

Loewenberg J. Joseph, and Michael H. Moskow, eds. *Collective Bargaining in Government: Readings and Cases.* Englewood Cliffs, N.J.: Prentice-Hall, 1972.

Nigro, Felix A. *Management-Employee Relations in the Public Service.* Chicago: International Personnel Management Association, 1969.

Research and Policy Committee of the Committee for Economic Development. *Improving Management of the Public Work Force: The Challenge to State and Local Government.* New York: Committee for Economic Development, 1978.

Roberts, Harold S., ed. *Labor-Management Relations in the Public Service.* Honolulu: University of Hawaii Press, 1970.

Smith, Russel A., Harry T. Edwards, and R. Theodore Uark, Jr. *Labor Relations in the Public Sector: Cases and Materials.* Indianapolis, Ind.: Bobbs-Merrill, 1974.

Spero, Sterling, and John M. Capozzola. *The Urban Community and Its Unionized Bureaucracies.* New York: Dunellen, 1973.

Stanley, David T. *Managing Local Government Under Union Pressure.* Washington, D.C.: The Brookings Institution, 1972.

Stenberg, Carl W. "Labor-Management Relations in State and Local Government: Progress and Prospects." *Public Administration Review* 32, no. 2 (March–April 1972):102–07.

Stieber, Jack. *Public Employee Unionism: Structure, Growth, Policy.* Washington, D.C.: The Brookings Institution, 1973.

Sulzner, George T. "The Impact of Labor Relations upon the Administration of Federal Personnel Policies and Practices: The View from Twenty Bargaining Units." *Public Personnel Management* 8, no. 4 (July–August 1979):228–40.

Twentieth Century Fund. *Pickets at City Hall: Reports and Recommendations of the Twentieth Century Fund: Task Force on Labor Disputes in Public Employment.* New York, 1970.

Zagoria, Sam, ed. *Public Workers and Public Unions.* Englewood Cliffs, N.J.: Prentice-Hall, 1972.

8 Organization Change and Job Design

The structure of an organization and the design of individual jobs can significantly affect the overall capability of an organization to attain its goals as well as the motivation and job satisfaction of its employees. Contemplated changes, therefore, should be analyzed concerning their potential impact upon organizational effectiveness and employee motivation. The implementation of any changes must also be carefully planned to minimize disruption to organizational programs and employee resistance. Moreover, the internal as well as external environment in which a change is expected to occur must be assessed and taken into account. Any significant change must have the support of top management, and this support must be clearly evident to all of those people who are likely to be affected by the change. The most carefully thought-out program for change is likely to fail in the absence of support from top management.

Even if top-level management support is present, a new program may founder if the feelings and perceptions of those people being affected by it are not considered. If those people being affected by the proposed change desire it or welcome it because it meets certain of their needs, the new program is more likely to be implemented successfully. However, if the change is viewed as an interference or hindrance, then it will be resisted or perhaps ignored. Also, change is threatening to most people. It is therefore important to set employees' fears at rest by taking them into management's confidence, by inviting their suggestions, and by keeping them informed. The need for this kind of collaboration and consultation is even more critical if employees are represented by unions. Management can do much to cultivate an organizational climate that supports change.

In many circumstances employee participation in the planning and implementation of change can be extremely beneficial. On the one hand, organizational members are frequently in the best position to make a positive contribution to the planning of change. All too often, the expertise and knowledge of organizational members is ignored. The organization should endeavor to draw whenever possible upon its own internal resources. On the other hand, participation can be a very effective method of eliciting employee commitment to a proposed change. Organizational members are more likely to feel personally committed to a change if they play a role in formulating that change. In order for people to feel a real commitment to change, however, they must believe that the program is necessary and desirable, not only from the organizational viewpoint, but also from the viewpoint of their own needs and goals.

A popular view holds that public organizations are more resistant to change than private organizations are. This may be true. In public organizations most actions and decisions are closely circumscribed by rules, laws, regulations, and procedures. Indeed, one of the characteristics of bureaucracy is the extensive use of formal, written, and reviewable records for specific actions and decisions. This bureaucratic reality, combined with federal laws, state or local merit system requirements, union contract provisions, and competing political forces, may severely limit the ability of public organizations to absorb change easily.

The systems view of organizations emphasizes that a change that is aimed at one area or subsystem of a organization also has an impact on other areas or subsystems. This view is not intended as an argument against change; it simply recognizes that organizations that are considering change should anticipate and be prepared to deal with a broad range of possible consequences. For example, the restructuring of jobs to provide more autonomy, discretion, and variety to employees raises new issues in the areas of selection, compensation, assignment, training, and labor relations. Horizontal expansion of jobs (i.e., adding a greater variety and number of tasks to a job) and/or vertical expansion (i.e., providing opportunity for planning the work and for checking on the results) may:

> Make the selection process more complex and more difficult because it becomes necessary to test for a wider range of duties;
>
> Make it necessary to offer incentives in the form of salary increments for employees to accept increased levels of responsibility;
>
> Imply a need for the increased training of workers if they are expected to perform a wider range of duties;
>
> Require a program that places and assigns those workers who are not able to perform all of the duties that are associated with the expanded job;
>
> Complicate relations with unions if, as a result of combining two or more titles, unions lose membership or jurisdiction over the titles that have been combined.

Public organizations must often maintain a delicate balance between and among internal and external forces such as employee organizations, interest groups, political leaders, and the community at large. Sometimes it takes very little to disturb the balance, and public organizations may not be able to absorb radical changes without the massive disruption of their ability to provide services. The most meaningful kind of changes often requires a commitment from top management that spans several years; yet, top leadership in public organizations is political and tends to focus on programs and activities that will bear tangible fruit in the short term. This is not to say that public organizations are free to reject radical changes; but it is doubtful whether such changes will be truly absorbed into the organization's subsystems over the short run. It is possible for an organization to absorb only the form of an externally imposed change while subverting the substance. Thus, changes may exist only on paper and receive lip service but may not exist in reality. The very nature of public organizations would appear therefore to call for gradual, incremental change.

Cases in Organization Change and Job Design

Reorganizing the Personnel Department

The Executive Orientation

Job Redesign for Pothole Repairers

The Police Department's Civilianization Program

The Commissioner's Management by Objectives Program

Reorganizing the
Personnel Department

On January 1, Leon Brown was appointed Director of the central Personnel Department that serviced the more than fifty agencies and 35,000 employees of a major western state. The Personnel Department, which comprised a staff of approximately 200 employees, was organized on a functional basis. The Examinations Bureau prepared tests for all of the agencies and job titles; the Training Bureau had state-wide training responsibilities; the Classification Bureau performed classification studies and classified all titles for all state agencies, and so forth. Each bureau employed personnel technicians that specialized in their particular area of operation. For example, technicians of the Examinations Bureau specialized in preparing civil service tests; they did little else. Since most of the personnel technicians had been working in their respective bureaus for some time, they had developed considerable expertise as well as a professional identification with their particular specialties.

After he took office, Brown began receiving numerous complaints from officials of other agencies about the effects of the highly specialized organization of work in the Personnel Department. They complained that the resolution of one personnel problem with several interrelated aspects sometimes required contacting five separate specialists in the Personnel Department. The agencies found the process to be frustrating, inefficient, and time consuming. Although the Personnel Department might view the establishment of a new class of positions, the allocation of specific positions to the new class, the filling of the vacancies on a temporary basis, the preparation of an examination, and the certification of a list of eligibles as five separate and distinct activities, an agency might view these as one issue—that is, the issue of getting people into the job.

The new Personnel Director was determined to do something about this problem. The solution, as he saw it, was to reorganize the Personnel Department so that an operating agency could get action on all of its personnel problems by contacting only one location in the Personnel Department. Brown was also concerned about what he perceived to be the overspecialization of the staff. He felt that the specialized role of the personnel technicians led to rigidities in their thinking, adversely affected their level of job satisfaction, limited their career growth opportunities, limited management's flexibility in assigning and utilizing staff, and was generally not in the best interests of the Department, the other agencies, or the technicians themselves.

In order to formulate a reorganization plan, Brown consulted with two management specialists whom he obtained on loan from another agency. He also called in the Department's six bureau chiefs, explained the goals of his reorganization, and asked for their suggestions about how these goals could be reached.

All six bureau chiefs, who submitted written proposals, suggested a client (or customer) form of organization (i.e., each new unit would be responsible for handling most of the personnel problems of a particular group of agencies) but argued that certain functions such as examinations, because of their highly specialized nature and the required level of expertise, should remain centralized in one unit. The Personnel Director rejected the proposed exceptions because he felt they could compromise the key concepts of his scheme. After considerable thought Brown adopted a new organization structure.

Department staff had an inkling that a major change was in the wind, but beyond vague rumors no one was able to confirm anything. The Personnel Director, who feared that a premature release of information about the reorganization might cause alarm, had instructed the bureau chiefs to discuss the reorganization with no one, not even with their key assistants.

The Director's plan called for a restructuring of the Department's staff into six new service groups. Each service group would be responsible for providing the entire range of personnel services for a particular group of related agencies (e.g., one service group would take care of all agencies in the state's criminal justice system—police, courts, public prosecutors, prisons, and so forth). Within each service group one personnel technician would be assigned to serve as a contact officer for each agency. All of the personnel technicians assigned to each service group would have to learn to carry out all phases of the personnel function. Specialists would have to become generalists. Thus, the technician assigned as contact officer to the Mental Health Department would have to be capable of providing classification, examination, training, recruitment, and other services to the agency.

Brown recognized that at the initial stages of the reorganization and until the staff learned the various hitherto specialized tasks, each service group would have to include some staff from each of the six specialized units. Accordingly, he asked one of his assistants to assign at least some staff from each specialty to each new service group. The assistant assigned an approximately equal number of personnel technicians from each specialty to each of the new groups.

On March 1, Brown called the entire staff of the Department together for a general meeting and issued to each employee a document that outlined the reorganization plan, its goals, and the nature of the assignments. He also announced that the new plan was to go into effect on March 15 and that all employees were to take up their new assignments by that date. Brown explained that he understood their natural fear of change but that they would all eventually come to see that the changes were in their own best interests. The announcements were greeted by most staff members in stunned silence.

1. Evaluate Brown's idea of changing the organization structure from a functional basis to a client.
2. Evaluate Brown's approach in carrying out the reorganization.
3. How is the staff likely to react to the reorganization?
4. How would the employees' professional identification with particular specialties affect their work motivation under the new structure?
5. How are the operating agencies likely to react to the new structure?
6. In addition to assigning some staff from each of the six specialized units to each new service unit, what else might be done to ease the transition?
7. What problems are likely to arise under the new structure?
8. Is the reorganization likely to succeed? Explain.

The Executive Orientation

As a means of increasing managerial effectiveness in city agencies, the Department of Personnel of the city of Bradleigh had developed at the direction of the Mayor a new results-based managerial performance appraisal system that was to be implemented in all city agencies. The new system was to be used as the basis for decisions on assignment, advancement, and salary increases as well as for identification of training needs.

The Personnel Director, George Adams, felt that it was essential to obtain the support of agencies' top management if the program was to succeed. He therefore decided to hold an executive briefing for top agency officials during which the elements of the new program would be explained. A date and time were selected, and the following letter was sent to each of the city's twenty agency heads:

> Our new managerial performance appraisal system is one of the cornerstones of our city's productivity improvement program. The system, which was developed at the Mayor's request, is designed to assist an agency in translating its overall mission statements into defined objectives and standards of managerial performance. Periodic appraisal of your managers should help you to improve your agency's overall performance.
>
> An initial orientation session for agency heads and top management is scheduled for Thursday, June 22, from 9:30 A.M. to 12 noon in the main conference room at City Hall. I am requesting that your agency be represented at this orientation by you as agency head, your First Deputy, and your Director of Administrative Services.
>
> The success of the managerial performance appraisal system is contingent on your agency's commitment, and we are counting on your active participation.
>
> I look forward to seeing you at the orientation.
>
> Sincerely,
> George Adams
> Personnel Director
> City of Bradleigh

Adams went to the orientation on June 22 with two of his staff specialists. Of the twenty agency heads who had received the invitations, only three appeared in person. Ten of the other heads sent lower-ranking officials to represent them. Seven agency heads were not represented at all. Adams convened the session with an introductory presentation and then turned the meeting over to his staff specialists. He left at 10 A.M. in disgust.

1. Why did so many agency heads fail to attend?
2. If you were Adams, how would you have gone about briefing the agency heads?
3. Should Adams have turned the meeting over to his specialists and then left? Explain.
4. What can Adams do now?
5. Do you think that attendance would have been better if the subject of the orientation was different? Explain.
6. Do some types of programs require more evidence of top-level support than others?
7. What is the Mayor's reaction likely to be when he learns of the attendance at the meeting?

Job Redesign for Pothole Repairers

An uproar was heard in the state capital when reporters photographed several members of the state's pothole repair crews who were standing by idly and drinking coffee during working hours. The Governor immediately ordered the state's Department of Highway Maintenance and the central Department of Personnel to undertake a study of the crews' assignments and to make appropriate recommendations.

The study revealed that each member of the pothole repair crew functioned as a specialist in repairing the potholes in the state's asphalt roads. One member was responsible for mixing the asphalt, another for spreading it, a third for tamping the mixture, a fourth for paving, and so forth. At the work site each member of the crew performed a set of specific tasks in turn while the other members stood by awaiting their turn. The driver of the crew, whose sole function was to drive the truck that carried the other members and their tools to and from the work site, stood by idly during the entire repair process. If the driver did not appear for work on a particular day and if a replacement was not available, the repair crew could not go out since the other members of the crew were not permitted to drive.

After consulting with the unions that represented the pothole crews (there were several unions who represented the various occupational specialties in the crews), the Department of Highway Maintenance and the Department of Personnel devised a job-enlargement plan that would overcome the inefficiencies of the existing system. Under the new plan all of the members of the pothole crew would be called pothole repairers, and all were expected to perform all aspects of street maintenance work, which included that of driving. The job of the pothole repairer was expected to become more varied and interesting.

The new plan was enthusiastically approved by the Governor and was very favorably received by the public at large. As an integral part of the new plan, specific performance standards were established for each crew in terms of the amount of asphalt spread and the number of potholes repaired.

In the first month of operation, the Department of Highway Maintenance was able to double the number of crews available for pothole repair. The size of each crew was reduced from five to three members. Productivity in terms of the total number of potholes repaired was tripled. In the second month of operation, ten trucks were either burned or seriously damaged, three asphalt spreaders were damaged, and one-third of all pothole repairs had to be done over again because of faulty workmanship. The Commissioner of the Department of Highway Maintenance suspected sabotage by the pothole crews.

1. Assuming the Commissioner's suspicions were confirmed, what might have led to the acts of sabotage?
2. If you were the Commissioner, what would you have done when your suspicions became confirmed?
3. Assuming that the Commissioner's suspicions were confirmed, what could have been done to make such acts of sabotage less likely?
4. What might be the effect of job-enlargement or job-enrichment programs on other personnel decisions such as testing, training, and compensation?
5. In general, would workers be likely to favor or oppose programs of job enlargement? Explain.
6. What is likely to be the position of unions toward job-enlargement programs?

The Police Department's
Civilianization Program

Helen Czyzewski, Mayor of the city of East-on, met with Louis Langley, the city's Police Commissioner. The following conversation took place during the meeting:

Mayor: Louis, I want to talk about how your department is staffed. Three years ago, your agency agreed to replace police officers who were doing clerical and other non-police-type jobs with civilians; the objective was to make the uniformed staff available for actual police duty. At the end of the first year of the program, 50 percent of the positions that our personnel technicians classified as being essentially civilian in nature were turned over to civilians. I just received the report for last year and it shows that the civilianization trend has been reversed. Seventy-five percent of these civilian-type jobs are now held by uniformed police officers. Why has this happened?

Langley: Frankly, the civilianization program has not been working out. My superior officers and precinct commanders have been telling me that although civilians may have the skills needed to do their jobs, they just aren't as reliable or dependable as police officers are. You know that we are a semimilitary organization and that discipline is critical in emergency situations. We have found that if you tell a police officer to do something, it generally gets done and done right. Police officers are trained and expected to obey orders. If you tell a civilian to do something, it may or may not get done. Also, civilians just don't seem to understand our operating procedures. For example, when we put civilians on the emergency telephone system, the system got overloaded. They just did not seem able to judge which calls were real emergencies and which could be handled through normal channels.

Mayor: What you are saying may have a certain amount of validity, but the City Council and the taxpayers may not understand why we are paying a police officer's salary to someone who answers the phone, types, or fills out forms. Police officers are paid high salaries to face dangers, take risks, and exercise judgment in difficult or sensitive community relations situations. We've been trying to keep expenditures down and civilianization will certainly help. I want you to submit a plan for replacing all police officers in civilian-type jobs with civilians over the next year. By that time all police officers should be doing strictly police work that civilians cannot do.

Langley: I'll do as you say, but I want you to understand that the Police Department's effectiveness will probably suffer as a result of this changeover.

1. Evaluate the Mayor's and Langley's arguments for and against civilianization of the Police Department.

2. Evaluate Langley's concluding statement.

3. What are likely to be the relations between the civilian and uniformed members of the Police Department?

4. Is the Mayor's timetable for civilianization likely to be met? Explain.

5. For what other occupations is "civilianization" a possible strategy to employ?

The Commissioner's Management by Objectives Program

The Police Commissioner of the city of Urbia (a major metropolis in the Southeast) decided to install a management by objectives (MBO) program in the Police Department as a method of raising the Department's productivity and of identifying those managers who deserved monetary rewards. The new Mayor had campaigned on a platform of sound management and high productivity for municipal services, and the Commissioner felt that the MBO approach would be very much in keeping with the policy of the new administration.

The Commissioner met with the Mayor in order to identify the high-priority goals of the city administration that in turn would guide the Department in formulating its own goals. He then consulted with the Management Planning Division within the Department. Several improvement projects consistent with city administration goals and specific accompanying performance indicators were identified by the Commissioner. These projects and indicators were incorporated into the Department's MBO plan. They included a 10 percent increase in the number of traffic citations issued, a 10 percent increase in the number of arrests made in each precinct, a 15 percent decrease in the use of overtime, and a 5 percent reduction in the use of sick leave on a Department-wide basis.

The Commissioner obtained the services of a prominent management consulting firm that would conduct briefing sessions for the Department's division commanders (the highest ranking line officers in the Department). At the briefing sessions the division commanders were informed of the Department's goals as they were contained in its MBO plan and were shown movies that demonstrated how managers and subordinates met, discussed, negotiated, and agreed on objectives. They were told to hold negotiating sessions with each of their subordinate precinct commanders. The Commissioner, who was present at the sessions, announced that after six months had gone by, his representatives would be visiting all of the precincts to review their records to determine the degree to which they were achieving the preselected objectives. He further stated that the performance of each division and precinct commander would be judged on the basis of these reviews; monetary awards would be based on achievement of objectives.

1. Evaluate the approach used to install the MBO program in the Department.
2. Comment on the method by which goals were established throughout the Department.
3. What was the likely reaction of the division and precinct commanders? Of their subordinate officers?
4. What were the precinct reviews likely to demonstrate?
5. How successful is the Commissioner's MBO program likely to be in the short run? In the long run? Explain.

Suggested Readings for Chapter 8

Alber, Antone F. "How (and How Not) to Approach Job Enrichment." *Personnel Journal* 58, no. 12 (December 1979):837–41.

Allan, Peter, and Stephen Rosenberg. "Establishing a Personnel System for Managers: The New York City Approach." *Public Personnel Management* 7, no. 4 (July–August 1978):236–42.

_____. "New York City's Approach to Civil Service Reform: Implications for State and Local Governments." *Public Administration Review* 38, no. 6 (November–December 1978):579–84.

_____. "Overcoming the Inefficiencies of an Overspecialized Title Structure." *Personnel Journal* 58, no. 3 (March 1979):164–67, 179, and 181.

Baker, H. Kent. "The Hows and Whys of Team Building." *Personnel Journal* 58, no. 6 (June 1979):367–70.

Brady, Rodney H. "MBO Goes to Work in the Public Sector." *Harvard Business Review* 51, no. 2 (March–April 1973):65–74.

Fien, Mitchell. "Job Enrichment: A Reevaluation." *Sloan Management Review* 15, no. 2 (Winter 1974):1–24.

Ford, Robert N. "Job Enrichment Lessons from A. T. & T." *Harvard Business Review* 51, no. 1 (January–February 1973).

Foulkes, Fred K. *Creating More Meaningful Work.* New York: American Management Association, 1969.

French, Wendell. "Organization Development: Objectives, Assumptions, and Strategies." *California Management Review* 12, no. 2 (1969):23–46.

Gibson, James L., John M. Ivancevich, and James H. Donnelly, Jr. *Organizations: Behavior, Structure, Process.* Dallas, Tex.: Business Publications, 1976.

Hackman, Richard J. "Is Job Enrichment Just a Fad?" *Harvard Business Review* 53, no. 5 (September–October 1975):129–38.

Hersey, Paul, and Kenneth H. Blanchard. "The Management of Change." *Training and Development Journal* 26, nos. 1, 2, and 3 (January, February, and March 1972):6–10, 20–24, and 28–33.

Hollmann, Robert W. "Applying MBO Research to Practice." *Human Resource Management* 15, no. 4 (Winter 1978):28–36.

Kotter, John P., and Leonard A. Schlesinger. "Choosing Strategies for Change." *Harvard Business Review* 57, no. 2 (March–April 1979):106–14.

Latham, Gary P., and Gary A. Yukl. "A Review of Research on the Application of Goal Setting in Organizations." *Academy of Management Journal* 18, no. 4 (December 1975):824–45.

Levinson, Harry. "Management by Whose Objectives." *Harvard Business Review* 48, no. 4 (July–August 1970):125–34.

Maher, John R., ed. *New Perspectives in Job Enrichment.* New York: Van Nostrand Reinhold, 1971.

Myers, M. Scott. "Overcoming Union Opposition to Job Enrichment." *Harvard Business Review* 49, no. 3 (May–June 1971):37–49.

Odiorne, George S. "How to Succeed in MBO Goal Setting." *Personnel Journal* 57, no. 8 (August 1978):427–29.

Patten, Thomas H., Jr. "Linking Financial Rewards to Employee Performance: The Roles of OD and MBO." *Human Resource Management* 15, no. 4 (Winter 1976):2–17.

Raia, Anthony P. *Managing by Objectives.* Glenview, Ill.: Scott, Foresman, 1974.

Steers, Richard M. "Achievement Needs and MBO Goal Setting." *Personnel Journal* 57, no. 1 (January 1978):26–28.

Strauss, George. "Managerial Practices." In J. Richard Hackman and J.L. Suttle, eds., *Improving Life at Work: Behavioral Science Approaches to Organizational Change.* Santa Monica, Calif.: Goodyear, 1977.

Tosi, Henry L., and Stephen Carroll. "Management by Objectives." *Personnel Administration* 33, no. 3 (July–August 1970):44–48.

Whitsett, David A. "Where Are Your Unenriched Jobs?" *Harvard Business Review* 53, no. 1 (January–February 1975):74–80.

Wikstrom, Walter S. *Managing by- and with-Objectives.* New York: The Conference Board, 1968.

Wool, Harold. "What's Wrong with Work in America?—A Review Essay." *Monthly Labor Review* 96, no. 3 (March 1973):38–44.

U.S. Department of Health, Education and Welfare. *Work in America: Report of a Special Task Force to the Secretary of Health, Education and Welfare.* Cambridge, Mass.: MIT Press, 1973.

Appendixes

Appendix

A: Uniform Guidelines on Employee Selection Procedures, 1978

Agencies: Equal Employment Opportunity Commission, Civil Service Commission, Department of Justice, and Department of Labor.

Action: Adoption of uniform guidelines on employee selection procedures as final rules by four agencies.

Summary: This document sets forth the uniform guidelines on employee selection procedures adopted by the Equal Employment Opportunity Commission, Civil Service Commission, Department of Justice, and the Department of Labor. At present two different sets of guidelines exist. The guidelines are intended to establish a uniform Federal position in the area of prohibiting discrimination in employment practices on grounds of race, color, religion, sex, or national origin. Cross reference documents are published at 5 CFR 300.103(c) (Civil Service Commission), 28 CFR 50.14 (Department of Justice), 29 CFR Part 1607 (Equal Employment Opportunity Commission), and 41 CFR Part 60–3 (Department of Labor). . . .

Effective date: September 25, 1978.

Source: *Federal Register,* 43, no. 166 (August 25, 1978).

I. Background

One problem that confronted the Congress which adopted the Civil Rights Act of 1964 involved the effect of written preemployment tests on equal employment opportunity. The use of these test scores frequently denied employment to minorities in many cases without evidence that the tests were related to success on the job. Yet employers wished to continue to use such tests as practical tools to assist in the selection of qualified employees. Congress sought to strike a balance which would proscribe discrimination, but otherwise permit the use of tests in the selection of employees. Thus, in title VII, Congress authorized the use of "any professionally developed ability test provided that such test, its administration or action upon the results is not designed, intended or used to discriminate. . .".[1]

At first, some employers contended that, under this section, they could use any test which had been developed by a professional so long as they did not intend to exclude minorities, even if such exclusion was the consequence of the use of the test. In 1966, the Equal Employment Opportunity Commission (EEOC) adopted guidelines to advise employers and other users what the law and good industrial psychology practice required.[2] The Department of Labor adopted the same approach in 1968 with respect to tests used by Federal contractors under Executive Order 11246 in a more detailed regulation. The Government's view was that the employer's intent was irrelevant. If tests or other practices had an adverse impact on protected groups, they were unlawful unless they could be justified. To justify a test which screened out a higher proportion of minorities, the employer would have to show that it fairly measured or predicted performance on the job. Otherwise, it would not be considered to be "professionally developed."

In succeeding years, the EEOC and the Department of Labor provided more extensive guidance which elaborated upon these principles and expanded the guidelines to emphasize all selection procedures. In 1971 in *Griggs* v. *Duke Power Co.*,[3] the Supreme Court announced the principle that employer practices which had an adverse impact on minorities and were not justified by business necessity constituted illegal discrimination under title VII. Congress confirmed this interpretation in the 1972 amendments to title VII. The elaboration of these principles by courts and agencies continued into the mid-1970's,[4] but differences between the EEOC and the other agencies (Justice, Labor, and Civil Service Commission) produced two different sets of guidelines by the end of 1976.

With the advent of the Carter administration in 1977, efforts were intensified to produce a unified government position. The following document represents the result of that effort. This introduction is intended to assist those not familiar with these matters to understand the basic approach of the uniform guidelines. While the guidelines are complex and technical, they are based upon the principles which have been consistently upheld by the courts, the Congress, and the agencies.

The following discussion will cite the sections of the Guidelines which embody these principles.

II. Adverse Impact

The fundamental principle underlying the guidelines is that employer policies or practices which have an adverse impact on employment opportunities of any race, sex, or ethnic group are illegal under title VII and the Executive order unless justified by business necessity.[5] A selection procedure which has no adverse impact generally does not violate title VII or the Executive order.[6] This means that an employer may usually avoid the application of the guidelines by use of procedures which have no adverse impact.[7] If adverse impact exists, it must be justified on grounds of business necessity. Normally, this means by validation which demonstrates the relation between the selection procedure and performance on the job.

The guidelines adopt a "rule of thumb" as a practical means of determining adverse impact for use in enforcement proceedings. This rule is known as the "4/5ths" or "80 percent" rule.[8] It is not a legal definition of discrimination, rather it is a practical device to keep the attention of enforcement agencies on serious discrepancies in hire or promotion rates or other employment decisions. To determine whether a selection procedure violates the "4/5ths rule", an employer compares its hiring rates for different groups.[9] But this rule of thumb cannot be applied automatically. An employer who has conducted an extensive recruiting campaign may have a larger than normal pool of applicants, and the "4/5ths rule" might unfairly expose it to enforcement proceedings.[10] On the other hand, an employer's reputation may have discouraged or "chilled" applicants of particular groups from applying because they believed application would be futile. The application of the "4/5ths" rule in that situation would allow an employer to evade scrutiny because of its own discrimination.[11]

III. Is Adverse Impact to Be Measured by the Overall Process?

In recent years some employers have eliminated the overall adverse impact of a selection procedure and employed sufficient numbers of minorities or women to meet this "4/5ths rule of thumb". However, they might continue use of a component which does have an adverse impact. For example, an employer might insist on a minimum passing score on a written test which is not job related and which has an adverse impact on minorities.[12] However the employer might compensate for this adverse impact by hiring a sufficient proportion of minorities who do meet its standards, so that its overall hiring is on a par with or higher than the applicant flow. Employers have argued that as long as their "bottom line" shows no overall adverse impact, there is no violation at all, regardless of the operation of a particular component of the process.

Employee representatives have argued that rights under equal employment opportunity laws are individual, and the fact that an employer has hired some minorities does not justify discrimination against other minorities. Therefore, they argue that adverse impact is to be determined by examination of each component of the selection procedure, regardless of the "bottom line." This question has not been answered definitively by the courts. There are decisions pointing in both directions.

These guidelines do not address the underlying question of law. They discuss only the exercise of prosecutorial discretion by the Government agencies themselves.[13] The agencies have decided that, generally, their resources to combat discrimination should be used against those respondents whose practices have restricted or excluded the opportunities of minorities and women. If an employer is appropriately including all groups in the work force, it is not sensible to spend Government time and effort on such a case, when there are so many employers whose practices do have adverse effects which should be challenged. For this reason, the guidelines provide that, in considering whether to take enforcement action, the Government will take into account the general posture of the employer concerning equal employment opportunity, including its affirmative action plan and results achieved under the plan.[14] There are some circumstances where the government may intervene even though the "bottom line" has been satisfied. They include the case where a component of a selection procedure restricts promotional opportunities of minorities or women who were discriminatorily assigned to jobs, and where a component, such as a height requirement, has been declared unlawful in other situations.[15]

What of the individual who is denied the job because of a particular component in a procedure which otherwise meets the "bottom line" standard? The individual retains the right to proceed through the appropriate agencies, and into Federal court.[16]

IV. Where Adverse Impact Exists: The Basic Options

Once an employer has established that there is adverse impact, what steps are required by the guidelines? As previously noted, the employer can modify or eliminate the procedure which produces the adverse impact, thus taking the selection procedure from the coverage of these guidelines. If the employer does not do that, then it must justify the use of the procedure on grounds of "business necessity."[17] This normally means that it must show a clear relation between performance on the selection procedure and performance on the job. In the language of industrial psychology, the employer must validate the selection procedure. Thus the bulk of the guidelines consist of the Government's interpretation of standards for validation.

V. Validation: Consideration of Alternatives

The concept of validation as used in personnel psychology involves the establishment of the relationship between a test instrument or other selection procedure and performance on the job. Federal equal employment opportunity law has added a requirement to the process of validation. In conducting a validation study, the employer should consider available alternatives which will achieve its legitimate business purpose with lesser adverse impact.[18] The employer cannot concentrate solely on establishing the validity of the instrument or procedure which it has been using in the past.

This same principle of using the alternative with lesser adverse impact is applicable to the manner in which an employer uses a valid selection procedure.[19] The guidelines assume that there are at least three ways in which an employer can use scores on a selection procedure: (1) To screen out of consideration those who are not likely to be able to perform the job successfully; (2) to group applicants in accordance with the likelihood of their successful performance on the job; and (3) to rank applicants, selecting those with the highest scores for employment.[20]

The setting of a "cutoff score" to determine who will be screened out may have an adverse impact. If so, an employer is required to justify the initial cutoff score by reference to its need for a trustworthy and efficient work force.[21] Similarly, use of results for grouping or for rank ordering is likely to have a greater adverse effect than use of scores solely to screen out unqualified candidates. If the employer chooses to use a rank order method, the evidence of validity must be sufficient to justify that method of use.[22]

VI. Testing for Higher Level Jobs

Normally, employers test for the job for which people are hired. However, there are situations where the first job is temporary or transient, and the workers who remain are promoted to work which involves more complex activities. The guidelines restrict testing for higher level jobs to users who promote a majority of the employees who remain with them to the higher level job within a reasonable period of time.[23]

VII. How Is Validation to Be Conducted?

Validation has become highly technical and complex, and yet is constantly changing as a set of concepts in industrial psychology. What follows here is a simple introduction to a highly complex field. There are three concepts which can be used to validate a selection procedure. These concepts reflect different approaches to investigating the job relatedness of selection procedures and may be interrelated in practice. They are (1) criterion-related validity,[24] (2) content validity,[25] and (3) construct validity.[26] In criterion-related validity, a selection procedure is justified by a statistical relationship between scores on the test or other selection procedure and measures of job performance. In content validity, a selection procedure is justified by showing that it representatively samples significant parts of the job, such as a typing test for a typist. Construct validity involves identifying the psychological trait (the construct) which underlies successful performance on the job and then devising a selection procedure to measure the presence and degree of the construct. An example would be a test of "leadership ability."

The guidelines contain technical standards and documentation requirements for the application of each of the three approaches.[27] One of the problems which the guidelines attempt to meet is the "borderline" between "content validity" and "construct validity." The extreme cases are easy to understand. A secretary, for example, may have to type. Many jobs require the separation of important matters which must be handled immediately from those which can be handled routinely. For the typing function, a typing test is appropriate. It is justifiable on the basis of content validity because it is a sample of an important or critical part of the job. The second function can be viewed as involving a capability to exercise selective judgment in light of the surrounding circumstances, a mental process which is difficult to sample.

In addressing this situation, the guidelines attempt to make it practical to validate the typing test by a content strategy,[28] but do not allow the validation of a test measuring a construct such as "judgment" by a content validity strategy.

The bulk of the guidelines deals with questions such as those discussed in the above paragraphs. Not all such questions can be answered simply, nor can all problems be addressed in the single document. Once the guidelines are issued, they will have to be interpreted in light of changing factual, legal, and professional circumstances.

VIII. Simplification of Reporting and Recordkeeping Requirements

The reporting and recordkeeping provisions which appeared in the December 30 draft which was published for comment have been carefully reviewed in light of comments received and President Carter's direction to limit paperwork burdens on those regulated by Government to the minimum necessary for effective regulation. As a result of this review, two major changes have been made in the documentation requirements of the guidelines:

1. A new section 15A(1) provides a simplified record-keeping option for employers with fewer than 100 employees:

2. Determinations of the adverse impact of selection procedures need not be made for groups which constitute less than 2 percent of the relevant labor force.

Also, the draft has been changed to make clear that users can assess adverse impact on an annual basis rather than on a continuing basis.

Analysis of comments. The uniform guidelines published today are based upon the proposition that the Federal Government should speak to the public and to those whom it regulates with one voice on this important subject; and that the Federal Government ought to impose upon itself obligations for equal employment opportunity which are at least as demanding as those it seeks to impose on others. These guidelines state a uniform Federal position on this subject, and are intended to protect the rights created by title VII of the Civil Rights Act of 1964, as amended, Executive Order 11246, as amended, and other provisions of Federal law. The uniform guidelines are also intended to represent "professionally acceptable methods" of the psychological profession for demonstrating whether a selection procedure validly predicts or measures performance for a particular job. *Albemarle Paper Co.* v. *Moody*, 442 U.S. 405, 425. They are also intended to be consistent with the decisions of the Supreme Court and authoritative decisions of other appellate courts.

Although the development of these guidelines preceded the issuance by President Jimmy Carter of Executive Order 12044 designed to improve the regulatory process, the spirit of his Executive order was followed in their development. Initial agreement among the Federal agencies was reached early in the fall of 1977, and the months from October 1977 until today have been spent in extensive consultation with civil rights groups whose clientele are protected by these guidelines; employers, labor unions, and State and local governments whose employment practices are affected by these guidelines; State and local government antidiscrimination agencies who share with the Federal Government enforcement responsibility for discriminatory practices; and appropriate members of the general public. For example, an earlier draft of these guidelines was circulated informally for comment on October 28, 1977, pursuant to OMB Circular A–85. Many comments were received from representatives of State and local governments, psychologists, private employers, and civil rights groups. Those comments were taken into account in the draft of these guidelines which was published for comment December 30, 1977, 42 FR 66542.

More than 200 organizations and individuals submitted written comments on the December 30, 1977, draft. These comments were from representatives of private industry, public employers, labor organizations, civil rights groups, the American Psychological Association and components thereof, and many individual employers, psychologists, and personnel specialists. On March 3, 1978, notice was given of a public hearing and meeting to be held on April 10, 1978, 43 FR 9131. After preliminary review of the comments, the agencies identified four issues of particular interest, and invited testimony particularly on those issues, 43 FR 11812 (March 21, 1978). In the same notice the agencies published questions and answers on four issues of concern to the commenters. The questions and answers were designed to clarify the intent of the December 30, 1977, draft, so as to provide a sharper focus for the testimony at the hearing.

At a full day of testimony on April 10, 1978, representatives of private industry, State and local governments, labor organizations, and civil rights groups, as well as psychologists, personnel specialists, and others testified at the public hearing and meeting. The written comments, testimony, and views expressed in subsequent informal consultations have been carefully considered by the four agencies. We set forth below a summary of the comments, and the major issues raised in the comments and testimony, and attempt to explain how we have resolved those issues.

The statement submitted by the American Psychological Association (A.P.A.) stated that "these guidelines represent a major step forward and with careful interpretation can provide a sound basis for concerned professional work." Most of the A.P.A. comments were directed to clarification and interpretation of the present language of the proposal. However, the A.P.A. recommended substantive change in the construct validity section and in the definition of work behavior.

Similarly, the Division of Industrial and Organizational Psychology (division 14) of the A.P.A. described the technical standards of the guidelines as "superior" in terms of congruence with professional standards to "most previous orders and guidelines but numerous troublesome aspects remain." Division 14 had substantial concerns with a number of the provisions of the general principles of the draft.

Civil rights groups generally found the uniform guidelines far superior to the FEA guidelines, and many urged their adoption, with modifications concerning ranking and documentation. Others raised concerns about the "bottom line" concept and other provisions of the guidelines.

The Ad Hoc Group on Employee Selection Procedures representing many employers in private industry supported the concept of uniform guidelines, but had a number of problems with particular provisions, some of which are described below. The American Society for Personnel Administration (ASPA) and the International Personnel Management Association, which represents State and local governments, generally took the same position as the ad hoc group. Major industrial unions found that the draft guidelines were superior to the FEA guidelines, but they perceived them to be inferior to the EEOC guidelines. They challenged particularly the bottom line concept and the construct validity section.

The building trade unions urged an exclusion of apprenticeship programs from coverage of the guidelines. The American Council on Education found them inappropriate for employment decisions concerning faculty at institutions of higher education. Other particular concerns were articulated by organizations representing the handicapped, licensing and certifying agencies, and college placement offices.

General Principles

1. *Relationship between validation and elimination of adverse impact, and affirmative action.* Federal equal employment opportunity law generally does not require evidence of validity for a selection procedure if there is no adverse impact; e.g., *Griggs* v. *Duke Power Co.,* 401 U.S. 424. Therefore, a user has the choice of complying either by providing evidence of validity (or otherwise justifying use in accord with Federal law), or by eliminating the adverse impact. These options have always been present under Federal law, 29 CFR 1607.3; 41 CFR 60-3.3(a); and the Federal Executive Agency Guidelines, 41 FR 51734 (November 23, 1976). The December 30 draft guidelines, however, clarified the nature of the two options open to users.

Psychologists expressed concern that the December 30 draft of section 6A encouraged the use of invalid procedures as long as there is no adverse impact. Employers added the concern that the section might encourage the use of illegal procedures not having an adverse impact against the groups who have historically suffered discrimination (minorities, women), even if they have an adverse impact on a different group (whites, males).

Section 6A was not so intended, and we have revised it to clarify the fact that illegal acts purporting to be affirmative action are not the goal of the agencies or of the guidelines; and that any employee selection procedure must be lawful and should be as job related as possible. The delineation of examples of alternative procedures was eliminated to avoid the implication that particular procedures are either prescribed or are necessarily appropriate. The basic thrust of section 6A, that elimination of adverse impact is an alternative to validation, is retained.

The inclusion of excerpts from the 1976 Equal Employment Opportunity Coordinating Council Policy Statement on Affirmative Action in section 13B of the December 30 draft was criticized as not belonging in a set of guidelines for the validation of selection procedures. Section 13 has been revised. The general statement of policy in support of voluntary affirmative action, and the reaffirmation of the policy statement have been retained, but this statement itself is now found in the appendix to the guidelines.

2. *The "bottom line" (section 4C).* The guidelines provide that when the overall selection process does not have an adverse impact the Government will usually not examine the individual components of that process for adverse impact or evidence of validity. The concept is based upon the view that the Federal Government should not generally concern itself with individual components of a selection process, if the overall effect of that process is nonexclusionary. Many commenters criticized the ambiguity caused by the word "generally" in the December 30 draft of section 4C which provided, "the Federal enforcement agencies . . . generally will not take enforcement action based upon adverse impact of any component" of a process that does not have an overall adverse impact. Employer groups stated the position that the "bottom line" should be a rule prohibiting enforcement action by Federal agencies with respect to all or any part of a selection process where the bottom line does not show adverse impact. Civil rights and some labor union representatives expressed the opposing concerns that the concept may be too restrictive, that it may be interpreted as a matter of law, and that it might allow certain discriminatory conditions to go unremedied.

The guidelines have been revised to clarify the intent that the bottom line concept is based upon administrative and prosecutorial discretion. The Federal agencies cannot accept the recommendation that they never inquire into or take enforcement action with respect to any component procedure unless the whole process of which it is a part has an adverse impact. The Federal enforcement agencies believe that enforcement action may be warranted in unusual circumstances, such as those involving other discriminatory practices, or particular selection procedures which have no validity and have a clear adverse impact on a national basis. Other unusual circumstances may warrant a high level agency decision to proceed with enforcement actions although the "bottom line" has been satisfied. At the same time the agencies adhere to the bottom line concept of allocating resources primarily to those users whose overall selection processes have an adverse impact. See overview, above, part III.

3. *Investigation of alternative selection procedures and alternative methods of use (section 3B).* The December 30 draft included an obligation on the user, when conducting a validity study, to investigate alternative procedures and uses, in order to determine whether there are other procedures which are substantially equally valid, but which have less adverse impact. The American Psychological Association stated:

> *We would concur with the drafters of the guidelines that it is appropriate in the determination of a selection strategy to consider carefully a variety of possible procedures and to think carefully about the question of adverse impact with respect to each of these procedures. Nevertheless, we feel it appropriate to note that a rigid enforcement of these sections, particularly for smaller employers, would impose a substantial and expensive burden on these employers.*

Since a reasonable consideration of alternatives is consistent with the underlying principle of minimizing adverse impact consistent with business needs, the provision is retained.

Private employer representatives challenged earlier drafts of these guidelines as being inconsistent with the decision of the Supreme Court in *Albemarle Paper Co.* v. *Moody,* 422 U.S. 405. No such inconsistency was intended. Accordingly, the first sentence of section 3B was revised to paraphrase the opinion in the *Albemarle* decision, so as to make it clear that section 3B is in accord with the principles of the *Albemarle* decision.

Section 3B was further revised to clarify the intent of the guidelines that the obligation to investigate alternative procedures is a part of conducting a validity study, so that alternative procedures should be evaluated in light of validity studies meeting professional standards, and that section 3B does not impose an obligation to search for alternatives if the user is not required to conduct a validity study.

Just as, under section 3B of the guidelines, a user should investigate alternative selection procedures as a part of choosing and validating a procedure, so should the user investigate alternative uses of the selection device chosen to find the use most appropriate to his needs. The validity study should address the question of what method of use (screening, grouping, or rank ordering) is appropriate for a procedure based on the kind and strength of the validity evidence shown, and the degree of adverse impact of the different uses.

4. *Establishment of cutoff scores and rank ordering.* Some commenters from civil rights groups believed that the December 30 draft guidelines did not provide sufficient guidance as to when it was permissible to use a selection procedure on a ranking basis rather than on a pass-fail basis. They also objected to section 5G in terms of setting cutoff scores. Other comments noted a lack of clarity as to how the determination of a cutoff score or the use of a procedure for ranking candidates relates to adverse impact.

As we have noted, users are not required to validate procedures which do not have an adverse impact. However, if one way of using a procedure (e.g., for ranking) results in greater adverse impact than another way (e.g., pass/fail), the procedure must be validated for that use. Similarly, cutoff scores which result in adverse impact should be justified. If the use of a validated procedure for ranking results in greater adverse impact than its use as a screening device, the evidence of validity and utility must be sufficient to warrant use of the procedures as a ranking device.

A new section 5G has been added to clarify these concepts. Section 5H (formerly section 5G) addresses the choice of a cutoff score when a procedure is to be used for ranking.

5. *Scope: Requests for exemptions for certain classes of users.* Some employer groups and labor organizations (e.g., academic institutions, large public employers, apprenticeship councils) argued that they should be exempted from all or some of the provisions of these guidelines because of their special needs. The intent of Congress as expressed in Federal equal employment opportunity law is to apply the same standards to all users, public and private.

These guidelines apply the same principles and standards to all employers. On the other hand, the nature of the procedures which will actually meet those principles and standards may be different for different employers, and the guidelines recognize that fact. Accordingly, the guidelines are applicable to all employers and other users who are covered by Federal equal employment opportunity law.

Organizations of handicapped persons objected to excluding from the scope of these guidelines the enforcement of laws prohibiting discrimination on the basis of handicap, in particular the Rehabilitation Act of 1973, sections 501, 503, and 504. While this issue has not been addressed in the guidelines, nothing precludes the adoption of the principles set forth in these guidelines for other appropriate situations.

Licensing and certification boards raised the question of the applicability of the guidelines to their licensing and certification functions. The guidelines make it clear that licensing and certification are covered "to the extent" that licensing and certification may be covered by Federal equal employment opportunity law.

Voluntary certification boards, where certification is not required by law, are not users as defined in section 16 with respect to their certifying functions and therefore are not subject to these guidelines. If an employer relies upon such certification in making employment decisions, the employer is the user and must be prepared to justify, under Federal law, that reliance as it would any other selection procedure.

6. *The "Four-Fifths Rule of Thumb" (section 4D).* Some representatives of employers and some professionals suggest that the basic test for adverse impact should be a test of statistical significance, rather than the four-fifths rule. Some civil rights groups, on the other hand, still regard the four-fifths rule as permitting some unlawful discrimination.

The Federal agencies believe that neither of these positions is correct. The great majority of employers do not hire, promote, or assign enough employees for most jobs to warrant primary reliance upon statistical significance. Many decisions in day-to-day life are made on the basis of information which does not have the justification of a test of statistical significance. Courts have found adverse impact without a showing of statistical significance. *Griggs v. Duke Power Co.*, supra; *Vulcan Society of New York v. CSC of N.Y.*, 490 F. 2d 387, 393 (2d Cir. 1973); *Kirkland v. New York St. Dept. of Corr. Serv.*, 520 F. 2d 420, 425 (2d Cir. 1975).

Accordingly, the undersigned believe that while the four-fifths rule does not define discrimination and does not apply in all cases, it is appropriate as a rule of thumb in identifying adverse impact.

Technical Standards

7. *Criterion-related validity (section 14B).* This section of the guidelines found general support among the commenters from the psychological profession and, except for the provisions concerning test fairness (sometimes mistakenly equated with differential prediction or differential validity), generated relatively little comment.

The provisions of the guidelines concerning criterion-related validity studies call for studies of fairness of selection procedures where technically feasible.

Section 14B(8). Some psychologists and employer groups objected that the concept of test fairness or unfairness has been discredited by professionals and pointed out that the term is commonly misused. We recognize that there is serious debate on the question of test fairness; however, it is accepted professionally that fairness should be examined where feasible. The A.P.A. standards for educational and psychological tests, for example, direct users to explore the question of fairness on finding a difference in group performances (section E9; pp. 43–44). Similarly the concept of test fairness is one which is closely related to the basic thrust of Federal equal employment opportunity law; and that concept was endorsed by the Supreme Court in *Albemarle Paper Co. v. Moody*, 422 U.S. 405.

Accordingly, we have retained in the guidelines the obligation upon users to investigate test fairness where it is technically feasible to do so.

8. *Content validity.* The Division of Industrial and Organizational Psychology of A.P.A. correctly perceived that the provisions of the draft guidelines concerning content validity, with their emphasis on observable work behaviors or work products, were "greatly concerned with minimizing the inferential leap between test and performance." That division expressed the view that the draft guidelines neglected situations where a knowledge, skill or ability is necessary to an outcome but where the work behavior cannot be replicated in a test. They recommended that the section be revised.

We believe that the emphasis on observable work behaviors or observable work products is appropriate; and that in order to show content validity, the gap between the test and performance on the job should be a small one. We recognize, however, that content validity may be appropriate to support a test which measures a knowledge, skill, or ability which is a necessary prerequisite to the performance of the job, even though the test might not be close enough to the work behavior to be considered a work sample, and the guidelines have been revised appropriately. On the other hand, tests of mental processes which are not directly observable and which may be difficult to determine on the basis of observable work behaviors or work products should not be supported by content validity.

Thus, the Principles for the Validation and Use of Personnel Selection Procedures (Division of Industrial and Organizational Psychology, American Psychological Association, 1975, p. 10), discuss the use of content validity to support tests of "specific items of knowledge, or specific job skills," but call attention to the inappropriateness of attempting to justify tests for traits or constructs on a content validity basis.

9. *Construct validity (section 14D).* Business groups and professionals expressed concern that the construct validity requirements in the December 30 draft were confusing and technically inaccurate. As section 14D indicates, construct validity is a relatively new procedure in the field of personnel selection and there is not yet substantial guidance in the professional literature as to its use in the area of employment practices. The provisions on construct validity have been revised to meet the concerns expressed by the A.P.A. The construct validity section as revised clarifies what is required by the Federal enforcement agencies at this stage in the development of construct validity. The guidelines leave open the possibility that different evidence of construct validity may be accepted in the future, as new methodologies develop and become incorporated in professional standards and other professional literature.

10. *Documentation (section 15).* Commenters stated that the documentation section did not conform to the technical requirements of the guidelines or was otherwise inadequate. Section 15 has been clarified and two significant changes have been made to minimize the recordkeeping burden. (See overview, part VIII.)

11. *Definitions (section 16).* The definition of work behavior in the December 30, 1977 draft was criticized by the A.P.A. and others as being too vague to provide adequate guidance to those using the guidelines who must identify work behavior as a part of any validation technique. Other comments criticized the absence or inadequacies of other definitions, especially "adverse impact." Substantial revisions of and additions to this section were therefore made.

Uniform Guidelines on Employee Selection Procedures (1978)

Note.—These guidelines are issued jointly by four agencies. Separate official adoptions follow the guidelines in this part IV as follows: Civil Service Commission, Department of Justice, Equal Employment Opportunity Commission, Department of Labor.

For official citation see section 18 of these guidelines.

Table of Contents

General principles

A. Use of Alternate Selection Procedures to Eliminate Adverse Impact
B. Where Validity Studies Cannot or Need Not Be Performed
    (1) Where Informal or Unscored Procedures are Used
    (2) Where Formal and Scored Procedures Are Used
7. Use of Other Validity Studies
    A. Validity Studies Not Conducted by the User
    B. Use of Criterion-related Validity Evidence from Other Sources
        (1) Validity Evidence
        (2) Job Similarity
        (3) Fairness Evidence
    C. Validity Evidence from Multi-Unit Study
    D. Other Significant Variables
8. Cooperative Studies
    A. Encouragement of Cooperative Studies
    B. Standards for Use of Cooperative Studies
9. No Assumption of Validity
    A. Unacceptable Substitutes for Evidence of Validity
    B. Encouragement of Professional Supervision
10. Employment Agencies and Employment Services
    A. Where Selection Procedures Are Devised by Agency
    B. Where Selection Procedures Are Devised Elsewhere
11. Disparate Treatment
12. Retesting of Applicants
13. Affirmative Action
    A. Affirmative Action Obligations
    B. Encouragement of Voluntary Affirmative Action Programs

Technical standards

14. Technical Standards for Validity Studies
    A. Validity Studies Should Be Based on Review of Information about the Job
    B. Technical Standards for Criterion-related Validity Studies
        (1) Technical Feasibility
        (2) Analysis of the Job
        (3) Criterion Measures

Documentation of impact and validity evidence

(3) Documentation of Validity Evidence
    (a) Type of Evidence
    (b) Form of Report
    (c) Completeness

B. Criterion-related Validity Studies
  (1) User(s), Location(s), and Date(s) of Study
  (2) Problem and Setting
  (3) Job Analysis or Review of Job Information
  (4) Job Titles and Codes
  (5) Criterion Measures
  (6) Sample Description
  (7) Description of Selection Procedures
  (8) Techniques and Results
  (9) Alternative Procedures Investigated
  (10) Uses and Applications
  (11) Source Data
  (12) Contact Person
  (13) Accuracy and Completeness

C. Content Validity Studies
  (1) User(s), Location(s), and Date(s) of Study
  (2) Problem and Setting
  (3) Job Analysis—Content of the Job
  (4) Selection Procedure and Its Content
  (5) Relationship between Selection Procedure and the Job
  (6) Alternative Procedures Investigated
  (7) Uses and Applications
  (8) Contact Person
  (9) Accuracy and Completeness

D. Construct Validity Studies
  (1) User(s), Location(s), and Date(s) of Study
  (2) Problem and Setting
  (3) Construct Definition
  (4) Job Analysis
  (5) Job Titles and Codes
  (6) Selection Procedure
  (7) Relationship to Job Performance
  (8) Alternative Procedures Investigated
  (9) Uses and Applications
  (10) Accuracy and Completeness
  (11) Source Data
  (12) Contact Person

E. Evidence of Validity from Other Studies
  (1) Evidence from Criterion-related Validity Studies
    (a) Job Information
    (b) Relevance of Criteria
    (c) Other Variables

Definitions

Appendix

General Principles

Section 1. *Statement of purpose.—A. Need for uniformity—Issuing agencies.* The Federal government's need for a uniform set of principles on the question of the use of tests and other selection procedures has long been recognized. The Equal Employment Opportunity Commission, the Civil Service Commission, the Department of Labor, and the Department of Justice jointly have adopted these uniform guidelines to meet that need, and to apply the same principles to the Federal Government as are applied to other employers.

B. *Purpose of guidelines.* These guidelines incorporate a single set of principles which are designed to assist employers, labor organizations, employment agencies, and licensing and certification boards to comply with requirements of Federal law prohibiting employment practices which discriminate on grounds of race, color, religion, sex, and national origin. They are designed to provide a framework for determining the proper use of tests and other selection procedures. These guidelines do not require a user to conduct validity studies of selection procedures where no adverse impact results. However, all users are encouraged to use selection procedures which are valid, especially users operating under merit principles.

C. *Relation to prior guidelines.* These guidelines are based upon and supersede previously issued guidelines on employee selection procedures. These guidelines have been built upon court decisions, the previously issued guidelines of the agencies, and the practical experience of the agencies, as well as the standards of the psychological profession. These guidelines are intended to be consistent with existing law.

Section 2. *Scope.—A. Application of guidelines.* These guidelines will be applied by the Equal Employment Opportunity Commission in the enforcement of title VII of the Civil Rights Act of 1964, as amended by the Equal Employment Opportunity Act of 1972 (hereinafter "Title VII"); by the Department of Labor, and the contract compliance agencies until the transfer of authority contemplated by the President's Reorganization Plan No. 1 of 1978, in the administration and enforcement of Executive Order 11246, as amended by Executive Order 11375 (hereinafter "Executive Order 11246"); by the Civil Service Commission and other Federal agencies subject to section 717 of Title VII; by the Civil Service Commission in exercising its responsibilities toward State and local governments under section 208(b)(1) of the Intergovernmental-Personnel Act; by the Department of Justice in exercising its responsibilities under Federal law; by the Office of Revenue Sharing of the Department of the Treasury under the State and Local Fiscal Assistance Act of 1972, as amended; and by any other Federal agency which adopts them.

B. *Employment decisions.* These guidelines apply to tests and other selection procedures which are used as a basis for any employment decision. Employment decisions include but are not limited to hiring, promotion, demotion, membership (for example, in a labor organization), referral, retention, and licensing and certification, to the extent that licensing and certification may be covered by Federal equal employment opportunity law. Other selection decisions, such as selection for training or transfer, may also be considered employment decisions if they lead to any of the decisions listed above.

C. *Selection procedures.* These guidelines apply only to selection procedures which are used as a basis for making employment decisions. For example, the use of recruiting procedures designed to attract members of a particular race, sex, or ethnic group, which were previously denied employment opportunities or which are currently underutilized, may be necessary to bring an employer into compliance with Federal law, and is frequently an essential element of any effective affirmative action program; but recruitment practices are not considered by these guidelines to be selection procedures. Similarly, these guidelines do not pertain to the question of the lawfulness of a seniority system within the meaning of section 703(h), Executive Order 11246 or other provisions of Federal law or regulation, except to the extent that such systems utilize selection procedures to determine qualifications or abilities to perform the job. Nothing in these guidelines is intended or should be interpreted as discouraging the use of a selection procedure for the purpose of determining qualifications or for the purpose of selection on the basis of relative qualifications, if the selection procedure had been validated in accord with these guidelines for each such purpose for which it is to be used.

D. *Limitations.* These guidelines apply only to persons subject to Title VII, Executive Order 11246, or other equal employment opportunity requirements of Federal law. These guidelines do not apply to responsibilities under the Age Discrimination in Employment Act of 1967, as amended, not to discriminate on the basis of age, or under sections 501, 503, and 504 of the Rehabilitation Act of 1973, not to discriminate on the basis of handicap.

E. *Indian preference not affected.* These guidelines do not restrict any obligation imposed or right granted by Federal law to users to extend a preference in employment to Indians living on or near an Indian reservation in connection with employment opportunities on or near an Indian reservation.

Section 3. *Discrimination defined: Relationship between use of selection procedures and discrimination.*—A. *Procedure having adverse impact constitutes discrimination unless justified.* The use of any selection procedure which has an adverse impact on the hiring, promotion, or other employment or membership opportunities of members of any race, sex, or ethnic group will be considered to be discriminatory and inconsistent with these guidelines, unless the procedure has been validated in accordance with these guidelines, or the provisions of section 6 below are satisfied.

B. *Consideration of suitable alternative selection procedures.* Where two or more selection procedures are available which serve the user's legitimate interest in efficient and trustworthy workmanship, and which are substantially equally valid for a given purpose, the user should use the procedure which has been demonstrated to have the lesser adverse impact. Accordingly, whenever a validity study is called for by these guidelines, the user should include, as part of the validity study, an investigation of suitable alternative selection procedures and suitable alternative methods of using the selection procedure which have as little adverse impact as possible, to determine the appropriateness of using or validating them in accord with these guidelines. If a user has made a reasonable effort to become aware of such alternative procedures and validity has been demonstrated in accord with these guidelines, the use of the test or other selection procedure may continue until such time as it should reasonably be reviewed for currency. Whenever the user is shown an alternative selection procedure with evidence of less adverse impact and substantial evidence of validity for the same job in similar circumstances, the user should investigate it to determine the appropriateness of using or validating it in accord with these guidelines. This subsection is not intended to preclude the combination of procedures into a significantly more valid procedure, if the use of such a combination has been shown to be in compliance with the guidelines.

Section 4. *Information on impact.*—A. *Records concerning impact.* Each user should maintain and have available for inspection records or other information which will disclose the impact which its tests and other selection procedures have upon employment opportunities of persons by identifiable race, sex, or ethnic group as set forth in subparagraph B below in order to determine compliance with these guidelines. Where there are large numbers of applicants and procedures are administered frequently, such information may be retained on a sample basis, provided that the sample is appropriate in terms of the applicant population and adequate in size.

B. *Applicable race, sex, and ethnic groups for recordkeeping.* The records called for by this section are to be maintained by sex, and the following races and ethnic groups: Blacks (Negroes), American Indians (including Alaskan Natives), Asians (including Pacific Islanders), Hispanic (including persons of Mexican, Puerto Rican, Cuban, Central or South American, or other Spanish origin or culture regardless of race), whites (Caucasians) other than Hispanic, and totals. The race, sex, and ethnic classifications called for by this section are consistent with the Equal Employment Opportunity Standard Form 100, Employer Information Report EEO–1 series of reports. The user should adopt safeguards to insure that the records required by this paragraph are used for appropriate purposes such as determining adverse impact, or (where required) for developing and monitoring affirmative action programs, and that such records are not used improperly. See sections 4E and 17(4), below.

C. *Evaluation of selection rates: The "bottom line."* If the information called for by sections 4A and B above shows that the total selection process for a job has an adverse impact, the individual components of the selection process should be evaluated for adverse impact. If this information shows that the total selection process does not have an adverse impact, the Federal enforcement agencies, in the exercise of their administrative and prosecutorial discretion, in usual circumstances, will not expect a user to evaluate the individual components for adverse impact, or to validate such individual components, and will not take enforcement action based upon adverse impact of any component of that process, including the separate parts of a multipart selection procedure or any separate procedure that is used as an alternative method of selection. However, in the following circumstances the Federal enforcement agencies will expect a user to evaluate the individual components for adverse impact and may, where appropriate, take enforcement action with respect to the individual components: (1) where the selection procedure is a significant factor in the continuation of patterns of assignments of incumbent employees caused by prior discriminatory employment practices, (2) where the weight of court decisions or administrative interpretations hold that a specific procedure (such as height or weight requirements or no-arrest records) is not job related in the same or similar circumstances. In unusual circumstances, other than those listed in (1) and (2) above, the Federal enforcement agencies may request a user to evaluate the individual components for adverse impact and may, where appropriate, take enforcement action with respect to the individual component.

D. *Adverse impact and the "four-fifths rule."* A selection rate for any race, sex, or ethnic group which is less than four-fifths (4/5) (or eighty percent) of the rate for the group with the highest rate will generally be regarded by the Federal enforcement agencies as evidence of adverse impact, while a greater than four-fifths rate will generally not be regarded by Federal enforcement agencies as evidence of adverse impact. Smaller differences in selection rate may nevertheless constitute adverse impact, where they are significant in both statistical and practical terms or where a user's actions have discouraged applicants disproportionately on grounds of race, sex, or ethnic group. Greater differences in selection rate may not constitute adverse impact where the differences are based on small numbers and are not statistically significant, or where special recruiting or other programs cause the pool of minority or female candidates to be atypical of the normal pool of applicants from that group. Where the user's evidence concerning the impact of a selection procedure indicates adverse impact but is based upon numbers which are too small to be reliable, evidence concerning the impact of the procedure over a longer period of time and/or evidence concerning the impact which the selection procedure had when used in the same manner in similar circumstances elsewhere may be considered in determining adverse impact. Where the user has not maintained data on adverse impact as required by the documentation section of applicable guidelines, the Federal enforcement agencies may draw an inference of adverse impact of the selection process from the failure of the user to maintain such data, if the user has an underutilization of a group in the job category, as compared to the group's representation in the relevant labor market or, in the case of jobs filled from within, the applicable work force.

E. *Consideration of user's equal employment opportunity posture.* In carrying out their obligations, the Federal enforcement agencies will consider the general posture of the user with respect to the equal employment opportunity for the job or group of jobs in question. Where a user has adopted an affirmative action program, the Federal enforcement agencies will consider the provisions of that program, including the goals and timetables which the user has adopted and the progress which the user has made in carrying out that program and in meeting the goals and timetables. While such affirmative action programs may in design and execution be race, color, sex, or ethnic conscious, selection procedures under such programs should be based upon the ability or relative ability to do the work.

Section 5. *General standards for validity studies.*—A. *Acceptable types of validity studies.* For the purposes of satisfying these guidelines, users may rely upon criterion-related validity studies, content validity studies or construct validity studies, in accordance with the standards set forth in the technical standards of these guidelines, section 14 below. New strategies for showing the validity of selection procedures will be evaluated as they become accepted by the psychological profession.

B. *Criterion-related, content, and construct validity.* Evidence of the validity of a test or other selection procedure by a criterion-related validity study should consist of empirical data demonstrating that the selection procedure is predictive of or significantly correlated with important elements of job performance. See section 14B below. Evidence of the validity of a test or other selection procedure by a content validity study should consist of data showing that the content of the selection procedure is representative of important aspects of performance on the job for which the candidates are to be evaluated. See section 14C below. Evidence of the validity of a test or other selection procedure through a construct validity study should consist of data showing that the procedure measures the degree to which candidates have identifiable characteristics which have been determined to be important in successful performance in the job for which the candidates are to be evaluated. See section 14D below.

C. *Guidelines are consistent with professional standards.* The provisions of these guidelines relating to validation of selection procedures are intended to be consistent with generally accepted professional standards for evaluating standardized tests and other selection procedures, such as those described in the Standards for Educational and Psychological Tests prepared by a joint committee of the American Psychological Association, the American Educational Research Association, and the National Council on Measurement in Education (American Psychological Association, Washington, D.C., 1974) (hereinafter "A.P.A. Standards") and standard textbooks and journals in the field of personnel selection.

D. *Need for documentation of validity.* For any selection procedure which is part of a selection process which has an adverse impact and which selection procedure has an adverse impact, each user should maintain and have available such documentation as is described in section 15 below.

E. *Accuracy and standardization.* Validity studies should be carried out under conditions which assure insofar as possible the adequacy and accuracy of the research and the report. Selection procedures should be administered and scored under standardized conditions.

F. *Caution against selection on basis of knowledges, skills, or ability learned in brief orientation period.* In general, users should avoid making employment decisions on the basis of measures of knowledges, skills, or abilities which are normally learned in a brief orientation period, and which have an adverse impact.

G. *Method of use of selection procedures.* The evidence of both the validity and utility of a selection procedure should support the method the user chooses for operational use of the procedure, if that method of use has a greater adverse impact than another method of use. Evidence which may be sufficient to support the use of a selection procedure on a pass/fail (screening) basis may be insufficient to support the use of the same procedure on a ranking basis under these guidelines. Thus, if a user decides to use a selection procedure on a ranking basis, and that method of use has a greater adverse impact than use of an appropriate pass/fail basis (see section 5H below), the user should have sufficient evidence of validity and utility to support the use on a ranking basis. See sections, 3B, 14B (5) and (6), and 14C (8) and (9).

H. *Cutoff scores.* Where cutoff scores are used, they should normally be set so as to be reasonable and consistent with normal expectations of acceptable proficiency within the work force. Where applicants are ranked on the basis of properly validated selection procedures and those applicants scoring below a higher cutoff score than appropriate in light of such expectations have little or no chance of being selected for employment, the higher cutoff score may be appropriate, but the degree of adverse impact should be considered.

I. *Use of selection procedures for higher level jobs.* If job progression structures are so established that employees will probably, within a reasonable period of time and in a majority of cases, progress to a higher level, it may be considered that the applicants are being evaluated for a job or jobs at the higher level. However, where job progression is not so nearly automatic, or the time span is such that higher level jobs or employees' potential may be expected to change in significant ways, it should be considered that applicants are being evaluated for a job at or near the entry level. A "reasonable period of time" will vary for different jobs and employment situations but will seldom be more than 5 years. Use of selection procedures to evaluate applicants for a higher level job would not be appropriate:

1. If the majority of those remaining employed do not progress to the higher level job;

2. If there is a reason to doubt that the higher level job will continue to require essentially similar skills during the progression period;

3. If the selection procedures measure knowledges, skills, or abilities required for advancement which would be expected to develop principally from the training or experience on the job.

J. *Interim use of selection procedures.* Users may continue the use of a selection procedure which is not at the moment fully supported by the required evidence of validity, provided: (1) The user has available substantial evidence of validity, and (2) the user has in progress, when technically feasible, a study which is designed to produce the additional evidence required by these guidelines within a reasonable time. If such a study is not technically feasible, see section 6B. If the study does not demonstrate validity, this provision of these guidelines for interim use shall not constitute a defense in any action, nor shall it relieve the user of any obligations arising under Federal law.

K. *Review of validity studies for currency.* Whenever validity has been shown in accord with these guidelines for the use of a particular selection procedure for a job or group of jobs, additional studies need not be performed until such time as the validity study is subject to review as provided in section 3B above. There are no absolutes in the area of determining the currency of a validity study. All circumstances concerning the study, including the validation strategy used, and changes in the relevant labor market and the job should be considered in the determination of when a validity study is outdated.

Section. 6. *Use of selection procedures which have not been validated.*—A. *Use of alternate selection procedures to eliminate adverse impact.* A user may choose to utilize alternative selection procedures in order to eliminate adverse impact or as part of an affirmative action program. See section 13 below. Such alternative procedures should eliminate the adverse impact in the total selection process, should be lawful and should be as job related as possible.

B. *Where validity studies cannot or need not be performed.* There are circumstances in which a user cannot or need not utilize the validation techniques contemplated by these guidelines. In such circumstances, the user should utilize selection procedures which are as job related as possible and which will minimize or eliminate adverse impact, as set forth below.

1. *Where informal or unscored procedures are used.* When an informal or unscored selection procedure which has an adverse impact is utilized, the user should eliminate the adverse impact, or modify the procedure to one which is a formal, scored or quantified measure or combination of measures and then validate the procedure in accord with these guidelines, or otherwise justify continued use of the procedure in accord with Federal law.

2. *Where formal and scored procedures are used.* When a formal and scored selection procedure is used which has an adverse impact, the validation techniques contemplated by these guidelines usually should be followed if technically feasible. Where the user cannot or need not follow the validation techniques anticipated by these guidelines, the user should either modify the procedure to eliminate adverse impact or otherwise justify continued use of the procedure in accord with Federal law.

Section 7. *Use of other validity studies.*—A. *Validity studies not conducted by the user.* Users may, under certain circumstances, support the use of selection procedures by validity studies conducted by other users or conducted by test publishers or distributors and described in test manuals. While publishers of selection procedures have a professional obligation to provide evidence of validity which meets generally accepted professional standards (see section 5C above), users are cautioned that they are responsible for compliance with these guidelines. Accordingly, users seeking to obtain selection procedures from publishers and distributors should be careful to determine that, in the event the user becomes subject to the validity requirements of these guidelines, the necessary information to support validity has been determined and will be made available to the user.

B. *Use of criterion-related validity evidence from other sources.* Criterion-related validity studies conducted by one test user, or described in test manuals and the professional literature, will be considered acceptable for use by another user when the following requirements are met:

1. *Validity evidence.* Evidence from the available studies meeting the standards of section 14B below clearly demonstrates that the selection procedure is valid;

2. *Job similarity.* The incumbents in the user's job and the incumbents in the job or group of jobs on which the validity study was conducted perform substantially the same major work behaviors, as shown by appropriate job analyses both on the job or group of jobs on which the validity study was performed and on the job for which the selection procedure is to be used; and

3. *Fairness evidence.* The studies include a study of test fairness for each race, sex, and ethnic group which constitutes a significant factor in the borrowing user's relevent labor market for the job or jobs in question. If the studies under consideration satisfy (1) and (2) above but do not contain an investigation of test fairness, and it is not technically feasible for the borrowing user to conduct an internal study of test fairness, the borrowing user may utilize the study until studies conducted elsewhere meeting the requirements of these guidelines show test unfairness, or until such time as it becomes technically feasible to conduct an internal study of test fairness and the results of that study can be acted upon. Users obtaining selection procedures from publishers should consider, as one factor in the decision to purchase a particular selection procedure, the availability of evidence concerning test fairness.

C. *Validity evidence from multi-unit study.* If validity evidence from a study covering more than one unit within an organization satisfies the requirements of section 14B below, evidence of validity specific to each unit will not be required unless there are variables which are likely to affect validity significantly.

D. *Other significant variables.* If there are variables in the other studies which are likely to affect validity significantly, the user may not rely upon such studies, but will be expected either to conduct an internal validity study or to comply with section 6 above.

Section 8. *Cooperative studies.*—A. *Encouragement of cooperative studies.* The agencies issuing these guidelines encourage employers, labor organizations, and employment agencies to cooperate in research, development, search for lawful alternatives, and validity studies in order to achieve procedures which are consistent with these guidelines.

B. *Standards for use of cooperative studies.* If validity evidence from a cooperative study satisfies the requirements of section 14 below, evidence of validity specific to each user will not be required unless there are variables in the user's situation which are likely to affect validity significantly.

Section 9. *No assumption of validity.*—A. *Unacceptable substitutes for evidence of validity.* Under no circumstances will the general reputation of a test or other selection procedures, its author or its publisher, or casual reports of its validity be accepted in lieu of evidence of validity. Specifically ruled out are: assumptions of validity based on a procedure's name or descriptive labels; all forms of promotional literature; data bearing on the frequency of a procedure's usage; testimonial statements and credentials of sellers, users, or consultants; and other nonempirical or anecdotal accounts of selection practices or selection outcomes.

B. *Encouragement of professional supervision.* Professional supervision of selection activities is encouraged but is not a substitute for documented evidence of validity. The enforcement agencies will take into account the fact that a thorough job analysis was conducted and that careful development and use of a selection procedure in accordance with professional standards enhance the probability that the selection procedure is valid for the job.

Section 10. *Employment agencies and employment services.*—A. *Where selection procedures are devised by agency.* An employment agency, including private employment agencies and State employment agencies, which agrees to a request by an employer or labor organization to devise and utilize a selection procedure should follow the standards in these guidelines for determining adverse impact. If adverse impact exists the agency should comply with these guidelines. An employment agency is not relieved of its obligation herein because the user did not request such validation or has requested the use of some lesser standard of validation than is provided in these guidelines. The use of an employment agency does not relieve an employee or labor organization or other user of its responsibilities under Federal law to provide equal employment opportunity or its obligations as a user under these guidelines.

B. *Where selection procedures are devised elsewhere.* Where an employment agency or service is requested to administer a selection procedure which has been devised elsewhere and to make referrals pursuant to the results, the employment agency or service should maintain and have available evidence of the impact of the selection and referral procedures which it administers. If adverse impact results the agency of service should comply with these guidelines. If the agency or service seeks to comply with these guidelines by reliance upon validity studies or other data in the possession of the employer, it should obtain and have available such information.

Section 11. *Disparate treatment.* The principles of disparate or unequal treatment must be distinguished from the concepts of validation. A selection procedure—even though validated against job performance in accordance with these guidelines—cannot be imposed upon members of a race, sex, or ethnic group where other employees, applicants, or members have not been subjected to that standard. Disparate treatment occurs where members of a race, sex, or ethnic group have been denied the same employment, promotion, membership, or other employment opportunities as have been available to other employees or applicants. Those employees or applicants who have been denied equal treatment, because of prior discriminatory practices or policies, must at least be afforded the same opportunities as had existed for other employees or applicants during the period of discrimination. Thus, the persons who were in the class of persons discriminated against during the period the user followed the discriminatory practices should be allowed the opportunity to qualify under less stringent selection procedures previously followed, unless the user demonstrates that the increased standards are required by business necessity. This section does not prohibit a user who has not previously followed merit standards from adopting merit standards which are in compliance with these guidelines; nor does it preclude a user who has previously used invalid or unvalidated selection procedures from developing and using procedures which are in accord with these guidelines.

Section 12. *Retesting of applicants.* Users should provide a reasonable opportunity for retesting and reconsideration. Where examinations are administered periodically with public notice, such reasonable opportunity exists, unless persons who have previously been tested are precluded from retesting. The user may however take reasonable steps to preserve the security of its procedures.

Section 13. *Affirmative action.*—A. *Affirmative action obligations.* The use of selection procedures which have been validated pursuant to these guidelines does not relieve users of any obligations they may have to undertake affirmative action to assure equal employment opportunity. Nothing in these guidelines is intended to preclude the use of lawful selection procedures which assist in remedying the effects of prior discriminatory practices, or the achievement of affirmative action objectives.

B. *Encouragement of voluntary affirmative action programs.* These guidelines are also intended to encourage the adoption and implementation of voluntary affirmative action programs by users who have no obligation under Federal law to adopt them; but are not intended to impose any new obligations in that regard. The agencies issuing and endorsing these guidelines endorse for all private employers and reaffirm for all governmental employers the Equal Employment Opportunity Coordinating Council's "Policy Statement on Affirmative Action Programs for State and Local Government Agencies" (41 FR 38814, September 13, 1976). That policy statement is attached hereto as appendix, section 17.

Technical Standards

Section 14. *Technical standards for validity studies.* The following minimum standards, as applicable, should be met in conducting a validity study. Nothing in these guidelines is intended to preclude the development and use of other professionally acceptable techniques with respect to validation of selection procedures. Where it is not technically feasible for a user to conduct a validity study, the user has the obligation otherwise to comply with these guidelines. See sections 6 and 7 above.

A. *Validity studies should be based on review of information about the job.* Any validity study should be based upon a review of information about the job for which the selection procedure is to be used. The review should include a job analysis except as provided in section 14B(3) below with respect to criterion-related validity. Any method of job analysis may be used if it provides the information required for the specific validation strategy used.

B. *Technical standards for criterion-related validity studies.*—1. *Technical feasibility.* Users choosing to validate a selection procedure by a criterion-related validity strategy should determine whether it is technically feasible (as defined in section 16) to conduct such a study in the particular employment context. The determination of the number of persons necessary to permit the conduct of a meaningful criterion-related study should be made by the user on the basis of all relevant information concerning the selection procedure, the potential sample and the employment situation. Where appropriate, jobs with substantially the same major work behaviors may be grouped together for validity studies, in order to obtain an adequate sample. These guidelines do not require a user to hire or promote persons for the purpose of making it possible to conduct a criterion-related study.

2. *Analysis of the job.* There should be a review of job information to determine measures of work behavior(s) or performance that are relevant to the job or group of jobs in question. These measures or criteria are relevant to the extent that they represent critical or important job duties, work behaviors or work outcomes as developed from the review of job information. The possibility of bias should be considered both in selection of the criterion measures and their application. In view of the possibility of bias in subjective evaluations, supervisory rating techniques and instructions to raters should be carefully developed. All criterion measures and the methods for gathering data need to be examined for freedom from factors which would unfairly alter scores of members of any group. The relevance of criteria and their freedom from bias are of particular concern when there are significant differences in measures of job performance for different groups.

3. *Criterion measures.* Proper safeguards should be taken to insure that scores on selection procedures do not enter into any judgments of employee adequacy that are to be used as criterion measures. Whatever criteria are used should represent important or critical work behavior(s) or work outcomes. Certain criteria may be used without a full job analysis if the user can show the importance of the criteria to the particular employment context. These criteria include but are not limited to production rate, error rate, tardiness, absenteeism, and length of service. A standardized rating of overall work performance may be used where a study of the job shows that it is an appropriate criterion. Where performance in training is used as a criterion, success in training should be properly measured and the relevance of the training should be shown either through a comparison of the content of the training program with the critical or important work behavior(s) of the job(s), or through a demonstration of the relationship between measures of performance in training and measures of job performance. Measures of relative success in training

include but are not limited to instructor evaluations, performance samples, or tests. Criterion measures consisting of paper and pencil tests will be closely reviewed for job relevance.

4. *Representativeness of the sample.* Whether the study is predictive or concurrent, the sample subjects should insofar as feasible be representative of the candidates normally available in the relevant labor market for the job or group of jobs in question, and should insofar as feasible include the races, sexes, and ethnic groups normally available in the relevant job market. In determining the representativeness of the sample in a concurrent validity study, the user should take into account the extent to which the specific knowledges or skills which are the primary focus of the test are those which employees learn on the job.

Where samples are combined or compared, attention should be given to see that such samples are comparable in terms of the actual job they perform, the length of time on the job where time on the job is likely to affect performance, and other relevant factors likely to affect validity differences; or that these factors are included in the design of the study and their effects identified.

5. *Statistical relationships.* The degree of relationship between selection procedure scores and criterion measures should be examined and computed, using professionally acceptable statistical procedures. Generally, a selection procedure is considered related to the criterion, for the purposes of these guidelines, when the relationship between performance on the procedure and performance on the criterion measure is statistically significant at the 0.05 level of significance, which means that it is sufficiently high as to have a probability of no more than one (1) in twenty (20) to have occurred by chance. Absence of a statistically significant relationship between a selection procedure and job performance should not necessarily discourage other investigations of the validity of that selection procedure.

6. *Operational use of selection procedures.* Users should evaluate each selection procedure to assure that it is appropriate for operational use, including establishment of cutoff scores or rank ordering. Generally, if other factors remain the same, the greater the magnitude of the relationship (e.g., correlation coefficient) between performance on a selection procedure and one or more criteria of performance on the job, and the greater the importance and number of aspects of job performance covered by the criteria, the more likely it is that the procedure will be appropriate for use. Reliance upon a selection procedure which is significantly related to a criterion measure, but which is based upon a study involving a large number of subjects and has a low correlation coefficient will be subject to close review if it has a large adverse impact. Sole reliance upon a single selection instrument which is related to only one of many job duties or aspects of job performance will also be subject to close review. The appropriateness of a selection procedure is best evaluated in each particular situation and there are no minimum correlation coefficients applicable to all employment situations. In determining whether a selection procedure is appropriate for operational use the following considerations should also be taken into account: The degree of adverse impact of the

procedure, the availability of other selection procedures of greater or substantially equal validity.

7. *Overstatement of validity findings.* Users should avoid reliance upon techniques which tend to overestimate validity findings as a result of capitalization on chance unless an appropriate safeguard is taken. Reliance upon a few selection procedures or criteria of successful job performance when many selection procedures or criteria of performance have been studied, or the use of optimal statistical weights for selection procedures computed in one sample, are techniques which tend to inflate validity estimates as a result of chance. Use of a large sample is one safeguard: cross-validation is another.

8. *Fairness.* This section generally calls for studies of unfairness where technically feasible. The concept of fairness or unfairness of selection procedures is a developing concept. In addition, fairness studies generally require substantial numbers of employees in the job or group of jobs being studied. For these reasons, the Federal enforcement agencies recognize that the obligation to conduct studies of fairness imposed by the guidelines generally will be upon users or groups of users with a large number of persons in a job class, or test developers; and that small users utilizing their own selection procedures will generally not be obligated to conduct such studies because it will be technically infeasible for them to do so.

a. *Unfairness defined.* When members of one race, sex, or ethnic group characteristically obtain lower scores on a selection procedure than members of another group and the differences in scores are not reflected in differences in a measure of job performance, use of the selection procedure may unfairly deny opportunities to members of the group that obtains the lower scores.

b. *Investigation of fairness.* Where a selection procedure results in an adverse impact on a race, sex, or ethnic group identified in accordance with the classifications set forth in section 4 above and that group is a significant factor in the relevant labor market, the user generally should investigate the possible existence of unfairness for that group if it is technically feasible to do so. The greater the severity of the adverse impact on a group, the greater the need to investigate the possible existence of unfairness. Where the weight of evidence from other studies shows that the selection procedure predicts fairly for the group in question and for the same or similar jobs, such evidence may be relied on in connection with the selection procedure at issue.

c. *General considerations in fairness investigations.* Users conducting a study of fairness should review the A.P.A. Standards regarding investigation of possible bias in testing. An investigation of fairness of a selection procedure depends on both evidence of validity and the manner in which the selection procedure is to be used in a particular employment context. Fairness of a selection procedure cannot necessarily be specified in advance without investigating these factors. Investigation of fairness of a selection procedure in samples where the range of scores on selection procedures or criterion measures is severely restricted for any subgroup sample (as compared to other subgroup samples) may produce misleading evidence of unfairness. That factor should accordingly be taken into account in conducting such studies and before reliance is placed on the results.

d. *When unfairness is shown.* If unfairness is demonstrated through a showing that members of a particular group perform better or poorer on the job than their scores on the selection procedure would indicate through comparison with how members of other groups perform, the user may either revise or replace the selection instrument in accordance with these guidelines, or may continue to use the selection instrument operationally with appropriate revisions in its use to assure compatibility between the probability of successful job performance and the probability of being selected.

e. *Technical feasibility of fairness studies.* In addition to the general conditions needed for technical feasibility for the conduct of a criterion-related study (see section 16, below) an investigation of fairness requires the following:

    i.   An adequate sample of persons in each group available for the study to achieve findings of statistical significance. Guidelines do not require a user to hire or promote persons on the basis of group classifications for the purpose of making it possible to conduct a study of fairness; but the user has the obligation otherwise to comply with these guidelines.

    ii.   The samples for each group should be comparable in terms of the actual job they perform, length of time on the job where time on the job is likely to affect performance, and other relevant factors likely to affect validity differences; or such factors should be included in the design of the study and their effects identified.

f. *Continued use of selection procedures when fairness studies not feasible.* If a study of fairness should otherwise be performed, but is not technically feasible, a selection procedure may be used which has otherwise met the validity standards of these guidelines, unless the technical infeasibility resulted from discriminatory employment practices which are demonstrated by facts other than past failure to conform with requirements for validation of selection procedures. However, when it becomes technically feasible for the user to perform a study of fairness and such a study is otherwise called for, the user should conduct the study of fairness.

C. *Technical standards for content validity studies.* —1. *Appropriateness of content validity studies.* Users choosing to validate a selection procedure by a content validity strategy should determine whether it is appropriate to conduct such a study in the particular employment context. A selection procedure can be supported by a content validity strategy to the extent that it is a representative sample of the content of the job. Selection procedures which purport to measure knowledges, skills, or abilities may in certain circumstances be justified by content validity, although they may not be representative samples, if the knowledge, skill, or ability measured by the selection procedure can be operationally defined as provided in section 14C(4) below, and if that knowledge, skill, or ability is a necessary prerequisite to successful job performance.

A selection procedure based upon inferences about mental processes cannot be supported solely or primarily on the basis of content validity. Thus, a content strategy is not appropriate for demonstrating the validity of selection procedures which purport to measure traits or constructs, such as intelligence, aptitude, personality, commonsense, judgment, leadership, and spatial ability. Content validity is also not an appropriate strategy when the selection procedure involves knowledges, skills, or abilities which an employee will be expected to learn on the job.

2. *Job analysis for content validity.* There should be a job analysis which includes an analysis of the important work behavior(s) required for successful performance and their relative importance and, if the behavior results in work product(s), an analysis of the work product(s). Any job analysis should focus on the work behavior(s) and the tasks associated with them. If work behavior(s) are not observable, the job analysis should identify and analyze those aspects of the behavior(s) that can be observed and the observed work products. The work behavior(s) selected for measurement should be critical work behavior(s) and/or important work behavior(s) constituting most of the job.

3. *Development of selection procedures.* A selection procedure designed to measure the work behavior may be developed specifically from the job and job analysis in question, or may have been previously developed by the user, or by other users or by a test publisher.

4. *Standards for demonstrating content validity.* To demonstrate the content validity of a selection procedure, a user should show that the behavior(s) demonstrated in the selection procedure are a representative sample of the behavior(s) of the job in question or that the selection procedure provides a representative sample of the work product of the job. In the case of a selection procedure measuring a knowledge, skill, or ability, the knowledge, skill, or ability being measured should be operationally defined. In the case of a selection procedure measuring a knowledge, the knowledge being measured should be operationally defined as that body of learned information which is used in and is a necessary prerequisite for observable aspects of work behavior of the job. In the case of skills or abilities, the skill or ability being measured should be operationally defined in terms of observable aspects of work behavior of the job. For any selection procedure measuring a knowledge, skill, or ability the user should show that (a) the selection procedure measures and is a representative sample of that knowledge, skill, or ability; and (b) that knowledge, skill, or ability is used in and is a necessary prerequisite to performance of critical or important work behavior(s). In addition, to be content valid, a selection procedure measuring a skill or ability should either closely approximate an observable work behavior, or its product should closely approximate an observable work product. If a test purports to sample a work behavior or to provide a sample of a work product, the manner and setting of the selection procedure and its level and complexity should closely approximate the work situation. The closer the content and the context of the selection procedure are to

work samples or work behaviors, the stronger is the basis for showing content validity. As the content of the selection procedure less resembles a work behavior, or the setting and manner of the administration of the selection procedure less resemble the work situation, or the result less resembles a work product, the less likely the selection procedure is to be content valid, and the greater the need for other evidence of validity.

5. *Reliability.* The reliability of selection procedures justified on the basis of content validity should be a matter of concern to the user. Whenever it is feasible, appropriate statistical estimates should be made of the reliability of the selection procedure.

6. *Prior training or experience.* A requirement for or evaluation of specific prior training or experience based on content validity, including a specification of level or amount of training or experience, should be justified on the basis of the relationship between the content of the training or experience and the content of the job for which the training or experience is to be required or evaluated. The critical consideration is the resemblance between the specific behaviors, products, knowledges, skills, or abilities in the experience or training and the specific behaviors, products, knowledges, skills, or abilities required on the job, whether or not there is close resemblance between the experience or training as a whole and the job as a whole.

7. *Content validity of training success.* Where a measure of success in a training program is used as a selection procedure and the content of a training program is justified on the basis of content validity, the use should be justified on the relationship between the content of the training program and the content of the job.

8. *Operational use.* A selection procedure which is supported on the basis of content validity may be used for a job if it represents a critical work behavior (i.e., behavior that is necessary for performance of the job) or work behaviors which constitute most of the important parts of the job.

9. *Ranking based on content validity studies.* If a user can show, by a job analysis or otherwise, that a higher score on a content valid selection procedure is likely to result in better job performance, the results may be used to rank persons who score above minimum levels. Where a selection procedure supported solely or primarily by content validity is used to rank job candidates, the selection procedure should measure those aspects of performance which differentiate among levels of job performance.

D. *Technical standards for construct validity studies.*—1. *Appropriateness of construct validity studies.* Construct validity is a more complex strategy than either criterion-related or content validity. Construct validation is a relatively new and developing procedure in the employment field, and there is at present a lack of substantial literature extending the concept to employment practices. The user should be aware that the effort to obtain sufficient empirical support for construct validity is both an extensive and arduous effort involving a series of research studies, which include criterion-related validity studies and which may include content validity studies. Users choosing to justify use of a selection procedure by this strategy should therefore take particular care to assure that the validity study meets the standards set forth below.

2. *Job analysis for construct validity studies.* There should be a job analysis. This job analysis should show the work behavior(s) required for successful performance of the job, or the groups of jobs being studied, the critical or important work behavior(s) in the job or group of jobs being studied, and an identification of the construct(s) believed to underlie successful performance of these critical or important work behaviors in the job or jobs in question. Each construct should be named and defined, so as to distinguish it from other constructs. If a group of jobs is being studied the jobs should have in common one or more critical or important work behaviors at a comparable level of complexity.

3. *Relationship to the job.* A selection procedure should then be identified or developed which measures the construct identified in accord with subparagraph (2) above. The user should show by empirical evidence that the selection procedure is validly related to the construct and that the construct is validly related to the performance of critical or important work behavior(s). The relationship between the construct as measured by the selection procedure and the related work behavior(s) should be supported by empirical evidence from one or more criterion-related studies involving the job or jobs in question which satisfy the provisions of section 14B above.

4. *Use of construct validity study without new criterion-related evidence.—a. Standards for use.* Until such time as professional literature provides more guidance on the use of construct validity in employment situations, the Federal agencies will accept a claim of construct validity without a criterion-related study which satisfies section 14B above only when the selection procedure has been used elsewhere in a situation in which a criterion-related study has been conducted and the use of a criterion-related validity study in this context meets the standards for transportability of criterion-related validity studies as set forth above in section 7. However, if a study pertains to a number of jobs having common critical or important work behaviors at a comparable level of complexity, and the evidence satisfies subparagraphs 14B (2) and (3) above for those jobs with criterion-related validity evidence for those jobs, the selection procedure may be used for all the jobs to which the study pertains. If construct validity is to be generalized to other jobs or groups of jobs not in the group studied, the Federal enforcement agencies will expect at a minimum additional empirical research evidence meeting the standards of subparagraphs section 14B (2) and (3) above for the additional jobs or groups of jobs.

b. *Determination of common work behaviors.* In determining whether two or more jobs have one or more work behavior(s) in common, the user should compare the observed work behavior(s) in each of the jobs and should compare the observed work product(s) in each of the jobs. If neither the observed work behavior(s) in each of the jobs nor the observed work product(s) in each of the jobs are the same, the Federal enforcement agencies will presume that the work behavior(s) in each job are different. If the work behaviors are not observable, then evidence of similarity of work products and any other relevant research evidence will be considered in determining whether the work behavior(s) in the two jobs are the same.

Documentation of Impact
and Validity Evidence

Section 15. *Documentation of Impact and Validity Evidence.*—A. *Required information.* Users of selection procedures other than those users complying with section 15A(1) below should maintain and have available for each job information on adverse impact of the selection process for that job and, where it is determined a selection process has an adverse impact, evidence of validity as set forth below.

1. *Simplified recordkeeping for users with less than 100 employees.* In order to minimize recordkeeping burdens on employers who employ one hundred (100) or fewer employees, and other users not required to file EEO-1, et seq., reports, such users may satisfy the requirements of this section 15 if they maintain and have available records showing, for each year:

a.   The number of persons hired, promoted, and terminated for each job, by sex, and where appropriate by race and national origin;

b.   The number of applicants for hire and promotion by sex and where appropriate by race and national origin;

c.   The selection procedures utilized (either standardized or not standardized).

These records should be maintained for each race or national origin group (see section 4 above) constituting more than two percent (2%) of the labor force in the relevant labor area. However, it is not necessary to maintain records by race and/or national origin (see §4 above) if one race or national origin group in the relevant labor area constitutes more than ninety-eight percent (98%) of the labor force in the area. If the user has reason to believe that a selection procedure has an adverse impact, the user should maintain any available evidence of validity for that procedure (see sections 7A and 8).

2. *Information on impact.*—a. *Collection of information on impact.* Users of selection procedures other than those complying with section 15A(1) above should maintain and have available for each job records or other information showing whether the total selection process for that job has an adverse impact on any of the groups for which records are called for by sections 4B above. Adverse impact determinations should be made at least annually for each such group which constitutes at least 2 percent of the labor force in the relevant labor area or 2 percent of the applicable workforce. Where a total selection process for a job has an adverse impact, the user should maintain and have available records or other information showing which components have an adverse impact. Where the total selection process for a job does not have an adverse impact, information need not be maintained for individual components except in circumstances set forth in subsection 15A(2)(b) below. If the determination of adverse impact is made using a procedure other than the "four-fifths rule," as defined in the first sentence of section

4D above, a justification, consistent with section 4D above, for the procedure used to determine adverse impact should be available.

b. *When adverse impact has been eliminated in the total selection process.* Whenever the total selection process for a particular job has had an adverse impact, as defined in section 4 above, in any year, but no longer has an adverse impact, the user should maintain and have available the information on individual components of the selection process required in the preceding paragraph for the period in which there was adverse impact. In addition, the user should continue to collect such information for at least two (2) years after the adverse impact has been eliminated.

c. *When data insufficient to determine impact.* Where there has been an insufficient number of selections to determine whether there is an adverse impact of the total selection process for a particular job, the user should continue to collect, maintain and have available the information on individual components of the selection process required in section 15(A)(2)(a) above until the information is sufficient to determine that the overall selection process does not have an adverse impact as defined in section 4 above, or until the job has changed substantially.

3. *Documentation of validity evidence.—a. Types of evidence.* Where a total selection process has an adverse impact (see section 4 above) the user should maintain and have available for each component of that process which has an adverse impact, one or more of the following types of documentation evidence:

i. Documentation evidence showing criterion-related validity of the selection procedure (see section 15B);

ii. Documentation evidence showing content validity of the selection procedure (see section 15C);

iii. Documentation evidence showing construct validity of the selection procedure (see section 15D);

iv. Documentation evidence from other studies showing validity of the selection procedure in the user's facility (see section 15E);

v. Documentation evidence showing why a validity study cannot or need not be performed and why continued use of the procedure is consistent with Federal law.

b. *Form of report.* This evidence should be compiled in a reasonably complete and organized manner to permit direct evaluation of the validity of the selection procedure. Previously written employer or consultant reports of validity, or reports describing validity studies completed before the issuance of these guidelines are acceptable if they are complete in regard to the documentation requirements contained in this section, or if they satisfied requirements of guidelines which were in effect when the validity study was completed. If they are not complete, the required additional documentation should be appended. If necessary information is not available the report of the validity study may still be used as documentation, but its adequacy will be evaluated in terms of compliance with the requirements of these guidelines.

c. *Completeness.* In the event that evidence of validity is reviewed by an enforcement agency, the validation reports completed after the effective date of these guidelines are expected to contain the information set forth below. Evidence denoted by use of the word "(essential)" is considered critical. If information denoted essential is not included, the report will be considered incomplete unless the user affirmatively demonstrates either its unavailability due to circumstances beyond the user's control or special circumstances of the user's study which make the information irrelevant. Evidence not so denoted is desirable but its absence will not be a basis for considering a report incomplete. The user should maintain and have available the information called for under the heading "Source Data" in sections 15B(11) and 15D(11). While it is a necessary part of the study, it need not be submitted with the report. All statistical results should be organized and presented in tabular or graphic form to the extent feasible.

B. *Criterion-related validity studies.* Reports of criterion-related validity for a selection procedure should include the following information:

1. *User(s), location(s), and date(s) of study.* Dates and location(s) of the job analysis or review of job information, the date(s) and location(s) of the administration of the selection procedures and collection of criterion data, and the time between collection of data on selection procedures and criterion measures should be provided (essential). If the study was conducted at several locations, the address of each location, including city and State, should be shown.

2. *Problem and setting.* An explicit definition of the purpose(s) of the study and the circumstances in which the study was conducted should be provided. A description of existing selection procedures and cutoff scores, if any, should be provided.

3. *Job analysis or review of job information.* A description of the procedure used to analyze the job or group of jobs, or to review the job information should be provided (essential). Where a review of job information results in criteria which may be used without a full job analysis (see section 14B(3)), the basis for the selection of these criteria should be reported (essential). Where a job analysis is required a complete description of the work behavior(s) or work outcome(s), and measures of their criticality or importance should be provided (essential). The report should describe the basis on which the behavior(s) or outcome(s) were determined to be critical or important, such as the proportion of time spent on the respective behaviors, their level of difficulty, their frequency of performance, the consequences of error, or other appropriate factors (essential). Where two or more jobs are grouped for a validity study, the information called for in this subsection should be provided for each of the jobs, and the justification for the grouping (see section 14B(1)) should be provided (essential).

4. *Job titles and codes.* It is desirable to provide the user's job title(s) for the job(s) in question and the corresponding job title(s) and code(s) from U.S. Employment Service's Dictionary of Occupational Titles.

5. *Criterion measures.* The bases for the selection of the criterion measures should be provided, together with references to the evidence considered in making the selection of criterion measures (essential). A full description of all criteria on which data were collected and means by which they were observed, recorded, evaluated, and quantified, should be provided (essential). If rating techniques are used as criterion measures, the appraisal form(s) and instructions to the rater(s) should be included as part of the validation evidence, or should be explicitly described and available (essential). All steps taken to insure that criterion measures are free from factors which would unfairly alter the scores of members of any group should be described (essential).

6. *Sample description.* A description of how the research sample was identified and selected should be included (essential). The race, sex, and ethnic composition of the sample, including those groups set forth in section 4A above, should be described (essential). This description should include the size of each subgroup (essential). A description of how the research sample compares with the relevant labor market or work force, the method by which the relevant labor market or work force was defined, and a discussion of the likely effects on validity of differences between the sample and the relevant labor market or work force, are also desirable. Descriptions of educational levels, length of service, and age are also desirable.

7. *Description of selection procedures.* Any measure, combination of measures, or procedure studied should be completely and explicitly described or attached (essential). If commercially available selection procedures are studied, they should be described by title, form, and publisher (essential). Reports of reliability estimates and how they were established are desirable.

8. *Techniques and results.* Methods used in analyzing data should be described (essential). Measures of central tendency (e.g., means) and measures of dispersion (e.g., standard deviations and ranges) for all selection procedures and all criteria should be reported for each race, sex, and ethnic group which constitutes a significant factor in the relevant labor market (essential). The magnitude and direction of all relationships between selection procedures and criterion measures investigated should be reported for each relevant race, sex, and ethnic group and for the total group (essential). Where groups are too small to obtain reliable evidence of the magnitude of the relationship, need not be reported separately. Statements regarding the statistical significance of results should be made (essential). Any statistical adjustments, such as for less then perfect reliability or for restriction of score range in the selection procedure or criterion should be described and explained; and uncorrected correlation coefficients should also be shown (essential). Where the statistical technique categorizes continuous data, such as biserial correlation and the phi coefficient, the categories and the bases on which they were determined should be described and explained (essential). Studies of test fairness should be included where called for by the requirements of section 14B(8) (essential). These studies should include the rationale by which a selection procedure was determined to be fair to the group(s) in question. Where test fair-

ness or unfairness has been demonstrated on the basis of other studies, a bibliography of the relevant studies should be included (essential). If the bibliography includes unpublished studies, copies of these studies, or adequate abstracts or summaries, should be attached (essential). Where revisions have been made in a selection procedure to assure compatability between successful job performance and the probability of being selected, the studies underlying such revisions should be included (essential). All statistical results should be organized and presented by relevant race, sex, and ethnic group (essential).

9. *Alternative procedures investigated.* The selection procedures investigated and available evidence of their impact should be identified (essential). The scope, method, and findings of the investigation, and the conclusions reached in light of the findings, should be fully described (essential).

10. *Uses and applications.* The methods considered for use of the selection procedure (e.g., as a screening device with a cutoff score, for grouping or ranking, or combined with other procedures in a battery) and available evidence of their impact should be described (essential). This description should include the rationale for choosing the method for operational use, and the evidence of the validity and utility of the procedure as it is to be used (essential). The purpose for which the procedure is to be used (e.g., hiring, transfer, promotion) should be described (essential). If weights are assigned to different parts of the selection procedure, these weights and the validity of the weighted composite should be reported (essential). If the selection procedure is used with a cutoff score, the user should describe the way in which normal expectations of proficiency within the work force were determined and the way in which the cutoff score was determined (essential).

11. *Source data.* Each user should maintain records showing all pertinent information about individual sample members and raters where they are used, in studies involving the validation of selection procedures. These records should be made available upon request of a compliance agency. In the case of individual sample members these data should include scores on the selection procedure(s), scores on criterion measures, age, sex, race, or ethnic group status, and experience on the specific job on which the validation study was conducted, and may also include such things as education, training, and prior job experience, but should not include names and social security numbers. Records should be maintained which show the ratings given to each sample member by each rater.

12. *Contact person.* The name, mailing address, and telephone number of the person who may be contacted for further information about the validity study should be provided (essential).

13. *Accuracy and completeness.* The report should describe the steps taken to assure the accuracy and completeness of the collection, analysis, and report of data and results.

C. *Content validity studies.* Reports of content validity for a selection procedure should include the following information:

1. *User(s), location(s) and date(s) of study.* Dates and location(s) of the job analysis should be shown (essential).

2. *Problem and setting.* An explicit definition of the purpose(s) of the study and the circumstances in which the study was conducted should be provided. A description of existing selection procedures and cutoff scores, if any, should be provided.

3. *Job analysis—Content of the job.* A description of the method used to analyze the job should be provided (essential). The work behavior(s), the associated tasks, and, if the behavior results in a work product, the work products should be completely described (essential). Measures of criticality and/or importance of the work behavior(s) and the method of determining these measures should be provided (essential). Where the job analysis also identified the knowledges, skills, and abilities used in work behavior(s), an operational definition for each knowledge in terms of a body of learned information and for each skill and ability in terms of observable behaviors and outcomes, and the relationship between each knowledge, skill, or ability and each work behavior, as well as the method used to determine this relationship, should be provided (essential). The work situation should be described, including the setting in which work behavior(s) are performed, and where appropriate, the manner in which knowledges, skills, or abilities are used, and the complexity and difficulty of the knowledge, skill, or ability as used in the work behavior(s).

4. *Selection procedure and its content.* Selection procedures, including those constructed by or for the user, specific training requirements, composites of selection procedures, and any other procedure supported by content validity, should be completely and explicitly described or attached (essential). If commercially available selection procedures are used, they should be described by title, form, and publisher (essential). The behaviors measured or sampled by the selection procedure should be explicitly described (essential). Where the selection procedure purports to measure a knowledge, skill, or ability, evidence that the selection procedure measures and is a representative sample of the knowledge, skill, or ability should be provided (essential).

5. *Relationship between the selection procedure and the job.* The evidence demonstrating that the selection procedure is a representative work sample, a representative sample of the work behavior(s), or a representative sample of a knowledge, skill, or ability as used as a part of a work behavior and necessary for that behavior should be provided (essential). The user should identify the work behavior(s) which each item or part of the selection procedure is intended to sample or measure (essential). Where the selection procedure purports to sample a work behavior or to provide a sample of a work product, a comparison should be provided of the manner, setting, and the level of complexity of the selection procedure with those of the work situation (essential). If any steps were taken to reduce adverse impact on a race, sex, or ethnic group in the content of the procedure or in its administration, these steps should be described. Establishment of time limits, if any, and how these limits are related to the speed with which duties must be performed on the job, should be explained. Measures of central tendency (e.g., means) and measures of dispersion (e.g., standard deviations) and estimates of reliability should be reported for all selection procedures if available. Such reports should be made

for relevant race, sex, and ethnic subgroups, at least on a statistically reliable sample basis.

6. *Alternative procedures investigated.* The alternative selection procedures investigated and available evidence of their impact should be identified (essential). The scope, method, and findings of the investigation, and the conclusions reached in light of the findings, should be fully described (essential).

7. *Uses and applications.* The methods considered for use of the selection procedure (e.g., as a screening device with a cutoff score, for grouping or ranking, or combined with other procedures in a battery) and available evidence of their impact should be described (essential). This description should include the rationale for choosing the method for operational use, and the evidence of the validity and utility of the procedure as it is to be used (essential). The purpose for which the procedure is to be used (e.g., hiring, transfer, promotion) should be described (essential). If the selection procedure is used with a cutoff score, the user should describe the way in which normal expectations of proficiency within the work force were determined and the way in which the cutoff score was determined (essential). In addition, if the selection procedure is to be used for ranking, the user should specify the evidence showing that a higher score on the selection procedure is likely to result in better job performance.

8. *Contact person.* The name, mailing address, and telephone number of the person who may be contacted for further information about the validity study should be provided (essential).

9. *Accuracy and completeness.* The report should describe the steps taken to assure the accuracy and completeness of the collection, analysis, and report of data and results.

D. *Construct validity studies.* Reports of construct validity for a selection procedure should include the following information:

1. *User(s), location(s), and date(s) of study.* Date(s) and location(s) of the job analysis and the gathering of other evidence called for by these guidelines should be provided (essential).

2. *Problem and setting.* An explicit definition of the purpose(s) of the study and the circumstances in which the study was conducted should be provided. A description of existing selection procedures and cutoff scores, if any, should be provided.

3. *Construct definition.* A clear definition of the construct(s) which are believed to underlie successful performance of the critical or important work behavior(s) should be provided (essential). This definition should include the levels of construct performance relevant to the job(s) for which the selection procedure is to be used (essential). There should be a summary of the position of the construct in the psychological literature, or in the absence of such a position, a description of the way in which the definition and measurement of the construct was developed and the psychological theory underlying it (essential). Any quantitative data which identify or define the job constructs, such as factor analyses, should be provided (essential).

4. *Job analysis.* A description of the method used to analyze the job should be provided (essential). A complete description of

work behavior(s) and, to the extent appropriate, work outcomes and measures of their criticality and/or importance should be provided (essential). The report should also describe the basis on which the behavior(s) or outcomes were determined to be important, such as their level of difficulty, their frequency of performance, the consequences of error or other appropriate factors (essential). Where jobs are grouped or compared for the purposes of generalizing validity evidence, the work behavior(s) and work product(s) for each of the jobs should be described, and conclusions concerning the similarity of the jobs in terms of observable work behaviors or work products should be made (essential).

5. *Job titles and codes.* It is desirable to provide the selection procedure user's job title(s) for the job(s) in question and the corresponding job title(s) and code(s) from the United States Employment Service's dictionary of occupational titles.

6. *Selection procedure.* The selection procedure used as a measure of the construct should be completely and explicitly described or attached (essential). If commercially available selection procedures are used, they should be identified by title, form and publisher (essential). The research evidence of the relationship between the selection procedure and the construct, such as factor structure, should be included (essential). Measures of central tendency, variability and reliability of the selection procedure should be provided (essential). Whenever feasible, these measures should be provided separately for each relevant race, sex and ethnic group.

7. *Relationship to job performance.* The criterion-related study(ies) and other empirical evidence of the relationship between the construct measured by the selection procedure and the related work behavior(s) for the job or jobs in question should be provided (essential). Documentation of the criterion-related study(ies) should satisfy the provisions of section 15B above or section 15E(1) below, except for studies conducted prior to the effective date of these guidelines (essential). Where a study pertains to a group of jobs, and, on the basis of the study, validity is asserted for a job in the group, the observed work behaviors and the observed work products for each of the jobs should be described (essential). Any other evidence used in determining whether the work behavior(s) in each of the jobs is the same should be fully described (essential).

8. *Alternative procedures investigated.* The alternative selection procedures investigated and available evidence of their impact should be identified (essential). The scope, method, and findings of the investigation, and the conclusions reached in light of the findings should be fully described (essential).

9. *Uses and applications.* The methods considered for use of the selection procedure (e.g., as a screening device with a cutoff score, for grouping or ranking, or combined with other procedures in a battery) and available evidence of their impact should be described (essential). This description should include the rationale for choosing the method for operational use, and the evidence of the validity and utility of the procedure as it is to be used (essential). The purpose for which the procedure is to be used (e.g., hiring, transfer, promotion) should be described (essential). If weights are assigned to different parts of the selection procedure, these weights and the validity of the

weighted composite should be reported (essential). If the selection procedure is used with a cutoff score, the user should describe the way in which normal expectations of proficiency within the work force were determined and the way in which the cutoff score was determined (essential).

10. *Accuracy and completeness.* The report should describe the steps taken to assure the accuracy and completeness of the collection, analysis, and report of data and results.

11. *Source data.* Each user should maintain records showing all pertinent information relating to its study of construct validity.

12. *Contact person.* The name, mailing address, and telephone number of the individual who may be contacted for further information about the validity study should be provided (essential).

E. *Evidence of validity from other studies.* When validity of a selection procedure is supported by studies not done by the user, the evidence from the original study or studies should be compiled in a manner similar to that required in the appropriate section of this section 15 above. In addition, the following evidence should be supplied:

1. *Evidence from criterion-related validity studies.*—a. *Job information.* A description of the important job behavior(s) of the user's job and the basis on which the behaviors were determined to be important should be provided (essential). A full description of the basis for determining that these important work behaviors are the same as those of the job in the original study (or studies) should be provided (essential).

b. *Relevance of criteria.* A full description of the basis on which the criteria used in the original studies are determined to be relevant for the user should be provided (essential).

c. *Other variables.* The similarity of important applicant pool or sample characteristics reported in the original studies to those of the user should be described (essential). A description of the comparison between the race, sex and ethnic composition of the user's relevant labor market and the sample in the original validity studies should be provided (essential).

d. *Use of the selection procedure.* A full description should be provided showing that the use to be made of the selection procedure is consistent with the findings of the original validity studies (essential).

e. *Bibliography.* A bibliography of reports of validity of the selection procedure for the job or jobs in question should be provided (essential). Where any of the studies included an investigation of test fairness, the results of this investigation should be provided (essential). Copies of reports published in journals that are not commonly available should be described in detail or attached (essential). Where a user is relying upon unpublished studies, a reasonable effort should be made to obtain these studies. If these unpublished studies are the sole source of validity evidence they should be described in detail or attached (essential). If these studies are not available, the name and address of the source, an adequate abstract or summary of the validity study and data, and a contact person in the source organization should be provided (essential).

2. *Evidence from content validity studies.* See section 14C(3) and section 15C above.

3. *Evidence from construct validity studies.* See sections 14D(2) and 15D above.

F. *Evidence of validity from cooperative studies.* Where a selection procedure has been validated through a cooperative study, evidence that the study satisfies the requirements of sections 7, 8 and 15E should be provided (essential).

G. *Selection for higher level job.* If a selection procedure is used to evaluate candidates for jobs at a higher level than those for which they will initially be employed, the validity evidence should satisfy the documentation provisions of this section 15 for the higher level job or jobs, and in addition, the user should provide: (1) a description of the job progression structure, formal or informal; (2) the data showing how many employees progress to the higher level job and the length of time needed to make this progression; and (3) an identification of any anticipated changes in the higher level job. In addition, if the test measures a knowledge, skill or ability, the user should provide evidence that the knowledge, skill or ability is required for the higher level job and the basis for the conclusion that the knowledge, skill or ability is not expected to develop from the training or experience on the job.

H. *Interim use of selection procedures.* If a selection procedure is being used on an interim basis because the procedure is not fully supported by the required evidence of validity, the user should maintain and have available (1) substantial evidence of validity for the procedure, and (2) a report showing the date on which the study to gather the additional evidence commenced, the estimated completion date of the study, and a description of the data to be collected (essential).

Definitions

Section 16. *Definitions.* The following definitions shall apply throughout these guidelines:

A. *Ability.* A present competence to perform an observable behavior or a behavior which results in an observable product.

B. *Adverse impact.* A substantially different rate of selection in hiring, promotion, or other employment decision which works to the disadvantage of members of a race, sex, or ethnic group. See section 4 of these guidelines.

C. *Compliance with these guidelines.* Use of a selection procedure is in compliance with these guidelines if such use has been validated in accord with these guidelines (as defined below), or if such use does not result in adverse impact on any race, sex, or ethnic group (see section 4, above), or, in unusual circumstances, if use of the procedure is otherwise justified in accord with Federal law. See section 6B, above.

D. *Content validity.* Demonstrated by data showing that the content of a selection procedure is representative of important aspects of performance on the job. See section 5B and section 14C.

E. *Construct validity.* Demonstrated by data showing that the selection procedure measures the degree to which candidates have identifiable characteristics which have been determined to be important for successful job performance. See section 5B and section 14D.

F. *Criterion-related validity.* Demonstrated by empirical data showing that the selection procedure is predictive of or significantly correlated with important elements of work behavior. See sections 5B and 14B.

G. *Employer.* Any employer subject to the provisions of the Civil Rights Act of 1964, as amended, including State or local governments, and any Federal agency subject to the provisions of section 717 of the Civil Rights Act of 1964, as amended, and any Federal contractor or subcontractor or federally assisted construction contractor or subcontractor covered by Executive Order 11246, as amended.

H. *Employment agency.* Any employment agency subject to the provisions of the Civil Rights Act of 1964, as amended.

I. *Enforcement action.* For the purposes of section 4 a proceeding by a Federal enforcement agency such as a lawsuit or an administrative proceeding leading to debarment from or withholding, suspension, or termination of Federal Government contracts or the suspension or withholding of Federal Government funds; but not a finding of reasonable cause or a conciliation process or the issuance of right to sue letters under title VII or under Executive Order 11246 where such finding, conciliation, or issuance of notice of right to sue is based upon an individual complaint.

J. *Enforcement agency.* Any agency of the executive branch of the Federal Government which adopts these guidelines for purposes of the enforcement of the equal employment opportunity laws or which has responsibility for securing compliance with them.

K. *Job analysis.* A detailed statement of work behaviors and other information relevant to the job.

L. *Job description.* A general statement of job duties and responsibilities.

M. *Knowledge.* A body of information applied directly to the performance of a function.

N. *Labor organization.* Any labor organization subject to the provisions of the Civil Rights Act of 1964, as amended, and any committee subject thereto controlling apprenticeship or other training.

O. *Observable.* Able to be seen, heard, or otherwise perceived by a person other than the person performing the action.

P. *Race, sex, or ethnic group.* Any group of persons identifiable on the grounds of race, color, religion, sex, or national origin.

Q. *Selection procedure.* Any measure, combination of measures, or procedure used as a basis for any employment decision. Selection procedures include the full range of assessment techniques from traditional paper and pencil tests, performance tests, training programs, or probationary periods and physical, educational, and work experience requirements through informal or casual interviews and unscored application forms.

R. *Selection rate.* The proportion of applicants or candidates who are hired, promoted, or otherwise selected.

S. *Should.* The term "should" as used in these guidelines is intended to connote action which is necessary to achieve compliance with the guidelines, while recognizing that there are circumstances where alternative courses of action are open to users.

T. *Skill.* A present, observable competence to perform a learned psychomotor act.

U. *Technical feasibility.* The existence of conditions permitting the conduct of meaningful criterion-related validity studies. These conditions include: (1) An adequate sample of persons available for the study to achieve findings of statistical significance; (2) having or being able to obtain a sufficient range of scores on the selection procedure and job performance measures to produce validity results which can be expected to be representative of the results if the ranges normally expected were utilized; and (3) having or being able to devise unbiased, reliable and relevant measures of job performance or other criteria of employee adequacy. See section 14B(2). With respect to investigation of possible unfairness, the same considerations are applicable to each group for which the study is made. See section 14B(8).

V. *Unfairness of selection procedure.* A condition in which members of one race, sex, or ethnic group characteristically obtain lower scores on a selection procedure than members of another group, and the differences are not reflected in differences in measures of job performance. See section 14B(7).

W. *User.* Any employer, labor organization, employment agency, or licensing or certification board, to the extent it may be covered by Federal equal employment opportunity law, which uses a selection procedure as a basis for any employment decision. Whenever an employer, labor organization, or employment agency is required by law to restrict recruitment for any occupation to those applicants who have met licensing or certification requirements, the licensing or certifying authority to the extent it may be covered by Federal equal employment opportunity law will be considered the user with respect to those licensing or certification requirements. Whenever a State employment agency or service does no more than administer or monitor a procedure as permitted by Department of Labor regulations, and does so without making referrals or taking any other action on the basis of the results, the State employment agency will not be deemed to be a user.

X. *Validated in accord with these guidelines or properly validated.* A demonstration that one or more validity study or studies meeting the standards of these guidelines has been conducted, including investigation and, where appropriate, use of suitable alternative selection procedures as contemplated by section 3B, and has produced evidence of validity sufficient to warrant use of the procedure for the intended purpose under the standards of these guidelines.

Y. *Work behavior.* An activity performed to achieve the objectives of the job. Work behaviors involve observable (physical) components and unobservable (mental) components. A work behavior consists of the performance of one or more tasks. Knowledges, skills, and abilities are not behaviors, although they may be applied in work behaviors.

Appendix

[Section] 17. *Policy statement on affirmative action* (see section 13B). The Equal Employment Opportunity Coordinating Council was established by act of Congress in 1972, and charged with responsibility for developing and implementing agreements and policies designed, among other things, to eliminate conflict and inconsistency among the agencies of the Federal Government responsible for administering Federal law prohibiting discrimination on grounds of race, color, sex, religion, and national origin. This statement is issued as an initial response to the requests of a number of State and local officials for clarification of the Government's policies concerning the role of affirmative action in the overall equal employment opportunity program. While the Coordinating Council's adoption of this statement expresses only the views of the signatory agencies concerning this important subject, the principles set forth below should serve as policy guidance for other Federal agencies as well.

1. Equal employment opportunity is the law of the land. In the public sector of our society this means that all persons, regardless of race, color, religion, sex, or national origin shall have equal access to positions in the public service limited only by their ability to do the job. There is ample evidence in all sectors of our society that such equal access frequently has been denied to members of certain groups because of their sex, racial, or ethnic characteristics. The remedy for such past and present discrimination is twofold.

On the one hand, vigorous enforcement of the laws against discrimination is essential. But equally, and perhaps even more important are affirmative voluntary efforts on the part of public employers to assure that positions in the public service are genuinely and equally accessible to qualified persons, without regard to their sex, racial, or ethnic characteristics. Without such efforts equal employment opportunity is no more than a wish. The importance of voluntary affirmative action on the part of employers is underscored by title VII of the Civil Rights Act of 1964, Executive Order 11246, and related laws and regulations—all of which emphasize voluntary action to achieve equal employment opportunity.

As with most management objectives, a systematic plan based on sound organizational analysis and problem identification is crucial to the accomplishment of affirmative action objectives. For this reason, the Council urges all State and local governments to develop and implement results oriented affirmative action plans which deal with the problems so identified.

The following paragraphs are intended to assist State and local governments by illustrating the kinds of analyses and activities which may be appropriate for a public employer's voluntary affirmative action plan. This statement does not address remedies imposed after a finding of unlawful discrimination.

2. Voluntary affirmative action to assure equal employment opportunity is appropriate at any stage of the employment process. The first step in the construction of any affirmative action plan should be an analysis of the employers' work force to determine whether percentages of sex, race, or ethnic groups in individual job classifications are substantially similar to the percentages of those groups available in the relevant job market who possess the basic job-related qualifications.

When substantial disparities are found through such analyses, each element of the overall selection process should be examined to determine which elements operate to exclude persons on the basis of sex, race, or ethnic group. Such elements include, but are not limited to, recruitment, testing, ranking certification, interview, recommendations for selection, hiring, promotion, etc. The examination of each element of the selection process should at a minimum include a determination of its validity in predicting job performance.

3. When an employer has reason to believe that its selection procedures have the exclusionary effect described in paragraph 2 above, it should initiate affirmative steps to remedy the situation. Such steps, which in design and execution may be race, color, sex, or ethnic "conscious," include, but are not limited to, the following:

a. The establishment of a long-term goal, and short-range, interim goals and timetables for the specific job classifications, all of which should take into account the availability of basically qualified persons in the relevant job market;

b. A recruitment program designed to attract qualified members of the group in question;

c. A systematic effort to organize work and redesign jobs in ways that provide opportunities for persons lacking "journeyman" level knowledge or skills to enter and, with appropriate training, to progress in a career field;

d. Revamping selection instruments or procedures which have not yet been validated in order to reduce or eliminate exclusionary effects on particular groups in particular job classifications;

e. The initiation of measures designed to assure that members of the affected group who are qualified to perform the job are included within the pool of persons from which the selecting official makes the selection;

f. A systematic effort to provide career advancement training, both classroom and on-the-job, to employees locked into dead end jobs;

g. The establishment of a system for regularly monitoring the effectiveness of the particular affirmative action program, and procedures for making timely adjustments in this program where effectiveness is not demonstrated.

4. The goal of any affirmative action plan should be achievement of genuine equal employment opportunity for all qualified persons. Selection under such plans should be based upon the ability of the applicant(s) to do the work. Such plans should not require the selection of the unqualified, or the unneeded, nor should they require the selection of persons on

the basis of race, color, sex, religion, or national origin. Moreover, while the Council believes that this statement should serve to assist State and local employers, as well as Federal agencies, it recognizes that affirmative action cannot be viewed as a standardized program which must be accomplished in the same way at all times in all places.

Accordingly, the Council has not attempted to set forth here either the minimum or maximum voluntary steps that employers may take to deal with their respective situations. Rather, the Council recognizes that under applicable authorities, State and local employers have flexibility to formulate affirmative action plans that are best suited to their particular situations. In this manner, the Council believes that affirmative action programs will best serve the goal of equal employment opportunity.

Respectfully submitted, [Harold R. Tyler, Jr., *Deputy Attorney General and Chairman of the Equal Employment Coordinating Council.* Michael H. Moskow, *Under Secretary of Labor.* Ethel Bent Walsh, *Acting Chairman, Equal Employment Opportunity Commission.* Robert E. Hampton, *Chairman, Civil Service Commission.* Arthur E. Flemming, *Chairman, Commission on Civil Rights.*]

Because of its equal employment opportunity responsibilities under the State and Local Government Fiscal Assistance Act of 1972 (the revenue sharing act), the Department of Treasury was invited to participate in the formulation of this policy statement; and it concurs and joins in the adoption of this policy statement.

Done this 26th day of August 1976. [Richard Albrecht, *General Counsel, Department of the Treasury.*]

Section 18. *Citations.* The official title of these guidelines is "Uniform Guidelines on Employee Selection Procedures (1978)". The Uniform Guidelines on Employee Selection Procedures (1978) are intended to establish a uniform Federal position in the area of prohibiting discrimination in employment practices on grounds of race, color, religion, sex, or national origin. These guidelines have been adopted by the Equal Employment Opportunity Commission, the Department of Labor, the Department of Justice, and the Civil Service Commission.

The official citation is: "Section——, Uniform Guidelines on Employee Selection Procedure (1978); 43 FR—— (August 25, 1978)."

The short form citation is: "Section——, U.G.E.S.P. (1978); 43 FR—— (August 25, 1978)."

When the guidelines are cited in connection with the activities of one of the issuing agencies, a specific citation to the regulations of that agency can be added at the end of the above citation. The specific additional citations are as follows: Equal Employment Opportunity Commission, 29 CFR Part 1607; Department of Labor, Office of Federal Contract Compliance Programs, 41 CFR Part 60–3; Department of Justice, 28 CFR 50.14; Civil Service Commission, 5 CFR 300.103(c).

Normally when citing these guidelines, the section number immediately preceding the title of the guidelines will be from these guidelines series 1–18. If a section number from the codification for an individual agency is needed it can also be added at the end of the agency citation. For example, section 6A of these guidelines could be cited for EEOC as follows: "Section 6A, Uniform Guidelines on Employee Selection Procedures (1978); 43 FR——, (August 25, 1978); 29 CFR Part 1607, section 6A." [Eleanor Holmes Norton, *Chair, Equal Employment Opportunity Commission.* Alan K. Campbell, *Chairman, Civil Service Commission.* Ray Marshall, *Secretary of Labor.* Griffin B. Bell, *Attorney General.*]

Notes

1. Section 703(h), 42 U.S.C. 2000e(2)(h).
2. See 35 U.S.L.W. 2137 (1966).
3. 401 U.S. 424 (1971).
4. See, *e.g., Albermarle Paper Co.* v. *Moody,* 422 U.S. 405 (1975).
5. *Griggs,* note 3, supra; uniform guidelines on employee selection procedures (1978), section 3A, (hereinafter cited by section number only).
6. *Furnco* v. *Waters,* 98 S.Ct. 2943 (1978).
7. Section 6.
8. Section 4D.
9. Section 16R (definition of selection rate).
10. Section 4D (special recruiting programs).
11. *Ibid* (user's actions have discouraged applicants).
12. See, *e.g., Griggs* v. *Duke Power Co.,* 401 U.S. 424 (1971).
13. Section 4C.
14. Section 4E.
15. Section 4C.
16. The processing of individual cases is excluded from the operation of the bottom line concept by the definition of "enforcement action," section 16I. Under section 4C, where adverse impact has existed, the employer must keep records of the effect of each component for 2 years after the adverse effect has dissipated.
17. A few practices may be used without validation even if they have adverse impact. See, *e.g., McDonnell Douglas* v. *Green,* 411 U.S. 792 (1973) and section 6B.
18. *Albemarle Paper Co.* v. *Moody* 422 U.S. 405 (1975); *Robinson* v. *Lorillard Corp.,* 444 F. 2d 791 (4th Cir. 1971).
19. Sections 3B; 5G.
20. *Ibid.*
21. See sections 3B; 5H. See also sections 14B(6) (criterion-related validity); 14C(9) (content validity); 14D(1) (construct validity).

22. Sections 5G, 14B(6); 14C(9); 14D(1).

23. Section 5I.

24. Sections 5B, (General Standards); 14B (Technical Standards); 15B (Documentation); 16F (Definition).

25. Sections 5B (General Standards); 14C (Technical Standards); 15C (Documentation); 16D (Definition).

26. Sections 5B (General Standards); 14D (Technical Standards); 15D (Documentation); 16E (Definition).

27. Technical standards are in section 14; documentation requirements are in section 15.

28. Section 14C.

Appendix

B: Questions and Answers to Clarify and Provide a Common Interpretation of the Uniform Guidelines on Employee Selection Procedures

Agencies: Equal Employment Opportunity Commission, Office of Personnel Management, Department of Justice, Department of Labor and Department of Treasury.

Action: Adoption of questions and answers designed to clarify and provide a common interpretation of the Uniform Guidelines on Employee Selection Procedures.

Source: *Federal Register,* 44, no. 43 (March 2, 1979).

Summary: The Uniform Guidelines on Employee Selection Procedures were issued by the five Federal agencies having primary responsibility for the enforcement of Federal equal employment opportunity laws, to establish a uniform Federal government position. See 43 FR 38290, et seq. (August 25, 1978) and 43 FR 40223 (September 11, 1978). They became effective on September 25, 1978. The issuing agencies recognize the need for a common interpretation of the Uniform Guidelines, as well as the desirability of providing additional guidance to employers and other users, psychologists, and investigators, compliance officers and other Federal enforcement personnel. These Questions and Answers are intended to address that need and to provide such guidance.

Effective date: March 2, 1979.

Introduction

The problems addressed by the Uniform Guidelines on Employee Selection Procedures (43 FR, 38290 et seq., August 25, 1978) are numerous and important, and some of them are complex. The history of the development of those Guidelines is set forth in the introduction to them (43 FR 38290–95). The experience of the agencies has been that a series of answers to commonly asked questions is helpful in providing guidance not only to employers and other users, but also to psychologists and others who are called upon to conduct validity studies, and to investigators, compliance officers and other Federal personnel who have enforcement responsibilities.

The Federal agencies which issued the Uniform Guidelines—the Departments of Justice and Labor, the Equal Employment Opportunity Commission, the Civil Service Commission (which has been succeeded in relevant part by the Office of Personnel Management), and the Office of Revenue Sharing, Treasury Department—recognize that the goal of a uniform position on these issues can best be achieved through a common interpretation of the same guidelines. The following Questions and Answers are part of such a common interpretation. The material included is intended to interpret and clarify, but not to modify, the provisions of the Uniform Guidelines. The questions selected are commonly asked questions in the field and those suggested by the Uniform Guidelines themselves and by the extensive comments received on the various sets of proposed guidelines prior to their adoption. Terms are used in the questions and answers as they are defined in the Uniform Guidelines.

The agencies recognize that additional questions may be appropriate for similar treatment at a later date, and contemplate working together to provide additional guidance in interpreting the Uniform Guidelines. Users and other interested persons are invited to submit additional questions. [Eleanor Holmes Norton, *Chair, Equal Employment Opportunity Commission.* Alan K. Campbell, *Director, Office of Personnel Management.* Drew S. Days III, *Assistant Attorney General, Civil Rights Division, Department of Justice.* Welden Rougeau, *Director, Office of Federal Contract Compliance, Department of Labor.* Kent A. Peterson, *Acting Deputy Director, Office of Revenue Sharing.*]

I. Purpose and Scope

1. *Question:* What is the purpose of the Guidelines?

Answer: The guidelines are designed to aid in the achievement of our nation's goal of equal employment opportunity without discrimination on the grounds of race, color, sex, religion or national origin. The Federal agencies have adopted the Guidelines to provide a uniform set of principles governing use of employee selection procedures which is consistent with applicable legal standards and validation standards generally accepted by the psychological profession and which the Government will apply in the discharge of its responsibilities.

2. *Question:* What is the basic principle of the Guidelines?

Answer: A selection process which has an adverse impact on the employment opportunities of members of a race, color, religion, sex, or national origin group (referred to as "race, sex, and ethnic group," as defined in Section 16P) and thus disproportionately screens them out is unlawfully discriminatory unless the process or its component procedures have been validated in accord with the Guidelines, or the user otherwise justifies them in accord with Federal law. See Sections 3 and 6.[1] This principle was adopted by the Supreme Court unanimously in *Griggs* v. *Duke Power Co.*, 401 U.S. 424, and was ratified and endorsed by the Congress when it passed the Equal Employment Opportunity Act of 1972, which amended Title VII of the Civil Rights Act of 1964.

3. *Question:* Who is covered by the Guidelines?

Answer: The Guidelines apply to private and public employers, labor organizations, employment agencies, apprenticeship committees, licensing and certification boards (see Question 7), and contractors or subcontractors, who are covered by one or more of the following provisions of Federal equal employment opportunity law: Title VII of the Civil Rights Act of 1964, as amended by the Equal Employment Opportunity Act of 1972 (hereinafter Title VII); Executive Order 11246, as amended by Executive Orders 11375 and 12086 (hereinafter Executive Order 11246); the State and Local Fiscal Assistance Act of 1972, as amended; Omnibus Crime Control and Safe Streets Act of 1968, as amended; and the Intergovernmental Personnel Act of 1970, as amended. Thus, under Title VII, the Guidelines apply to the Federal Government with regard to Federal employment. Through Title VII they apply to most private employers who have 15 or more employees for 20 weeks or more a calendar year, and to most employment agencies, labor organizations and apprenticeship committees. They apply to state and local governments which employ 15 or more employees, or which receive revenue sharing funds, or which receive funds from the Law Enforcement Assistance Administration to impose and strengthen law enforcement and criminal justice, or which receive grants or other federal assistance under a program which requires maintenance of personnel standards on a merit basis. They apply through Executive Order 11246 to contractors and subcontractors of the Federal Government and to contractors and subcontractors under federally-assisted construction contracts.

4. *Question:* Are college placement officers and similar organizations considered to be users subject to the Guidelines?

Answer: Placement offices may or may not be subject to the Guidelines depending on what services they offer. If a placement office uses a selection procedure as a basis for any employment decision, it is covered under the definition of "user". Section 16. For example, if a placement office selects some students for referral to an employer but rejects others, it is covered. However, if the placement office refers all interested students to an employer, it is not covered, even though it may offer office space and provision for informing the students of job openings. The Guidelines are intended to cover all users of employee selection procedures, including employment agencies, who are subject to Federal equal employment opportunity law.

5. *Question:* Do the Guidelines apply only to written tests?

Answer: No. They apply to all selection procedures used to make employment decisions, including interviews, review of experience or education from application forms, work samples, physical requirements, and evaluations of performance. Sections 2B and 16Q, and see Question 6.

6. *Question:* What practices are covered by the Guidelines?

Answer: The Guidelines apply to employee selection procedures which are used in making employment decisions, such as hiring, retention, promotion, transfer, demotion, dismissal or referral. Section 2B. Employee selection procedures include job requirements (physical, education, experience), and evaluation of applicants or candidates on the basis of application forms, interviews, performance tests, paper and pencil tests, performance in training programs or probationary periods, and any other procedures used to make an employment decision whether administered by the employer or by an employment agency. See Section 2B.

7. *Question:* Do the Guidelines apply to the licensing and certification functions of state and local governments?

Answer: The Guidelines apply to such functions to the extent that they are covered by Federal law. Section 2B. The courts are divided on the issue of such coverage. The Government has taken the position that at least some kinds of licensing and certification which deny persons access to employment opportunity may be enjoined in an action brought pursuant to Section 707 of the Civil Rights Act of 1964, as amended.

8. *Question:* What is the relationship between Federal equal employment opportunity law, embodied in these Guidelines, and State and Local government merit system laws or regulations requiring rank ordering of candidates and selection from a limited number of the top candidates?

Answer: The Guidelines permit ranking where the evidence of validity is sufficient to support that method of use. State or local laws which compel rank ordering generally do so on the assumption that the selection procedure is valid. Thus, if there is adverse impact and the validity evidence does not adequately support that method of use, proper interpretation of such a state law would require validation prior to ranking. Accordingly, there is no necessary or inherent conflict between Federal law and State or local laws of the kind described.

Under the Supremacy Clause of the Constitution (Art. VI, Cl. 2), however, Federal law or valid regulation overrides any contrary provision of state or local law. Thus, if there is any conflict Federal equal opportunity law prevails. For example, in *Rosenfeld* v. *So. Pacific Co.*, 444 F. 2d 1219 (9th Cir., 1971), the court held invalid state protective laws which prohibited the employment of women in jobs entailing long hours or heavy labor, because the state laws were in conflict with Title VII. Where a State or local official believes that there is a possible conflict, the official may wish to consult with the State Attorney General, County or City attorney, or other legal official to determine how to comply with the law.

II. Adverse Impact: The Bottom
Line and Affirmative Action

9. *Question:* Do the Guidelines require that only validated selection procedures be used?

Answer: No. Although validation of selection procedures is desirable in personnel management, the Uniform Guidelines require users to produce evidence of validity only when the selection procedure adversely affects the opportunities of a race, sex, or ethnic group for hire, transfer, promotion, retention or other employment decision. If there is no adverse impact, there is no validation requirement under the Guidelines. Sections 1B and 3A. See also, Section 6A.

10. *Question:* What is adverse impact?

Answer: Under the Guidelines adverse impact is a substantially different rate of selection in hiring, promotion or other employment decision which works to the disadvantage of members of a race, sex or ethnic group. Sections 4D and 16B. See Questions 11 and 12.

11. *Question:* What is a substantially different rate of selection?

Answer: The agencies have adopted a rule of thumb under which they will generally consider a selection rate for any race, sex, or ethnic group which is less than four-fifths (4/5ths) or eighty percent (80%) of the selection rate for the group with the highest selection rate as a substantially different rate of selection. See Section 4D. This "4/5ths" or "80%" rule of thumb is not intended as a legal definition, but is a practical means of keeping the attention of the enforcement agencies on serious discrepancies in rates of hiring, promotion and other selection decisions.

For example, if the hiring rate for whites other than Hispanics is 60%, for American Indians 45%, for Hispanics 48%, and for Blacks 51%, and each of these groups constitutes more than 2% of the labor force in the relevant labor area (see Question 16), a comparison should be made of the selection rate for each group with that of the highest group (whites). These comparisons show the following impact ratios: American Indians 45/60 or 75%; Hispanics 48/60 or 80%; and Blacks 51/60 or 85%. Applying the 4/5ths or 80% rule of thumb, on the basis of the above information alone, adverse impact is indicated for American Indians but not for Hispanics or Blacks.

12. *Question:* How is adverse impact determined?

Answer: Adverse impact is determined by a four step process:

1. Calculate the rate of selection for each group (divide the number of persons selected from a group by the number of applicants from that group).
2. Observe which group has the highest selection rate.
3. Calculate the impact ratios, by comparing the selection rate for each group with that of the highest group (divide the selection rate for a group by the selection rate for the highest group).
4. Observe whether the selection rate for any group is substantially less (i.e., usually less than 4/5ths or 80%) than the selection rate for the highest group. If it is, adverse impact is indicated in most circumstances. See Section 4D.

For example:

Applicants	Hired	Selection rate percent hired
80 white	48	48/80 or 60%
40 black	12	12/40 or 30%

A comparison of the black selection rate (30%) with the white selection rate (60%) shows that the black rate is 30/60, or one-half (or 50%) of the white rate. Since the one-half (50%) is less than 4/5ths (80%) adverse impact is usually indicated.

The determination of adverse impact is not purely arithmetic however; and other factors may be relevant. See, Section 4D.

13. *Question:* Is adverse impact determined on the basis of the overall selection process or for the components in that process?

Answer: Adverse impact is determined first for the overall selection process for each job. If the overall selection process has an adverse impact, the adverse impact of the individual selection procedure should be analyzed. For any selection procedures in the process having an adverse impact which the user continues to use in the same manner, the user is expected to have evidence of validity satisfying the Guidelines. Sections 4C and 5D. If there is no adverse impact for the overall selection process, in most circumstances there is no obligation under the Guidelines to investigate adverse impact for the components, or to validate the selection procedures used for that job. Section 4C. But see Question 25.

14. *Question:* The Guidelines designate the "total selection process" as the initial basis for determining the impact of selection procedures. What is meant by the "total selection process"?

Answer: The "total selection process" refers to the combined effect of all selection procedures leading to the final employment decision such as hiring or promoting. For example, appraisal of candidates for administrative assistant positions in an organization might include initial screening based upon an application blank and interview, a written test, a medical examination, a background check, and a supervisor's interview. These in combination are the total selection process. Additionally, where there is more than one route to the particular kind of employment decision, the total selection process encompasses the combined results of all routes. For example, an employer may select some applicants for a particular kind of job through appropriate written and performance tests. Others may be selected through an internal upward mobility program, on the basis of successful performance in a directly related trainee type of position. In such a case, the impact of the total selection process would be the combined effect of both avenues of entry.

15. *Question:* What is meant by the terms "applicant" and "candidate" as they are used in the Uniform Guidelines?

Answer: The precise definition of the term "applicant" depends upon the user's recruitment and selection procedures. The concept of an applicant is that of a person who has indicated an interest in being considered for hiring, promotion, or other employment opportunities. This interest might be expressed by completing an application form, or might be expressed orally, depending upon the employer's practice.

The term "candidate" has been included to cover those situations where the initial step by the user involves consideration of current employees for promotion, or training, or other employment opportunities without inviting applications. The procedure by which persons are identified as candidates is itself a selection procedure under the Guidelines.

A person who voluntarily withdraws formally or informally at any stage of the selection process is no longer an applicant or candidate for purposes of computing adverse impact. Employment standards imposed by the user which discourage disproportionately applicants of a race, sex or ethnic group may, however, require justification. Records should be kept for persons who were applicants or candidates at any stage of the process.

16. *Question:* Should adverse impact determinations be made for all groups regardless of their size?

Answer: No. Section 15A(2) calls for annual adverse impact determinations to be made for each group which constitutes either 2% or more of the total labor force in the relevant labor area, or 2% or more of the applicable workforce. Thus, impact determinations should be made for any employment decision for each group which constitutes 2% or more of the labor force in the relevant labor area. For hiring, such determination should also be made for groups which constitute more than 2% of the applicants; and for promotions, determinations should also be made for those groups which constitute at least 2% of the user's workforce. There are record keeping obligations for all groups, even those which are less than 2%. See Question 86.

17. *Question:* In determining adverse impact, do you compare the selection rates for males and females, and blacks and whites, or do you compare selection rates for white males, white females, black males and black females?

Answer: The selection rates for males and females are compared, and the selection rates for the race and ethnic groups are compared with the selection rate of the race or ethnic group with the highest selection rate. Neutral and objective selection procedures free of adverse impact against any race, sex or ethnic group are unlikely to have an impact against a subgroup. Thus there is no obligation to make comparisons for subgroups (e.g., white male, white female, black male, black female). However, there are obligations to keep records (see Question 87), and any apparent exclusion of a subgroup may suggest the presence of discrimination.

18. *Question:* Is it usually necessary to calculate the statistical significance of differences in selection rates when investigating the existence of adverse impact?

Answer: No. Adverse impact is normally indicated when one selection rate is less than 80% of the other. The federal enforcement agencies normally will use only the 80% (4/5ths) rule of thumb, except where large numbers of selections are made. See Questions 20 and 22.

19. *Question:* Does the 4/5ths rule of thumb mean that the Guidelines will tolerate up to 20% discrimination?

Answer: No. The 4/5ths rule of thumb speaks only to the question of adverse impact, and is not intended to resolve the ultimate question of unlawful discrimination. Regardless of the amount of difference in selection rates, unlawful discrimination may be present, and may be demonstrated through appropriate evidence. The 4/5ths rule merely establishes a numerical basis for drawing an initial inference and for requiring additional information.

With respect to adverse impact, the Guidelines expressly state (section 4D) that differences in selection rates of less than 20% may still amount to adverse impact where the differences are significant in both statistical and practical terms. See Question 20. In the absence of differences which are large enough to meet the 4/5ths rule of thumb or a test of statistical significance, there is no reason to assume that the differences are reliable, or that they are based upon anything other than chance.

20. *Question:* Why is the 4/5ths rule called a rule of thumb?

Answer: Because it is not intended to be controlling in all circumstances. If, for the sake of illustration, we assume that nationwide statistics show that use of an arrest record would disqualify 10% of all Hispanic persons but only 4% of all whites other than Hispanic (hereafter non-Hispanic), the selection rate for that selection procedure is 90% for Hispanics and 96% for non-Hispanics. Therefore, the 4/5ths rule of thumb would not indicate the presence of adverse impact (90% is approximately 94% of 96%). But in this example, the information is based upon nationwide statistics, and the sample is large enough to yield statistically significant results, and the difference (Hispanics are 2½ times as likely to be disqualified as non-Hispanics) is large enough to be practically significant. Thus, in this example the enforcement agencies would consider a disqualification based on an arrest record alone as having an adverse impact. Likewise, in *Gregory v. Litton Industries*, 472 F. 2d 631 (9th Cir., 1972), the court held that the employer violated Title VII by disqualifying persons from employment solely on the basis of an arrest record, where that disqualification had an adverse impact on blacks and was not shown to be justified by business necessity.

On the other hand, a difference of more than 20% in rates of selection may not provide a basis for finding adverse impact if the number of persons selected is very small. For example, if the employer selected three males and one female from an applicant pool of 20 males and 10 females, the 4/5ths rule would indicate adverse impact (selection rate for women is 10%; for men 15%; 10/15 or 66⅔% is less than 80%), yet the number of selections is too small to warrant a determination of adverse impact. In these circumstances, the enforcement agency would not require validity evidence in the absence of additional information (such as selection rates for a longer period of time) indicating adverse impact. For recordkeeping requirements, see Section 15A(2)(c) and Questions 84 and 85.

21. *Question:* Is evidence of adverse impact sufficient to warrant a validity study or an enforcement action where the numbers involved are so small that it is more likely than not that the difference could have occurred by chance?

For example:

Applicants	Not hired	Hired	Selection rate percent hired
80 white	64	16	20
20 black	17	3	15

White selection rate	20
Black selection rate	15

15 divided by 20 = 75% (which is less than 80%).

Answer: No. If the numbers of persons and the difference in selection rates are so small that it is likely that the difference could have occurred by chance, the Federal agencies will not assume the existence of adverse impact, in the absence of other evidence. In this example, the difference in selection rates is too small, given the small number of black applicants, to constitute adverse impact in the absence of other information (see Section 4D). If only one more black had been hired instead of a white the selection rate for blacks (20%) would be higher than that for whites (18.7%). Generally, it is inappropriate to require validity evidence or to take enforcement action where the number of persons and the difference in selection rates are so small that the selection of one different person for one job would shift the result from adverse impact against one group to a situation in which that group has a higher selection rate than the other group.

On the other hand, if a lower selection rate continued over a period of time, so as to constitute a pattern, then the lower selection rate would constitute adverse impact, warranting the need for validity evidence.

22. *Question:* Is it ever necessary to calculate the statistical significance of differences, in selection rates to determine whether adverse impact exists?

Answer: Yes. Where large numbers of selections are made, relatively small differences in selection rates may nevertheless constitute adverse impact if they are both statistically and practically significant. See Section 4D and Question 20. For that reason, if there is a small difference in selection rates (one rate is more than 80% of the other), but large numbers of selections are involved, it would be appropriate to calculate the statistical significance of the difference in selection rates.

23. *Question:* When the 4/5ths rule of thumb shows adverse impact, is there adverse impact under the Guidelines?

Answer: There usually is adverse impact, except where the number of persons selected and the difference in selection rates are very small. See Section 4D and Questions 20 and 21.

24. *Question:* Why do the Guidelines rely primarily upon the 4/5ths rule of thumb, rather than tests of statistical significance?

Answer: Where the sample of persons selected is not large, even a large real difference between groups is likely not to be confirmed by a test of statistical significance (at the usual .05 level of significance). For this reason, the Guidelines do not rely primarily upon a test of statistical significance, but use the 4/5ths rule of thumb as a practical and easy-to-administer measure of whether differences in selection rates are substantial. Many decisions in day-to-day life are made without reliance upon a test of statistical significance.

25. *Question:* Are there any circumstances in which the employer should evaluate components of a selection process, even though the overall selection process results in no adverse impact?

Answer: Yes, there are such circumstances: (1) Where the selection procedure is a significant factor in the continuation of patterns of assignments of incumbent employees caused by prior discriminatory employment practices. Assume, for example, an employer who traditionally hired blacks as employees for the "laborer" department in a manufacturing plant, and traditionally hired only whites as skilled craftsmen. Assume further that the employer in 1962 began to use a written examination not supported by a validity study to screen incumbent employees who sought to enter the apprenticeship program for skilled craft jobs. The employer stopped making racial assignments in 1972. Assume further that for the last four years, there have been special recruitment efforts aimed at recent black high school graduates and that the selection process, which includes the written examination, has resulted in the selection of black applicants for apprenticeship in approximately the same rates as white applicants.

In those circumstances, if the written examination had an adverse impact, its use would tend to keep incumbent black employees in the laborer department, and deny them entry to apprenticeship programs. For that reason, the enforcement agencies would expect the user to evaluate the impact of the written examination, and to have validity evidence for the use of the written examination if it has an adverse impact.

(2) Where the weight of court decisions or administrative interpretations holds that a specific selection procedure is not job related in similar circumstances.

For example, courts have held that because an arrest is not a determination of guilt, an applicant's arrest record by itself does not indicate inability to perform a job consistent with the trustworthy and efficient operation of a business. Yet a no arrest record requirement has a nationwide adverse impact on some minority groups. Thus, an employer who refuses to hire applicants solely on the basis of an arrest record is on notice that this policy may be found to be discriminatory. *Gregory v. Litton Industries*, 472 F. 2d 631 (9th Cir., 1972) (excluding persons from employment solely on the basis of arrests, which has an adverse impact, held to violate Title VII). Similarly, a minimum height requirement disproportionately disqualifies women and some national origin groups, and has been held not to be job related in a number of cases. For example, in *Dothard v. Rawlinson*, 433 U.S. 321 (1977), the Court held that height and weight requirements not shown to be job related were violative of Title VII. Thus an employer using a minimum height requirement should have evidence of its validity.

(3) In addition, there may be other circumstances in which an enforcement agency may decide to request an employer to evaluate components of a selection process, but such circumstances would clearly be unusual. Any such decision will be made only at a high level in the agency. Investigators and compliance officers are not authorized to make this decision.

26. *Question:* Does the bottom line concept of Section 4C apply to the administrative processing of charges of discrimination filed with an issuing agency, alleging that a specific selection procedure is discriminatory?

Answer: No. The bottom line concept applies only to enforcement actions as defined in Section 16 of the Guidelines. Enforcement actions include only court enforcement actions and other similar proceedings as defined in Section 16I. The EEOC administrative processing of charges of discrimination (investigation, finding of reasonable cause/no cause, and conciliation) required by Section 706(b) of Title VII are specifically exempted from the bottom line concept by the definition of an enforcement action. The bottom line concept is a result of a decision by the various enforcement agencies that, as a matter of prosecutorial discretion, they will devote their limited enforcement resources to the most serious offenders of equal employment opportunity laws. Since the concept is not a rule of law, it does not affect the discharge by the EEOC of its statutory responsibilities to investigate charges of discrimination, render an administrative finding on its investigation, and engage in voluntary conciliation efforts. Similarly, with respect to the other issuing agencies, the bottom line concept applies not to the processing of individual charges, but to the initiation of enforcement action.

27. *Question:* An employer uses one test or other selection procedure to select persons for a number of different jobs. Applicants are given the test, and the successful applicants are then referred to different departments and positions on the basis of openings available and their interests. The Guidelines appear to require assessment of adverse impact on a job-by-job basis (Section 15A(2)(a)). Is there some way to show that the test as a whole does not have adverse impact even though the proportions of members of each race, sex or ethnic group assigned to different jobs may vary?

Answer: Yes, in some circumstances. The Guidelines require evidence of validity only for those selection procedures which have an adverse impact, and which are part of a selection process which has an adverse impact. If the test is administered and used in the same fashion for a variety of jobs, the impact of that test can be assessed in the aggregate. The records showing the results of the test, and the total number of persons selected, generally would be sufficient to show the impact of the test. If the test has no adverse impact, it need not be validated.

But the absence of adverse impact of the test in the aggregate does not end the inquiry. For there may be discrimination or adverse impact in the assignment of individuals to, or in the selection of persons for, particular jobs. The Guidelines call for records to be kept and determinations of adverse impact to be made of the overall selection process on a job by job basis. Thus, if there is adverse impact in the assignment or selection procedures for a job even though there is no adverse impact from the test, the user should eliminate the adverse impact from the assignment procedure or justify the assignment procedure.

28. *Question:* The Uniform Guidelines apply to the requirements of Federal law prohibiting employment practices which discriminate on the grounds of race, color, religion, sex or national origin. However, records are required to be kept only by sex and by specified race and ethnic groups. How can adverse impact be determined for religious groups and for national origin groups other than those specified in Section 4B of the Guidelines?

Answer: The groups for which records are required to be maintained are the groups for which there is extensive evidence of continuing discriminatory practices. This limitation is designed in part to minimize the burden on employers for recordkeeping which may not be needed.

For groups for which records are not required, the person(s) complaining may obtain information from the employer or others (voluntarily or through legal process) to show that adverse impact has taken place. When that has been done, the various provisions of the Uniform Guidelines are fully applicable.

Whether or not there is adverse impact, Federal equal employment opportunity law prohibits any deliberate discrimination or disparate treatment on grounds of religion or national origin, as well as on grounds of sex, color, or race.

Whenever "ethnic" is used in the Guidelines or in these Questions and Answers, it is intended to include national origin and religion, as set forth in the statutes, executive orders, and regulations prohibiting discrimination. See Section 16P.

29. *Question:* What is the relationship between affirmative action and the requirements of the Uniform Guidelines?

Answer: The two subjects are different, although related. Compliance with the Guidelines does not relieve users of their affirmative action obligations, including those of Federal contractors and subcontractors under Executive Order 11246. Section 13.

The Guidelines encourage the development and effective implementation of affirmative action plans or programs in two ways. First, in determining whether to institute action against a user on the basis of a selection procedure which has adverse impact and which has not been validated, the enforcement agency will take into account the general equal employment opportunity posture of the user with respect to the job classifications for which the procedure is used and the progress which has been made in carrying out any affirmative action program. Section 4E. If the user has demonstrated over a substantial period of time that it is in fact appropriately utilizing in the job or group of jobs in question the available race, sex or ethnic groups in the relevant labor force, the enforcement agency will generally exercise its discretion by not initiating enforcement proceedings based on adverse impact in relation to the applicant flow. Second, nothing in the Guidelines is intended to preclude the use of selection procedures, consistent with Federal law, which assist in the achievement of affirmative action objectives. Section 13A. See also, Questions 30 and 31.

30. *Question:* When may a user be race, sex or ethnic-conscious?

Answer: The Guidelines recognize that affirmative action programs may be race, sex or ethnic-conscious in appropriate circumstances, (See Sections 4E and 13; See also Section 17, Appendix). In addition to obligatory affirmative action programs (See Question 29), the Guidelines encourage the adoption of voluntary affirmative action programs. Users choosing to engage in voluntary affirmative action are referred to EEOC's Guidelines on Affirmative Action (44 F.R. 4422, January 19, 1979). A user may justifiably be race, sex or ethnic-conscious in circumstances where it has reason to believe that qualified persons of specified race, sex or ethnicity have been or may be subject to the exclusionary effects of its selection procedures or other employment practices in its work force or particular jobs therein. In establishing long and short range goals, the employer may use the race, sex, or ethnic classification as the basis for such goals (Section 17(3) (a)).

In establishing a recruiting program, the employer may direct its recruiting activities to locations or institutions which have a high proportion of the race, sex, or ethnic group which has been excluded or underutilized (section 17(3) (b)). In establishing the pool of qualified persons from which final selections are to be made, the employer may take reasonable steps to assure that members of the excluded or underutilized race, sex, or ethnic group are included in the pool (Section 17(3) (e)).

Similarly, the employer may be race, sex or ethnic-conscious in determining what changes should be implemented if the objectives of the programs are not being met (Section 17(3) (g)).

Even apart from affirmative action programs a user may be race, sex or ethnic-conscious in taking appropriate and lawful measures to eliminate adverse impact from selection procedures (Section 6A).

31. *Question:* Section 6A authorizes the use of alternative selection procedures to eliminate adverse impact, but does not appear to address the issue of validity. Thus, the use of alternative selection procedures without adverse impact seems to be presented as an option in lieu of validation. Is that its intent?

Answer: Yes. Under Federal equal employment opportunity law the use of any selection procedure which has an adverse impact on any race, sex or ethnic group is discriminatory unless the procedure has been properly validated, or the use of the procedure is otherwise justified under Federal law. *Griggs* v. *Duke Power Co.,* 401 U.S. 424 (1971); Section 3A. If a selection procedure has an adverse impact, therefore, Federal equal employment opportunity law authorizes the user to choose lawful alternative procedures which eliminate the adverse impact rather than demonstrating the validity of the original selection procedure.

Many users, while wishing to validate all of their selection procedures, are not able to conduct the validity studies immediately. Such users have the option of choosing alternative techniques which eliminate adverse impact, with a view to providing a basis for determining subsequently which selection procedures are valid and have as little adverse impact as possible.

Apart from Federal equal employment opportunity law, employers have economic incentives to use properly validated selection procedures. Nothing in Section 6A should be interpreted as discouraging the use of properly validated selection procedures; but Federal equal employment opportunity law does not require validity studies to be conducted unless there is adverse impact. See Section 2C.

III. General Questions Concerning Validity and the Use of Selection Procedures

32. *Question:* What is "validation" according to the Uniform Guidelines?

Answer: Validation is the demonstration of the job relatedness of a selection procedure. The Uniform Guidelines recognize the same three validity strategies recognized by the American Psychological Association:

1. Criterion-related validity—a statistical demonstration of a relationship between scores on a selection procedure and job performance of a sample of workers;

2. Content validity—a demonstration that the content of a selection procedure is representative of important aspects of performance on the job;

3. Construct validity—a demonstration that (a) a selection procedure measures a construct (something believed to be an underlying human trait or characteristic, such as honesty) and (b) the construct is important for successful job performance.

33. *Question:* What is the typical process by which validity studies are reviewed by an enforcement agency?

Answer: The validity study is normally requested by an enforcement officer during the course of a review. The officer will first determine whether the user's data show that the overall selection process has an adverse impact, and if so, which component selection procedures have an adverse impact. See Section 15A(3). The officer will then ask for the evidence of validity for each procedure which has an adverse impact. See Sections 15B, C, and D. This validity evidence will be referred to appropriate personnel for review. Agency findings will then be communicated to the user.

34. *Question:* Can a user send its validity evidence to an enforcement agency before a review, so as to assure its validity?

Answer: No. Enforcement agencies will not review validity reports except in the context of investigations or reviews. Even in those circumstances, validity evidence will not be reviewed without evidence of how the selection procedure is used and what impact its use has on various race, sex, and ethnic groups.

35. *Question:* May reports of validity prepared by publishers of commercial tests and printed in test manuals or other literature be helpful in meeting the Guidelines?

Answer: They may be. However, it is the user's responsibility to determine that the validity evidence is adequate to meet the Guidelines. See Section 7, and Questions 43 and 66. Users should not use selection procedures which are likely to have an adverse impact without reviewing the evidence of validity to make sure that the standards of the Guidelines are met.

The following questions and answers (36–81) assume that a selection procedure has an adverse impact and is part of a selection process that has an adverse impact.

36. *Question:* How can users justify continued use of a procedure on a basis other than validity?

Answer: Normally, the method of justifying selection procedures with an adverse impact and the method to which the Guidelines are primarily addressed, is validation. The method of justification of a procedure by means other than validity is one to which the Guidelines are not addressed. See Section 6B. In *Griggs* v. *Duke Power Co.,* 401 U.S. 424, the Supreme Court indicated that the burden on the user was a heavy one, but that the selection procedure could be used if there was a "business necessity" for its continued use; therefore, the Federal agencies will consider evidence that a selection procedure is necessary for the safe and efficient operation of a business to justify continued use of a selection procedure.

37. *Question:* Is the demonstration of a rational relationship (as that term is used in constitutional law) between a selection procedure and the job sufficient to meet the validation requirements of the Guidelines?

Answer: No. The Supreme Court in *Washington* v. *Davis,* 426 U.S. 229 (1976) stated that different standards would be applied to employment discrimination allegations arising under the Constitution than would be applied to employment discrimination allegations arising under Title VII. The *Davis* case arose under the Constitution, and no Title VII violation was alleged. The Court applied a traditional constitutional law standard of "rational relationship" and said that it would defer to the "seemingly reasonable acts of administrators and executives." However, it went on to point out that under Title VII, the appropriate standard would still be an affirmative demonstration of the relationship between the selection procedure and measures of job performance by means of accepted procedures of validation and it would be an "insufficient response to demonstrate some rational basis" for a selection procedure having an adverse impact. Thus, the mere demonstration of a rational relationship between a selection procedure and the job does not meet the requirement of Title VII of the Civil Rights Act of 1964, or of Executive Order 11246, or the State and Local Fiscal Assistance Act of 1972, as amended (the revenue sharing act) or the Omnibus Crime Control and Safe Streets Act of 1968, as amended, and will not meet the requirements of these Guidelines for a validity study. The three validity strategies called for by these Guidelines all require evidence that the selection procedure is related to successful performance on the job. That evidence may be obtained through local validation or through validity studies done elsewhere.

38. *Question:* Can a user rely upon written or oral assertions of validity instead of evidence of validity?

Answer: No. If a user's selection procedures have an adverse impact, the user is expected to produce evidence of the validity of the procedures as they are used. Thus, the unsupported assertion by anyone, including representatives of the Federal government or State Employment Services, that a test battery or other selection procedure has been validated is not sufficient to satisfy the Guidelines.

39. *Question:* Are there any formal requirements imposed by these Guidelines as to who is allowed to perform a validity study?

Answer: No. A validity study is judged on its own merits, and may be performed by any person competent to apply the principles of validity research, including a member of the user's staff or a consultant. However, it is the user's responsibility to see that the study meets validity provisions of the Guidelines, which are based upon professionally accepted standards. See Question 42.

40. *Question:* What is the relationship between the validation provisions of the Guidelines and other statements of psychological principles, such as the *Standards for Educational and Psychological Tests,* published by the American Psychological Association (Wash., D.C., 1974) (hereinafter "American Psychological Association Standards")?

Answer: The validation provisions of the Guidelines are designed to be consistent with the generally accepted standards of the psychological profession. These Guidelines also interpret Federal equal employment opportunity law, and embody some policy determinations of an administrative nature. To the extent that there may be differences between particular provisions of the Guidelines and expressions of validation principles found elsewhere, the Guidelines will be given precedence by the enforcement agencies.

41. *Question:* When should a validity study be carried out?

Answer: When a selection procedure has adverse impact on any race, sex or ethnic group, the Guidelines generally call for a validity study or the elimination of adverse impact. See Sections 3A and 6, and Questions 9, 31, and 36. If a selection procedure has adverse impact, its use in making employment decisions without adequate evidence of validity would be inconsistent with the Guidelines. Users who choose to continue the use of a selection procedure with an adverse impact until the procedure is challenged increase the risk that they will be found to be engaged in discriminatory practices and will be liable for back pay awards, plaintiffs' attorneys' fees, loss of Federal contracts, subcontracts or grants, and the like. Validation studies begun on the eve of litigation have seldom been found to be adequate. Users who choose to validate selection procedures should consider the potential benefit from having a validation study completed or well underway before the procedures are administered for use in employment decisions.

42. *Question:* Where can a user obtain professional advice concerning validation of selection procedures?

Answer: Many industrial and personnel psychologists validate selection procedures, review published evidence of validity and make recommendations with respect to the use of selection procedures. Many of these individuals are members or fellows of Division 14 (Industrial and Organizational Psychology) or Division 5 (Evaluation and Measurement) of the American Psychological Association. They can be identified in the membership directory of that organization. A high level of qualification is represented by a diploma in Industrial Psychology awarded by the American Board of Professional Psychology.

Individuals with the necessary competence may come from a variety of backgrounds. The primary qualification is pertinent training and experience in the conduct of validation research.

Industrial psychologists and other persons competent in the field may be found as faculty members in colleges and universities (normally in the departments of psychology or business administration) or working as individual consultants or as members of a consulting organization.

Not all psychologists have the necessary expertise. States have boards which license and certify psychologists, but not generally in a specialty such as industrial psychology. However, State psychological associations may be a source of information as to individuals qualified to conduct validation studies. Addresses of State psychological associations or other sources of information may be obtained from the American Psychological Association, 1200 Seventeenth Street, NW., Washington, D.C. 20036.

43. *Question:* Can a selection procedure be a valid predictor of performance on a job in a certain location and be invalid for predicting success on a different job or the same job in a different location?

Answer: Yes. Because of differences in work behaviors, criterion measures, study samples or other factors, a selection procedure found to have validity in one situation does not necessarily have validity in different circumstances. Conversely, a selection procedure not found to have validity in one situation may have validity in different circumstances. For these reasons, the Guidelines requires that certain standards be satisfied before a user may rely upon findings of validity in another situation. Section 7 and Section 14D. See also, Question 66. Cooperative and multi-unit studies are however encouraged, and, when those standards of the Guidelines are satisfied, validity evidence specific to each location is not required. See Section 7C and Section 8.

44. *Question:* Is the user of a selection procedure required to develop the procedure?

Answer: No. A selection procedure developed elsewhere may be used. However, the user has the obligation to show that its use for the particular job is consistent with the Guidelines. See Section 7.

45. *Question:* Do the Guidelines permit users to engage in cooperative efforts to meet the Guidelines?

Answer: Yes. The Guidelines not only permit but encourage such efforts. Where users have participated in a cooperative study which meets the validation standards of these Guidelines and proper account has been taken of variables which might affect the applicability of the study to specific users, validity evidence specific to each user will not be required. Section 8.

46. *Question:* Must the same method for validation be used for all parts of a selection process?

Answer: No. For example, where a selection process includes both a physical performance test and an interview, the physical test might be supported on the basis of content validity, and the interview on the basis of a criterion-related study.

47. *Question:* Is a showing of validity sufficient to assure the lawfulness of the use of a selection procedure?

Answer: No. The use of the selection procedure must be consistent with the validity evidence. For example, if a research study shows only that, at a given passing score the test satisfactorily screens out probable failures, the study would not justify the use of substantially different passing scores, or of ranked lists of those who passed. See Section 5G. Similarly, if the research shows that a battery is valid when a particular set of weights is used, the weights actually used must conform to those that were established by the research.

48. *Question:* Do the Guidelines call for a user to consider and investigate alternative selection procedures when conducting a validity study?

Answer: Yes. The Guidelines call for a user, when conducting a validity study, to make a reasonable effort to become aware of suitable alternative selection procedures and methods of use which have as little adverse impact as possible, and to investigate those which are suitable. Section 3B.

An alternative procedure may not previously have been used by the user for the job in question and may not have been extensively used elsewhere. Accordingly, the preliminary determination of the suitability of the alternative selection procedure for the user and job in question may have to be made on the basis of incomplete information. If on the basis of the evidence available, the user determines that the alternative selection procedure is likely to meet its legitimate needs, and is likely to have less adverse impact than the existing selection procedure, the alternative should be investigated further as a part of the validity study. The extent of the investigation should be reasonable. Thus, the investigation should continue until the user has reasonably concluded that the alternative is not useful or not suitable, or until a study of its validity has been completed. Once the full validity study has been completed, including the evidence concerning the alternative procedure, the user should evaluate the results of the study to determine which procedure should be used. See Section 3B and Question 50.

49. *Question:* Do the Guidelines call for a user *continually* to investigate "suitable alternative selection procedures and suitable alternative methods of using the selection procedure which have as little adverse impact as possible"?

Answer: No. There is no requirement for continual investigation. A reasonable investigation of alternatives is called for by the Guidelines as a part of any validity study. Once the study is complete and validity has been found, however, there is generally no obligation to conduct further investigations, until such time as a new study is called for. See, Sections 3B and 5K. If a government agency, complainant, civil rights organization or other person having a legitimate interest shows such a user an alternative procedure with less adverse impact and with substantial evidence of validity for the same job in similar circumstances, the user is obliged to investigate only the particular procedure which has been presented. Section 3B.

50. *Question:* In what circumstances do the Guidelines call for the use of an alternative selection procedure or an alternative method of using the procedure?

Answer: The alternative selection procedure (or method of use) should be used when it has less adverse impact and when the evidence shows that its validity is substantially the same or greater for the same job in similar circumstances. Thus, if under the original selection procedure the selection rate for black applicants was only one half (50 percent) that of the selection rate for white applicants, whereas under the alternative selection procedure the selection rate for blacks is two-thirds (67 percent) that of white applicants, the new alternative selection procedure should be used when the evidence shows substantially the same or greater validity for the alternative than for the original procedure. The same principles apply to a new user who is deciding what selection procedure to institute.

51. *Question:* What are the factors to be considered in determining whether the validity for one procedure is substantially the same as or greater than that of another procedure?

Answer: In the case of a criterion-related validity study, the factors include the importance of the criteria for which significant relationships are found, the magnitude of the relationship between selection procedure scores and criterion measures, and the size and composition of the samples used. For content validity, the strength of validity evidence would depend upon the proportion of critical and/or important job behaviors measured, and the extent to which the selection procedure resembles actual work samples or work behaviors. Where selection procedures have been validated by different strategies, or by construct validity, the determination should be made on a case by case basis.

52. *Question:* The Guidelines require consideration of alternative procedures and alternative methods of use, in light of the evidence of validity and utility and the degree of adverse impact of the procedure. How can a user know that any selection procedure with an adverse impact is lawful?

Answer: The Uniform Guidelines (Section 5G) expressly permit the use of a procedure in a manner supported by the evidence of validity and utility, even if another method of use has a lesser adverse impact. With respect to consideration of alternative selection procedures, if the user made a reasonable effort to become aware of alternative procedures, has considered them and investigated those which appear suitable as a part of the validity study, and has shown validity for a procedure, the user has complied with the Uniform Guidelines. The burden is then on the person challenging the procedure to show that there is another procedure with better or substantially equal validity which will accomplish the same legitimate business purposes with less adverse impact. Section 3 B. See also, *Albermarle Paper Co.* v. *Moody,* 422 U.S. 405.

53. *Question:* Are the Guidelines consistent with the decision of the Supreme Court in *Furnco Construction Corp.* v. *Waters,* ——U.S.——, 98 S. Ct. 2943 (1978) where the Court stated: "Title VII . . . does not impose a duty to adopt a hiring procedure that maximizes hiring of minority employees."

Answer: Yes. The quoted statement in *Furnco* v. *Waters* was made on a record where there was no adverse impact in the hiring process, no different treatment, no intentional discrimination, and no contractual obligations under E.O. 11246. Section 3B of the Guidelines is predicated upon a finding of adverse impact. Section 3B indicates that, when two or more selection procedures are available which serve a legitimate business purpose with substantially equal validity, the user should use the one which has been demonstrated to have the lesser adverse impact. Part V of the Overview of the Uniform Guidelines, in elaborating on this principle, states: "Federal equal employment opportunity law has added a requirement to the process of validation. In conducting a validation study, the employer should consider available alternatives which will achieve its legitimate purpose with lesser adverse impact."

Section 3B of the Guidelines is based on the principle enunciated in the Supreme Court decision in *Albermarle Paper Co.* v. *Moody,* 422 U.S. 405 (1975) that, even where job relatedness has been proven, the availability of other tests or selection devices which would also serve the employer's legitimate interest in "efficient and trustworthy workmanship" without a similarly undesirable racial effect would be evidence that the employer was using its tests merely as a pretext for discrimination.

Where adverse impact still exists, even though the selection procedure has been validated, there continues to be an obligation to consider alternative procedures which reduce or remove that adverse impact if an opportunity presents itself to do so without sacrificing validity. Where there is no adverse impact, the *Furnco* principle rather than the *Albermarle* principle is applicable.

IV. Technical Standards

54. *Question:* How does a user choose which validation strategy to use?

Answer: A user should select a validation strategy or strategies which are (1) appropriate for the type of selection procedure, the job, and the employment situation, and (2) technically and administratively feasible. Whatever method of validation is used, the basic logic is one of prediction; that is, the presumption that level of performance on the selection procedure will, on the average, be indicative of level of performance on the job after selection. Thus, a criterion-related study, particularly a predictive one, is often regarded as the closest to such an ideal. See American Psychological Association *Standards,* pp. 26–27.

Key conditions for a criterion-related study are a substantial number of individuals for inclusion in the study, and a considerable range of performance on the selection and criterion measures. In addition, reliable and valid measures of job performance should be available, or capable of being developed. Section 14B(1). Where such circumstances exist, a user should consider use of the criterion-related strategy.

Content validity is appropriate where it is technically and administratively feasible to develop work samples or measures of operationally defined skills, knowledges, or abilities which are a necessary prerequisite to observable work behaviors. Content validity is not appropriate for demonstrating the validity of tests of mental processes or aptitudes or characteristics; and is not appropriate for knowledges, skills or abilities which an employee will be expected to learn on the job. Section 14C(1)

The application of a construct validity strategy to support employee selection procedures is newer and less developed than criterion-related or content validity strategies. Continuing research may result in construct validity becoming more widely used. Because construct validity represents a generalization of findings, one situation in which construct validity might hold particular promise is that where it is desirable to use the same selection procedures for a variety of jobs. An overriding consideration in whether or not to consider construct validation is the availability of an individual with a high level of expertise in this field.

In some situations only one kind of validation study is likely to be appropriate. More than one strategy may be possible in other circumstances, in which case administrative considerations such as time and expense may be decisive. A combination of approaches may be feasible and desirable.

55. *Question:* Why do the Guidelines recognize only content, construct and criterion-related validity?

Answer: These three validation strategies are recognized in the Guidelines since they represent the current professional consensus. If the professional community recognizes new strategies or substantial modifications of existing strategies, they will be considered and, if necessary, changes will be made in the Guidelines. Section 5A.

56. *Question:* Why don't the Uniform Guidelines state a preference for criterion-related validity over content or construct validity?

Answer: Generally accepted principles of the psychological profession support the use of criterion-related, content or construct validity strategies as appropriate. American Psychological Association *Standards*, E, pp. 25–26. This use was recognized by the Supreme Court in *Washington v. Davis*, 426 U.S. 229, 247, fn. 13. Because the Guidelines describe the conditions under which each validity strategy is inappropriate, there is no reason to state a general preference for any one validity strategy.

57. *Question:* Are the Guidelines intended to restrict the development of new testing strategies, psychological theories, methods of job analysis or statistical techniques?

Answer: No. The Guidelines are concerned with the validity and fairness of selection procedures used in making employment decisions, and are not intended to limit research and new developments. See Question 55.

58. *Question:* Is a full job analysis necessary for all validity studies?

Answer: It is required for all content and construct studies, but not for all criterion-related studies. See Sections 14A and 14B(2). Measures of the results or outcomes of work behaviors such as production rate or error rate may be used without a full job analysis where a review of information about the job shows that these criteria are important to the employment situation of the user. Similarly, measures such as absenteeism, tardiness or turnover may be used without a full job analysis if these behaviors are shown by a review of information about the job to be important in the specific situation. A rating of overall job performance may be used without a full job analysis only if the user can demonstrate its appropriateness for the specific job and employment situation through a study of the job. The Supreme Court held in *Albemarle Paper Co.* v. *Moody*, 422 U.S. 405 (1975), that measures of overall job performance should be carefully developed and their use should be standardized and controlled.

59. *Question:* Section 5J on interim use requires the user to have available substantial evidence of validity. What does this mean?

Answer: For purposes of compliance with 5J, "substantial evidence" means evidence which may not meet all the validation requirements of the Guidelines but which raises a strong inference that validity pursuant to these standards will soon be shown. Section 5J is based on the proposition that it would not be an appropriate allocation of Federal resources to bring enforcement proceedings against a user who would soon be able to satisfy fully the standards of the Guidelines. For example, a criterion-related study may have produced evidence which meets almost all of the requirements of the Guidelines with the exception that the gathering of the data of test fairness is still in progress and the fairness study has not yet produced results. If the correlation coefficient for the group as a whole permits the strong inference that the selection procedure is valid, then the selection procedure may be used on an interim basis pending the completion of the fairness study.

60. *Question:* What are the potential consequences to a user when a selection procedure is used on an interim basis?

Answer: The fact that the Guidelines permit interim use of a selection procedure under some conditions does not immunize the user from liability for back pay, attorney fees and the like, should use of the selection procedure later be found to be in violation of the Guidelines. Section 5J. For this reason, users should take steps to come into full compliance with the Guidelines as soon as possible. It is also appropriate for users to consider ways of minimizing adverse impact during the period of interim use.

61. *Question:* Must provisions for retesting be allowed for job-knowledge tests, where knowledge of the test content would assist in scoring well on it the second time?

Answer: The primary intent of the provision for retesting is that an applicant who was not selected should be given another chance. Particularly in the case of job-knowledge tests, security precautions may preclude retesting with the same test after a short time. However, the opportunity for retesting should be provided for the same job at a later time, when the applicant may have acquired more of the relevant job knowledges.

62. *Question:* Under what circumstances may a selection procedure be used for ranking?

Answer: Criterion-related and construct validity strategies are essentially empirical, statistical processes showing a relationship between performance on the selection procedure and performance on the job. To justify ranking under such validity strategies, therefore, the user need show mathematical support for the proposition that persons who receive higher scores on the procedure are likely to perform better on the job.

Content validity, on the other hand, is primarily a judgmental process concerned with the adequacy of the selection procedure as a sample of the work behaviors. Use of a selection procedure on a ranking basis may be supported by content validity if there is evidence from job analysis or other empirical data that what is measured by the selection procedure is associated with differences in levels of job performance. Section 14C(9); see also Section 5G.

Any conclusion that a content validated procedure is appropriate for ranking must rest on an inference that higher scores on the procedure are related to better job performance. The more closely and completely the selection procedure approximates the important work behaviors, the easier it is to make such an inference. Evidence that better performance on the procedure is related to greater productivity or to performance of behaviors of greater difficulty may also support such an inference.

Where the content and context of the selection procedure are unlike those of the job, as, for example, in many paper-and-pencil job knowledge tests, it is difficult to infer an association between levels of performance on the procedure and on the job. To support a test of job knowledge on a content validity basis, there must be evidence of a specific tie-in between each item of knowledge tested and one or more work behaviors. See Question 79. To justify use of such a test for ranking, it would also have to be demonstrated from empirical evidence either that mastery of more difficult work behaviors, or that mastery of a greater scope of knowledge corresponds to a greater scope of important work behaviors.

For example, for a particular warehouse worker job, the job analysis may show that lifting a 50-pound object is essential, but the job analysis does not show that lifting heavier objects is essential or would result in significantly better job performance. In this case a test of ability to lift 50 pounds could be justified on a content validity basis for a pass/fail determination. However, ranking of candidates based on relative amount of weight that can be lifted would be inappropriate.

In another instance, a job analysis may reflect that, for the job of machine operator, reading of simple instructions is not a major part of the job but is essential. Thus, reading would be a critical behavior under the Guidelines. See Section 14C(8). Since the job analysis in this example did not also show that the ability to read such instructions more quickly or to understand more complex materials would be likely to result in better job performance, a reading test supported by content validity alone should be used on a pass/fail rather than a ranking basis. In such circumstances, use of the test for ranking would have to be supported by evidence from a criterion-related (or construct) validity study.

On the other hand, in the case of a person to be hired for a typing pool, the job analysis may show that the job consists almost entirely of typing from manuscript, and that productivity can be measured directly in terms of finished typed copy. For such a job, typing constitutes not only a critical behavior, but it constitutes most of the job. A higher score on a test which measured words per minute typed, with adjustments for errors, would therefore be likely to predict better job performance than a significantly lower score. Ranking or grouping based on such a typing test would therefore be appropriate under the Guidelines.

63. *Question:* If selection procedures are administered by an employment agency or a consultant for an employer, is the employer relieved of responsibilities under the Guidelines?

Answer: No. The employer remains responsible. It is therefore expected that the employer will have sufficient information available to show: (a) What selection procedures are being used on its behalf; (b) the total number of applicants for referral by race, sex and ethnic group; (c) the number of persons, by race, sex and ethnic group, referred to the employer; and (d) the impact of the selection procedures and evidence of the validity of any such procedure having an adverse impact as determined above.

A. Criterion-related Validity

64. *Question:* Under what circumstances may success in training be used as a criterion in criterion-related validity studies?

Answer: Success in training is an appropriate criterion when it is (1) necessary for successful job performance or has been shown to be related to degree of proficiency on the job and (2) properly measured. Section 14B(3). The measure of success in training should be carefully developed to ensure that factors which are not job related do not influence the measure of training success. Section 14B(3).

65. *Question:* When may concurrent validity be used?

Answer: A concurrent validity strategy assumes that the findings from a criterion-related validity study of current employees can be applied to applicants for the same job. Therefore, if concurrent validity is to be used, differences between the applicant and employee groups which might affect validity should be taken into account. The user should be particularly concerned with those differences between the applicant group and current employees used in the research sample which are caused by work experience or other work related events or by prior selection of employees and selection of the sample. See Section 14B(4).

66. *Question:* Under what circumstances can a selection procedure be supported (on other than an interim basis) by a criterion-related validity study done elsewhere?

Answer: A validity study done elsewhere may provide sufficient evidence if four conditions are met (Sec. 7B):

1. The evidence from the other studies clearly demonstrates that the procedure was valid in its use elsewhere.
2. The job(s) for which the selection procedure will be used closely matches the job(s) in the original study as shown by a comparison of major work behaviors as shown by the job analyses in both contexts.
3. Evidence of fairness from the other studies is considered for those groups constituting a significant factor in the user's labor market. Section 7B(3). Where the evidence is not available the user should conduct an internal study of test fairness, if technically feasibe. Section 7B(3).
4. Proper account is taken of variables which might affect the applicability of the study in the new setting, such as performance standards, work methods, representatives of the sample in terms of experience or other relevant factors, and the currency of the study.

67. *Question:* What does "unfairness of a selection procedure" mean?

Answer: When a specific score on a selection procedure has a different meaning in terms of expected job performance for members of one race, sex or ethnic group than the same score does for members of another group, the use of that selection procedure may be unfair for members of one of the groups. See Section 16V. For example, if members of one group have an average score of 40 on the selection procedure, but perform on the job as well as another group which has an average score of 50, then some uses of the selection procedure would be unfair to the members of the lower scoring group. See Question 70.

68. *Question:* When should the user investigate the question of fairness?

Answer: Fairness should be investigated generally at the same time that a criterion-related validity study is conducted, or as soon thereafter as feasible. Section 14B(8).

69. *Question:* Why do the Guidelines require that users look for evidence of unfairness?

Answer: The consequences of using unfair selection procedures are severe in terms of discriminating against applicants on the basis of race, sex or ethnic group membership. Accordingly, these studies should be performed routinely where technically feasible and appropriate, whether or not the probability of finding unfairness is small. Thus, the Supreme Court indicated in *Albemarle Paper Co.* v. *Moody,* 422 U.S. 405, that a validation study was "materially deficient" because, among other reasons, it failed to investigate fairness where it was not shown to be unfeasible to do so. Moreover, the American Psychological Association *Standards* published in 1974 call for the investigation of test fairness in criterion-related studies wherever feasible (pp. 43–44).

70. *Question:* What should be done if a selection procedure is unfair for one or more groups in the relevant labor market?

Answer: The Guidelines discuss three options. See Section 14B(8)(d). First, the selection instrument may be replaced by another validated instrument which is fair to all groups. Second, the selection instrument may be revised to eliminate the sources of unfairness. For example, certain items may be found to be the only ones which cause the unfairness to a particular group, and these items may be deleted or replaced by others. Finally, revisions may be made in the method of use of the selection procedure to ensure that the probability of being selected is compatible with the probability of successful job performance.

The Federal enforcement agencies recognize that there is serious debate in the psychological profession on the question of test fairness, and that information on that concept is developing. Accordingly, the enforcement agencies will consider developments in this field in evaluating actions occasioned by a finding of test unfairness.

71. *Question:* How is test unfairness related to differential validity and to differential prediction?

Answer: Test unfairness refers to use of selection procedures based on scores when members of one group characteristically obtain lower scores than members of another group, and the differences are not reflected in measures of job performance. See Sections 16V and 14B(8)(a), and Question 67.

Differential validity and test unfairness are conceptually distinct. Differential validity is defined as a situation in which a given instrument has significantly different validity coefficients for different race, sex or ethnic groups. Use of a test may be unfair to some groups even when differential validity is not found.

Differential prediction is a central concept for one definition of test unfairness. Differential prediction occurs when the use of the same set of scores systematically overpredicts or underpredicts job performance for members of one group as compared to members of another group.

Other definitions of test unfairness which do not relate to differential prediction may, however, also be appropriately applied to employment decisions. Thus these Guidelines are not intended to choose between fairness models as long as the model selected is appropriate to the manner in which the selection procedure is used.

72. *Question:* What options does a user have if a criterion-related study is appropriate but is not feasible because there are not enough persons in the job?

Answer: There are a number of options the user should consider, depending upon the particular facts and circumstances, such as:

1. Change the procedure so as to eliminate adverse impact (see Section 6A);

2. Validate a procedure through a content validity strategy, if appropriate (see Section 14C and Questions 54 and 74);

3. Use a selection procedure validated elsewhere in conformity with the Guidelines (see Sections 7–8 and Question 66);

4. Engage in a cooperative study with other facilities or users (in cooperation with such users either bilaterally or through industry or trade associations or governmental groups), or participate in research studies conducted by the state employment security system. Where different locations are combined, care is needed to insure that the jobs studied are in fact the same and that the study is adequate and in conformity with the Guidelines (see Sections 8 and 14 and Question 45).

5. Combine essentially similar jobs into a single study sample. See Section 14B(1).

B. Content Validity

73. *Question:* Must a selection procedure supported by content validity be an actual "on the job" sample of work behaviors?

Answer: No. The Guidelines emphasize the importance of a close approximation between the content of the selection procedure and the observable behaviors or products of the job, so as to minimize the inferential leap between performance on the selection procedure and job performance. However, the Guidelines also permit justification on the basis of content validity of selection procedures measuring knowledges, skills, or abilities which are not necessarily samples of work behaviors if: (1) The knowledge, skill, or ability being measured is operationally defined in accord with Section 14C(4); and (2) that knowledge, skill, or ability is a prerequisite for critical or important work behaviors. In addition users may justify a requirement for training, or for experience obtained from prior employment or volunteer work, on the basis of content validity, even though the prior training or experience does not duplicate the job. See Section 14B(6).

74. *Question:* Is the use of a content validity strategy appropriate for a procedure measuring skills or knowledges which are taught in training after initial employment?

Answer: Usually not. The Guidelines state (Section 14C(1)) that content validity is not appropriate where the selection procedure involves knowledges, skills, or abilities which the employee will be expected to learn "on the job". The phrase "on the job" is intended to apply to training which occurs after hiring, promotion or transfer. However, if an ability, such as speaking and understanding a language, takes a substantial length of time to learn, is required for successful job performance, and is not taught to those initial hires who possess it in advance, a test for that ability may be supported on a content validity basis.

75. *Question:* Can a measure of a trait or construct be validated on the basis of content validity?

Answer: No. Traits or constructs are by definition underlying characteristics which are intangible and are not directly observable. They are therefore not appropriate for the sampling approach of content validity. Some selection procedures, while labeled as construct measures, may actually be samples of observable work behaviors. Whatever the label, if the operational definitions are in fact based upon observable work behaviors, a selection procedure measuring those behaviors may be appropriately supported by a content validity strategy. For example, while a measure of the construct "dependability" should not be supported on the basis of content validity, promptness and regularity of attendance in a prior work record are frequently inquired into as a part of a selection procedure, and such measures may be supported on the basis of content validity.

76. *Question:* May a test which measures what the employee has learned in a training program be justified for use in employment decisions on the basis of content validity?

Answer: Yes. While the Guidelines (Section 14C(1)) note that content validity is not an appropriate strategy for knowledges, skills or abilities which an employee "will be expected to learn on the job", nothing in the Guidelines suggests that a test supported by content validity is not appropriate for determining what the employee has learned on the job, or in a training program. If the content of the test is relevant to the job, it may be used for employment decisions such as retention or assignment. See Section 14C(7).

77. *Question:* Is a task analysis necessary to support a selection procedure based on content validity?

Answer: A description of all tasks is not required by the Guidelines. However, the job analysis should describe all important work behaviors and their relative importance and their level of difficulty. Sections 14C(2) and 15C(3). The job analysis should focus on observable work behaviors and, to the extent appropriate, observable work products, and the tasks associated with the important observable work behaviors and/or work products. The job analysis should identify how the critical or important work behaviors are used in the job, and should support the content of the selection procedure.

78. *Question:* What is required to show the content validity of a paper-and-pencil test that is intended to approximate work behaviors?

Answer: Where a test is intended to replicate a work behavior, content validity is established by a demonstration of the similarities between the test and the job with respect to behaviors, products, and the surrounding environmental conditions. Section 14B(4).

Paper-and-pencil tests which are intended to replicate a work behavior are most likely to be appropriate where work behaviors are performed in paper and pencil form (e.g., editing and bookkeeping). Paper-and-pencil tests of effectiveness in interpersonal relations (e.g., sales or supervision), or of physical activities (e.g., automobile repair) or ability to function properly under danger (e.g., firefighters) generally are not close enough approximations of work behaviors to show content validity.

The appropriateness of tests of job knowledge, whether or not in pencil and paper form, is addressed in Question 79.

79: *Question:* What is required to show the content validity of a test of a job knowledge?

Answer: There must be a defined, well recognized body of information, and knowledge of the information must be prerequisite to performance of the required work behaviors. The work behavior(s) to which each knowledge is related should be identified on an item by item basis. The test should fairly sample the information that is actually used by the employee on the job, so that the level of difficulty of the test items should correspond to the level of difficulty of the knowledge as used in the work behavior. See Section 14C(1) and (4).

80: *Question:* Under content validity, may a selection procedure for entry into a job be justified on the grounds that the knowledges, skills or abilities measured by the selection procedure are prerequisites to successful performance in a training program?

Answer: Yes, but only if the training material and the training program closely approximate the content and level of difficulty of the job and if the knowledges, skills or abilities are not those taught in the training program. For example, if training materials are at a level of reading difficulty substantially in excess of the reading difficulty of materials used on the job, the Guidelines would not permit justification on a content validity basis of a reading test based on those training materials for entry into the job.

Under the Guidelines a training program itself is a selection procedure if passing it is a prerequisite to retention or advancement. See Section 2C and 14C(17). As such, the content of the training program may only be justified by the relationship between the program and critical or important behaviors of the job itself, or through a demonstration of the relationship between measures of performance in training and measures of job performance.

Under the example given above, therefore, where the requirements in the training materials exceed those on the job, the training program itself could not be validated on a content validity basis if passing it is a basis for retention or promotion.

C. Construct Validity

81. *Question:* In Section 5, "General Standards for Validity Studies," construct validity is identified as no less acceptable than criterion-related and content validity. However, the specific requirements for construct validity, in Section 14D, seem to limit the generalizability of construct validity to the rules governing criterion-related validity. Can this apparent inconsistency be reconciled?

Answer: Yes. In view of the developing nature of construct validation for employment selection procedures, the approach taken concerning the generalizability of construct validity (section 14D) is intended to be a cautious one. However, construct validity may be generalized in circumstances where transportability of tests supported on the basis of criterion-related validity would not be appropriate. In establishing transportability of criterion-related validity, the jobs should have substantially the same major work behaviors. Section 7E(2). Construct validity, on the other hand, allows for situations where only some of the important work behaviors are the same. Thus, well-established measures of the construct which underlie particular work behaviors and which have been shown to be valid for some jobs may be generalized to other jobs which have some of the same work behaviors but which are different with respect to other work behaviors. Section 14D(4).

As further research and professional guidance on construct validity in employment situations emerge, additional extensions of construct validity for employee selection may become generally accepted in the profession. The agencies encourage further research and professional guidance with respect to the approprite use of construct validity.

V. Records and Documentation

82. *Question:* Do the Guidelines have simplified recordkeeping for small users (employers who employ one hundred or fewer employees and other users not required to file EEO–1, *et seq.* reports)?

Answer: Yes. Although small users are fully covered by Federal equal employment opportunity law, the Guidelines have reduced their record-keeping burden. See option in Section 15A(1). Thus, small users need not make adverse impact determinations nor are they required to keep applicant data on a job-by-job basis. The agencies also recognize that a small user may find that some or all validation strategies are not feasible. See Question 54. If a small user has reason to believe that its selection procedures have adverse impact and validation is not feasible, it should consider other options. See Sections 7A and 8 and Questions 31, 36, 45, 66, and 72.

83. *Question:* Is the requirement in the Guidelines that users maintain records of the race, national origin, and sex of employees and applicants constitutional?

Answer: Yes. For example, the United States Court of Appeals for the First Circuit rejected a challenge on constitutional and other grounds to the Equal Employment Opportunity Commission regulations requiring State and local governmental units to furnish information as to race, national origin and sex of employees. *United States* v. *New Hampshire,* 539 F. 2d 277 (1st Cir. 1976), *cert. denied,* sub nom. *New Hampshire* v. *United States,* 429 U.S. 1023. The Court held that the recordkeeping and reporting requirements promulgated under Title VII of the Civil Rights Act of 1964, as amended, were reasonably necessary for the Federal agency to determine whether the state was in compliance with Title VII and thus were authorized and constitutional. The same legal principles apply to recordkeeping with respect to applicants.

Under the Supremacy Clause of the Constitution, the Federal law requiring maintenance of records identifying race, sex and national origin overrides any contrary provision of State law. See Question 8.

The agencies recognize, however, that such laws have been enacted to prevent misuse of this information. Thus, employers should take appropriate steps to ensure proper use of all data. See Question #88.

84. *Question:* Is the user obliged to keep records which show whether its selection processes have an adverse impact on race, sex, or ethnic groups?

Answer: Yes. Under the Guidelines users are obliged to maintain evidence indicating the impact which their selection processes have on identifiable race, sex or ethnic groups. Sections 4 A and B. If the selection process for a job does have an adverse impact on one or more such groups, the user is expected to maintain records showing the impact for the individual procedures. Section 15A(2).

85. *Question:* What are the recordkeeping obligations of a user who cannot determine whether a selection process for a job has adverse impact because it makes an insufficient number of selections for that job in a year?

Answer: In such circumstances the user should collect, maintain, and have available information on the impact of the selection process and the component procedures until it can determine that adverse impact does not exist for the overall process or until the job has changed substantially. Section 15A(2)(c).

86. *Question:* Should applicant and selection information be maintained for race or ethnic groups constituting less than 2% of the labor force and the applicants?

Answer: Small employers and other small users are not obliged to keep such records. Section 15A(1). Employers with more than 100 employees and other users required to file EEO-1 *et seq.* reports should maintain records and other information upon which impact determinations could be made, because section 15A2 requires the maintenance of such information for "any of the groups for which records are called for by section 4B above." See also, Section 4A.

No user, regardless of size, is required to make adverse impact determinations for race or ethnic groups constituting less than 2% of the labor force and the applicants. See Question 16.

87. *Question:* Should information be maintained which identifies applicants and persons selected both by sex and by race or ethnic group?

Answer: Yes. Although the Federal agencies have decided not to require computations of adverse impact by subgroups (white males, black males, white females, black females—see Question 17), the Guidelines call for record keeping which allows identification of persons by sex, combined with race or ethnic group, so as to permit the identification of discriminatory practices on any such basis. Section 4A and 4B.

88. *Question:* How should a user collect data on race, sex or ethnic classifications for purposes of determining the impact of selection procedures?

Answer: The Guidelines have not specified any particular procedure, and the enforcement agencies will accept different procedures that capture the necessary information. Where applications are made in person, a user may maintain a log or applicant flow chart based upon visual observation, identifying the number of persons expressing an interest, by sex and by race or national origin; may in some circumstances rely upon personal knowledge of the user; or may rely upon self-identification. Where applications are not made in person and the applicants are not personally known to the employer, self-identification may be appropriate. Wherever a self-identification form is used, the employer should advise the applicant that identification by race, sex and national origin is sought, not for employment decisions, but for record-keeping in compliance with Federal law. Such self-identification forms should be kept separately from the application, and should not be a basis for employment decisions; and the applicants should be so advised. See Section 4B.

89. *Question:* What information should be included in documenting a validity study for purposes of these Guidelines?

Answer: Generally, reports of validity studies should contain all the information necessary to permit an enforcement agency to conclude whether a selection procedure has been validated. Information that is critical to this determination is denoted in Section 15 of the Guidelines by the word "(essential)"

Any reports completed after September 25, 1978, (the effective date of the Guidelines) which do not contain this information will be considered incomplete by the agencies unless there is good reason for not including the information. Users should therefore prepare validation reports according to the format of Section 15 of the Guidelines, and should carefully document the reasons if any of the information labeled "(essential)" is missing.

The major elements for all types of validation studies include the following:

When and where the study was conducted.

A description of the selection procedure, how it is used, and the results by race, sex, and ethnic group.

How the job was analyzed or reviewed and what information was obtained from this job analysis or review.

The evidence demonstrating that the selection procedure is related to the job. The nature of this evidence varies, depending upon the strategy used.

What alternative selection procedures and alternative methods of using the selection procedure were studied and the results of this study.

The name, address and telephone number of a contact person who can provide further information about the study.

The documentation requirements for each validation strategy are set forth in detail in Section 15 B, C, D, E, F, and G. Among the requirements for each validity strategy are the following:

1. *Criterion-related Validity.* A description of the criterion measures of job performance, how and why they were selected, and how they were used to evaluate employees.

   A description of the sample used in the study, how it was selected, and the size of each race, sex, or ethnic group in it.

   A description of the statistical methods used to determine whether scores on the selection procedure are related to scores on the criterion measures of job performance, and the results of these statistical calculations.

2. *Content Validity.* The content of the job, as identified from the job analysis.

   The content of the selection procedure.

   The evidence demonstrating that the content of the selection procedure is a representative sample of the content of the job.

3. *Construct Validity.* A definition of the construct and how it relates to other constructs in the psychological literature.

The evidence that the selection procedure measures the construct.

The evidence showing that the measure of the construct is related to work behaviors which involve the construct.

90. *Question:* Although the records called for under "Source Data", Section 15B(11) and section 15D(11), are not listed as "Essential", the Guidelines state that each user should maintain such records, and have them available upon request of a compliance agency. Are these records necessary? Does the absence of complete records preclude the further use of research data compiled prior to the issuance of the Guidelines?

Answer: The Guidelines require the maintenance of these records in some form "as a necessary part of the study." Section 15A(3)(c). However, such records need not be compiled or maintained in any specific format. The term "Essential" as used in the Guidelines refers to information considered essential to the validity report. Section 15A(3)(b). The Source Data records need not be included with reports of validation or other formal reports until and unless they are specifically requested by a compliance agency. The absence of complete records does not preclude use of research data based on those records that are available. Validation studies submitted to comply with the requirements of the Guidelines may be considered inadequate to the extent that important data are missing or there is evidence that the collected data are inaccurate.

Note

1. Section references throughout these questions and answers are to the sections of the *Uniform Guidelines on Employee Selection Procedures* (herein referred to as "Guidelines") that were published by the Equal Employment Opportunity Commission, the Civil Service Commission, the Department of Labor, and the Department of Justice on Aug. 25, 1978, 43 FR 38290. The Uniform Guidelines were adopted by the Office of Revenue Sharing of the Department of Treasury on September 11, 1978, 43 FR 40223.